LITERARY NEO-ORIENTALISM AND THE ARAB UPRISINGS

Edinburgh Studies of the Globalised Muslim World

Series Editor: **Frédéric Volpi**, Director, Prince Alwaleed Bin Talal Centre for the Study of Contemporary Islam, University of Edinburgh

This innovative series investigates the dynamics of Muslim societies in a globalised world. It considers the boundaries of the contemporary Muslim world, their construction, their artificiality or durability. It sheds new light on what it means to be part of the Muslim world today, for both those individuals and communities who live in Muslim-majority countries and those who reside outside and are part of a globalised ummah. Its analysis encompasses the micro and the macro level, exploring the discourses and practices of individuals, communities, states and transnational actors who create these dynamics. It offers a multidisciplinary perspective on the salient contemporary issues and interactions that shape the internal and external relations of the Muslim world.

Published and forthcoming titles

Salafi Social and Political Movements: National and Transnational Contexts
Masooda Bano (ed.)

A Political Theory of Muslim Democracy
Ravza Altuntaş-Çakır

Political Islam in the Syrian Conflict and Tunisian Transition: The Contentious Practices of Islamist Movements
Teije J. Donker

Islamic Modernities in World Society: The Rise, Spread and Fragmentation of a Hegemonic Idea
Dietrich Jung

Why Islamists Go Green
Emmanuel Karagiannis

Literary Neo-Orientalism and the Arab Uprisings: Tensions in English, French and German Language Fiction
Julia Wurr

edinburghuniversitypress.com/series/esgmw

LITERARY NEO-ORIENTALISM AND THE ARAB UPRISINGS

Tensions in English, French and German Language Fiction

Julia Wurr

EDINBURGH
University Press

Edinburgh University Press is one of the leading presses in the UK. We publish academic books and journals in our selected subject areas across the humanities and social sciences, combining cutting-edge scholarship with high editorial and productions values to produce academic works of lasting importance. For more information visit our website: edinburghuniversitypress.com

© Julia Wurr, 2022, 2024

Edinburgh University Press
The Tun – Holyrood Road
12 (2f) Jackson's Entry
Edinburgh EH8 8PJ

First published in hardback by Edinburgh University Press 2022

Typeset in Adobe Garamond Pro by
Cheshire Typesetting Ltd, Cuddington, Cheshire

A CIP record is available from the British Library

ISBN 978 1 4744 8800 6 (hardback)
ISBN 978 1 4744 880B (paperback)
ISBN 978 1 4744 8802 0 (webready PDF)
ISBN 978 1 4744 8803 7 (epub)

The right of Julia Wurr to be identified as author of this work has been asserted in accordance with the Copyright, Designs and Patents Act 1988 and the Copyright and Related Rights
Regulations 2003 (SI No. 2498).

CONTENTS

Acknowledgements	vi
Series Editor's Foreword	viii
1 From Tahrir to Terror: Neo-Orientalism and the 'Arab Spring'	1
2 The Arab Uprisings and the Western Literary Market	33
3 Precarity Far and Near: The Arab Uprisings in Tahar Ben Jelloun's *Par le feu* and Jonas Lüscher's *Frühling der Barbaren*	53
4 Affective Masculinity and the Arab Uprisings: Adam Thirlwell's *Kapow!* and Jochen Beyse's *Rebellion*	101
5 Figurations of Terror: The Islamist Rage Boy in Karim Alrawi's *Book of Sands* and Mathias Énard's *Rue des voleurs*	154
6 The Arab Uprisings between Inequality, Insecurity and Identity	220
References	226
Index	245

ACKNOWLEDGEMENTS

In the summer of 2019, this study was accepted as a doctoral dissertation at the Faculty of Languages, Literatures and Media Studies at the University of Trier, Germany.

My sincere gratitude goes out to everyone who has been interested and involved in this project.

I would like to express my special thanks to the wonderful team of supervisors who have helped me along the way. I would like to thank Wolfgang Klooß, for his inspiring and constructive feedback, for his sense of humour and his trust. And for reminding me of the importance of full stops, both literal and metaphorical ones. A warm thank you to Frauke Matthes, for taking the time to work with me and for offering valuable comments and recommendations.

Merci, danke and thank you to all those at the International Research Group 'Diversity – Mediating Difference in Transcultural Spaces' who read, provided feedback on and helped me with my work in so many different ways (especially Ursula Lehmkuhl, Laurence McFalls, Hans-Jürgen Lüsebrink, Astrid Fellner, Ralf Hertel, Saaz Taher and Judith Lamberty). I wrote my dissertation as a doctoral researcher at the International Research Training Group and without the great interdisciplinary, organisational and financial support of the Group, this would have been much harder.

Moreover, I would like to acknowledge all those lively discussions I have had with a great number of colleagues and friends during the last few years. I am grateful to each and every one who shared their thoughts with me and encouraged me to continue my work. The conferences 'Représentations littéraires et culturelles – Orient, Maghreb et Afrique occidentale' (2017) and 'Orientalism and the Francophone Postcolonial World: Legacies of Edward W. Said' (2018) were particularly helpful for this project. In addition, I attended a fascinating workshop on 'Ethnosexism' with Gabriele Dietze, whom I would like to thank both for the useful discussions and for her suggestions concerning sources.

I also wish to thank all the people who devoted their time to reading earlier versions of this book. Special thanks go to Anna Stahlhofen, Anna Weinand, Lutz Schowalter and Werner Schäfer, who made time to read the first drafts of my chapters and who supported me from very early on, and to Anna Maria Duplang, for her enthusiastic and encouraging help with the proofreading. I would also like to thank Michael Banks for undertaking the challenging task of translating the German quotations in Chapter Four into English.

Furthermore, I would like to thank Frédéric Volpi, who kindly included my study in his book series 'Edinburgh Studies of the Globalised Muslim World', and the reviewers, whose thought-provoking feedback provided me with useful impulses when I started transforming my dissertation into this book. I am particularly grateful to Marilyn Booth for her careful reading of the manuscript and for her extremely helpful and constructive suggestions. In addition, I would like to express my thanks to Kirsty Woods, Louise Hutton, Eddie Clark and the entire team at Edinburgh University Press, and Lel Gillingwater, for their professional support in publishing this book.

Above all, I would like to thank my friends for being such warm-hearted people, and for all their love and laughs. A heartfelt thank you goes out to my mother, Sonja Fröhlich, for always thinking of ways to support me. I am profoundly grateful to Janin Geißler, for fighting off disease, for surviving, for our friendship. And thank you, Lucas Alt, for your patience – and for everything else.

Julia Wurr
August 2021

SERIES EDITOR'S FOREWORD

Edinburgh Studies of the Globalised Muslim World is a series that focuses on the contemporary transformations of Muslim societies. Globalisation is meant here to say that although the Muslim world was always interacting with other societal, religious, imperial or national forces over the centuries, the evolution of these interconnections constantly reshapes Muslim societies. The second half of the twentieth century has been characterised by the increasing number and diversity of exchanges on a global scale bringing people and societies 'closer', for better and for worse. The beginning of the twenty-first century confirmed the increasingly glocalised nature of these interactions and the challenges and opportunities that they bring to existing institutional, social and cultural orders.

The series is not a statement that everything is different in today's brave new world. Indeed, many 'old' ideas and practices still have much currency in the present, and undoubtedly will also have in the future. Rather, the series emphasises how our current globalised condition shapes and mediates how past worldviews and modes of being are transmitted between people and institutions. The contemporary Muslim world is not merely a reflection of past histories, but it is also a living process of creating a new order on the basis of what people want, desire, fear and hope. This creative endeavour can transform existing relations for the better, for example by reconsidering the relations between society and the environment. They can equally fan violence and hatred, as illustrated in the reignition of cycles of conflicts over sovereignties, ideologies or resources across the globe.

The Globalised Muslim World series arrives at a challenging time for any inquiry into Muslim societies. The new millennium began inauspiciously with a noticeable spike in transnational and international violence framed in 'civilisational' terms. A decade of 'war of terror' contributed to entrench negative mutual perceptions across the globe while reinforcing essentialist views. The ensuing decade hardly improved the situation with political and territorial conflicts multiplying in different parts of the Muslim world, and some of the most violent groups laid claim to the idea of a global caliphate to justify themselves. Yet, a focus on trajectories of violence gives a distorted picture of the evolution of Muslim societies and their relations with the rest of the world. This series is very much about the 'what else' is happening as we move further into the twenty-first century.

Literary Neo-Orientalism and the Arab Uprisings is unmistakably a most timely contribution by Julia Wurr to the contemporary debates about the representation of Muslim societies in a globalised literary culture. The successes and failures of the 2011 Arab uprisings have been crucial in shaping perceptions around the world of what Muslim Middle Eastern actors can do, individually and collectively, to change the states and societies in which they live. Beyond the political debates and role of the mass media at the time, the literary works that emerged during and in the aftermath of this tumultuous period contributed to transform the public understanding of these events. Wurr's book addresses this process directly and creatively.

The work considers the tension between Neo-Orientalist and post-Orientalist views of the Other that remains at the core of most narratives of the Arab uprisings. Wurr analyses how negative stereotypes of the dangerous Muslim and/or Arab that have gained momentum before the uprisings make their way directly or indirectly into the post-uprisings depictions of the region and its people. By considering different literary productions and markets in Europe and North America, Wurr illustrates some of the crucial trends in the globalisation of such narratives and their insertion in different cultural settings. Literary works both convey and transcend Orientalist views of the region in their own ways, creating new possibilities for understanding while remaining constrained by the demands of the globalised literary market.

Considering well-received recent works of English, French and German language fiction about the Arab uprisings, Wurr explores the tensions involving fears of the dangerous Muslim/Arab, insecurity about Western culture, and cosmopolitan hopes for the future. These narratives built by diasporic and non-diasporic writers reveal the depth of the stereotypes permeating the contemporary Western literary culture just as they set about challenging them each in their own ways. The work outlines some promising avenues for rethinking the Arab and Muslim referents in globalised cultural narratives still influenced by orientalism. Beyond the literary field, this work illustrates clearly the crucial challenges that face scholarly and public discourses about the region and its inhabitants.

Frédéric Volpi
Chair in the Politics of the Muslim World
The University of Edinburgh

1

FROM TAHRIR TO TERROR: NEO-ORIENTALISM AND THE 'ARAB SPRING'

> We, looking back on these events, see them through the perspective of our hard-won knowledge, and understand that the practice of extreme violence, known by the catch-all and often inexact term *terrorism*, was always of particular attraction to male individuals who were either virgins or unable to find sexual partners. Mind-altering frustration, and the damage to the male ego which accompanied it, found its release in rage and assaults. When lonely, hopeless young men were provided with loving, or at least desirous, or at the very least willing sexual partners, they lost interest in suicide belts, bombs and the virgins of heaven, and preferred to live. In the absence of the favourite pastime of every jinni, human males turned their thoughts to orgasmic endings. Death, being readily available everywhere, was often an alternative pursuit to unavailable sex.[1]

In *Two Years Eight Months & Twenty-Eight Nights* (2015), a fantasy set in the future, Salman Rushdie imagines a war between reason and religion – and uses hyperbolic irony to criticise a fundamentalist interpretation of both. Tinged by this irony, the novel's elucidation of terrorism mimics – by relying on stereotypes itself – the often-reductive representation not just of Islamist terrorism, but of the Islamicate Other more generally.[2] In this – albeit ironic – reliance on negative framings of the Islamicate Other, the text's representational approach is no exception on the Western literary market. In fact, and as this book argues, with few exceptions, the dependence on reductive sexualised and securitised modes of representing the Islamicate Other can frequently be found even in literature marketed as open-minded and cosmopolitan; in contrast, fundamental reframings in different contexts of meaning are much rarer.

What holds true for the literary market is a phenomenon which by far transcends the realm of fiction. Despite the existence of, for instance journalistic, attempts to provide a more nuanced picture, negative framings of the Islamicate Other mostly attract greater attention. From Donald Trump's 'Muslim ban' to Renaud Camus' Great Replacement theory to hate speech against alleged 'rapefugees': since the terrorist attacks of 9/11, the vilification of the Islamicate Other as a threat to the West has sharply intensified in public discourse. Stressing aspects such as an alleged backwardness, sexism, the propensity for violence or the inability to even fathom, let alone establish democracy or rule of law,[3] Western political and media discourse has portrayed the Islamicate Other mainly 'in terms of global terrorism, Islamic jihadism, fanatic Islamism, fundamentalism, fascism, and Islamic authoritarianism',[4] or 'as a problematic presence, troubling those values of individualism and freedom said to define Western nations'.[5] Not only do epithets pertaining to the broader semantic field of danger thus increasingly influence Western representations of the Islamicate world, but Muslims are also frequently presented as a threat to Western liberal-democratic values.

Such a predominance of negative framings as well as the attendant near absence of alternative depictions of the Islamicate world are indicative of how deeply Western public discourse is informed by Neo-Orientalist patterns of representation. Neo-Orientalism is a marketable, gendered and racialised system of representation and knowledge production which is complicit in translating global inequalities into affective, ahistorical and homogenising projections of the allegedly backward and dangerous Islamicate Other.[6] While also continuing to draw on established stereotypes and country-specific forms of Orientalist representation, Neo-Orientalism has found a transnational common denominator in its focus on securitising the Islamicate world – that is, on presenting people from an Islamicate background as an existential threat to Western security, freedom and identity.[7]

Although configurations of the dangerous Muslim have a long-established tradition,[8] Neo-Orientalism has not only revived, but has also reinforced and refocused the securitised dimension of Orientalism.[9] After a long phase in which the Islamicate Other was constructed mainly as a foil in Western colonial identity discourse, representations of the danger which allegedly emanates from the Islamicate Other and jeopardises the so-called Western way of life have proliferated massively in the wake of the oil and Iranian hostage crises in the 1970s, after the end of the Cold War and, in particular, after the 9/11 attacks.[10] Following the latest tectonic shifts associated with the Middle East and North Africa region – that is, the Arab uprisings and the rise of the self-proclaimed Islamic State as well as after the terrorist attacks in several Western cities and migration movements – this securitised dimension of Neo-Orientalism has gained further momentum.

In its sharper and at times almost exclusive focus on the danger allegedly emanating from the Islamicate Other – who, in a process of full identification, is often reduced to their religion[11] – Neo-Orientalism, although based on Orientalism, does not only differ from its predecessor in geographical and topical scope,[12] but also fulfils a different discursive function. While in its increased attention to the Arab and Islamic world, Neo-Orientalism is narrower in geographical scope than Orientalism, it simultaneously serves as a transnational discourse which is no longer propounded by Western Orientalists only, but which can also be found in the writing of 'Middle Eastern women and men who use their native subjectivity and newfound agency in the West to render otherwise biased accounts of the region seemly [sic] more authoritative and objective'.[13] If the geographical focus of Neo-Orientalism is thus clearly influenced by neo-imperial processes of globalisation, the same holds true for its discursive function. By presenting the Islamicate Other mainly as a threat to the West, Neo-Orientalism simplifies neo-imperial complexities according to its own hegemonic interests – and it projects the very insecurities which stem from the increasingly unstable political and economic conditions of Western countries into a fear of the Other. Thereby refracting the psychosocial consequences of neo-liberalism into the allegedly problematic Other, Neo-Orientalism serves as a neo-liberal proxy discourse. In this way, Neo-Orientalist representations do not only conceal the causes of widespread feelings of insecurity. What is more, as they are both informed by and inform anti-Muslim racism, ethnosexism and securitisation, Neo-Orientalist representations endanger those whom they present as a danger.[14]

Neo-Orientalism and the Arab Uprisings

At least for a short while, the Arab uprisings seemed to be a possible opening in – or even the end of – Neo-Orientalist discourse. In the predominantly negative media coverage on the Islamicate world since 2001, Tahrir – 'liberation' – was the odd one out. When the so-called Arab Spring began in 2011, Tahrir Square became an emblem of emancipation and transnational protest, and – in a world torn apart by neo-liberal competitiveness – the uprisings in several Arab countries were celebrated as the possible inception of an 'era and, indeed idea, of humanistic counter-culture'.[15] Not only did they inspire a cycle of global discontent which ranged from the Spanish Indignados to the Occupy Wall Street and Blockupy movements to the revolts in Taksim Gezi Park,[16] but by prioritising issues of social justice, they also fostered a transnational paradigm which challenged essentialised constructs underlying the alleged clash of civilisations:

> The insurrections have also performed a kind of ideological house-cleaning, sweeping away racist conceptions of a clash of civilisations that consign Arab politics to the past. The multitudes in Tunis, Cairo, Damascus, Sana'a, Manâma, Tripoli shatter the political stereotypes that Arabs are constrained to the choice between secular dictatorships and fanatical theocracies, or that Muslims are somehow incapable of freedom and democracy.[17]

In a first bout of optimism, Western media coverage of the uprisings consequently voiced the hope that the combined force of young people in countries such as Tunisia, Egypt, Libya and Syria would be potent enough to chase away Western-approved dictators; Nobel laureate Joseph E. Stiglitz declared the year 2011 as the new 1848 or 1968;[18] intellectuals such as Slavoj Žižek and Hamid Dabashi hailed the uprisings as the possible end of Orientalism as a Western system of constructing and dominating the Orient.[19] In Žižek's words, people had recommenced 'dreaming dangerously'.[20] For Dabashi, the uprisings engendered a completely new way of Post-Orientalist thinking devoid of ideology:

> The Arab Spring is not a fulfillment but a delivery. This is what I mean by its being the end of postcolonialism: the Arab Spring is not the final fulfillment of a set of ideologies but the exhaustion of all ideologies, a final delivery from them all.[21]

Within just a few years, however, the so-called Arab Spring itself was turned into yet another construct of Western representational power. Far from what, without the benefit of hindsight, Dabashi called 'the epistemic end of that violent autonormativity whereby the "West" kept reinventing itself and all its inferior others',[22] representations of the uprisings still abound with Orientalist and Neo-Orientalist stereotypes. Instead of deconstructing dichotomies presumed overcome, most Western political and media discourse continues to frame the uprisings with clichés of backwardness or as a source of insecurity.[23] Especially since the end of the revolts, in the wake of the rise of Islamist parties and of the self-proclaimed Islamic State and with several terrorist attacks in Europe, coverage of the Arab uprisings has frequently evoked a causal relationship between the region's alleged inability to establish democracy or the rule of law and the increase in Islamist terrorism.[24]

Neo-Orientalist modes of representation have consequently regained much of the ground which they appeared to have lost during 2011. If, at the time of the revolutions, a post-Orientalist paradigm tentatively stressed systemic similarities, Neo-Orientalist patterns have since returned in a more subtle, but no less pernicious form:

> The Arab uprisings seemed to herald a fatal rupture in orientalist narratives, challenging as they did essentialized renderings of the region as one mired by 'authoritarian resilience' and failures to democratize. However, four years after the uprisings, familiar forms of reductionist analysis about the regions persist, albeit more subtly.[25]

It is because of this tension between the initially optimistic reception and the ensuing Neo-Orientalist appropriation of the so-called Arab Spring that this book – in its endeavour to test the aesthetic functioning and confines of Neo-Orientalism – focuses on literary adaptations of the uprisings. By identifying recurring tropes, frames and figurations, the following chapters illustrate in what specific aestheticised forms Neo-Orientalism was able to gather such momentum. Moreover, the following chapters demonstrate how literary Neo-Orientalism helps to circulate, in the midst of society, a form of Othering which is complicit in translating societal insecurities into a transnational Othering. Thus, retracing how systemic socio-economic and sociopolitical problems are culturalised into questions of race and gender, the following analyses both contribute to exploring the significance of the uprisings for the postcolonial Middle East and to offering a reversal of perspectives which raises awareness for the insecurity of the securitised.[26]

Neo-Orientalism and its Others

Although Neo-Orientalism follows an ahistorical logic itself – neglecting centuries of imperialistic and epistemic violence – its representational power relies heavily on the long tradition of Orientalism. More than forty years ago, Edward Said defined Orientalism as 'a style of thought based upon an ontological and epistemological distinction made between "the Orient" and (most of the time) "the Occident"'.[27] Accordingly, Orientalism is 'a system of knowledge about the Orient [and] an accepted grid for filtering through the Orient into Western consciousness ...'[28] Given that most Western political and media discourse about people from an Islamicate background still features Orientalist stereotypes of backwardness, violence, irrationality and affect-driven behaviour or the inability to establish democracy or rule of law,[29] Said's observations have remained extremely relevant – all attacks on *Orientalism*'s methodological soundness notwithstanding.[30]

Besides this reliance on Orientalist frames, it is the increased focus on the securitisation and racialisation of Muslims which decisively informs Neo-Orientalism:[31] not only have 'Orientalist frames ... become common-sense and naturalized'[32] again after the 9/11 attacks, but they frequently manifest in combination with securitised and racialised homogenisations of Islam, such as: 'Islam is a monolithic religion, Islam is a uniquely sexist religion, the "Muslim mind" is incapable of rationality and science, Islam is inherently violent, the West spreads democracy, while Islam spawns terrorism.'[33] As a result, Neo-Orientalism is 'much more racially and ethnically tinged'[34] than earlier forms of Orientalism, and it projects Islam both as a threat and as a backward foil to Western civilisation:

The racialisation of Muslims in the process of securitisation permits Western politicians and many in the mainstream media to target Muslim women, associate Muslim males with terrorism, and criminalise migrants and refugees. One outcome of the process is that some intellectuals and media see Islam as the very antithesis of 'Western civilisation'. Taken together, these developments have become the signifiers of the new Orientalism.[35]

Islamicate Alterity Then and Now

If nowadays the construct of the Orient is closely interwoven with the racialisation of Muslims and Muslim look-alikes, this semantic proximity is a more recent development.[36] Although Said claims that in the Anglo-French experience up until the nineteenth century, the Orient encompassed 'only India and the Bible lands',[37] and that it was the 'experience of the Arabs and Islam which for almost a thousand years together stood for the Orient',[38] forms of Orientalism had existed long before this – and they included more than the Middle East and North Africa region. In fact,

> Orientalism as discourse is believed to have begun its formal existence with the decision of the Church Council of Vienne in 1312 to found a series of chairs in Arabic, Greek, Hebrew and Syriac at Oxford, Paris, Bologna, Avignon and Salamanca[39]

and authors such as Sir John Mandeville or Marco Polo stirred interest in what is now India and China as early as in the thirteenth and fourteenth centuries.

Not only did the geographical borders of the Orient thus significantly exceed the Islamicate world, but non-Islamicate elements also greatly inspired the Western imagination of the Orient.[40] For instance, and as Andrea Polaschegg demonstrates in her discussion of German Orientalism, the topos of the Orient as the cradle of humanity, that is, the Orient of antiquity rather than the increasingly Islamicate Orient, was prevalent up until the twentieth century.[41] For a long time, pharaonic Egypt, and also the Byzantine Empire, China and Japan were thus widely regarded as Oriental in the West; moreover, the Orient encompassed parts of Europe as eccentrically distributed as Andalusia, the Balkans or Sicily;[42] Vienna was regarded as the gateway not only to the geographical Orient, but also to Sigmund Freud's Orient of the unconscious.[43]

Up until the second half of the twentieth century, the conjoint weight of the constituents 'Arabs' and 'Muslims' in the Western imagination of the Orient was consequently much less prominent than today. Of course, Arabs informed representations of the Orient as influential as the *Arabian Nights* or the dangerous Saracen (a figure which originally designated Arabs living in the Western part of the Arabian Peninsula, but which acquired a *pars pro toto* meaning so as to signify 'Arab' or 'Mohammedan' more generally over time).[44] However, other configurations from areas which are now considered to be Islamicate featured more prominently. In addition to the Barbary pirate kidnapper, a recurring figure in the Mediterranean from the sixteenth to the nineteenth century,[45] the Ottoman Empire served as an important Oriental grid. In fact, from the beginning of the sixteenth century onwards, what is called the Near and Middle East today was part of the Ottoman Empire,[46] and Islam was mainly perceived as the religion of the Turks.[47] Although from the end of the eleventh to the thirteenth century, the Latin Church reacted to the spread of Islam in the region of today's Middle East by beginning the Crusades, the more direct encounters of the West with Islam happened in the context of the rise and fall of the Ottoman Empire. After the Turks won the Battle of Kosovo in 1389 and after Constantinople fell in 1453, Christianity lost its influence in Asia Minor and continued to feel threatened by the Ottoman Empire during the next two centuries:

> The gradual spread of Islam and the expansion of the Ottoman Empire threatened the West and Christianity even more ... The West became fearful of this encroachment, and to deal with it became a matter of urgent military necessity. Numerous city states (especially Venice) were actively involved in combating the Turks. By degrees the expansion ceased and over a period of some four hundred years or more the administration of the Empire became steadily more unwieldy, incompetent and corrupt. By the 18th century, travel through it, though often hazardous, became possible for the intrepid.[48]

In accordance with its long and varied history, the term 'Orient' has been ambivalent and subject to change from the very beginning.[49] Although it soon developed its own momentum as a proper name, the term's underlying Western-centric perspective had inscribed the construct with geo-discursive ambiguity from early on. While, during biblical times, the geographical reference to the Orient (from the Latin *oriens*: 'East', 'morning') was relatively unequivocal (it denoted the area lying east of the Holy Land), this deixis became blurred when the Christian-Occidental point of view wandered west. By the sixth century, Christianity had become the state religion in Rome and deictically shifted the area directly east of the Mediterranean into the Orient. At the same time, it preserved the biblical point of view and its specific deixis.[50] Nowadays, with the United States of America, Canada and Australia as important constituents of the global West, this early double perspective of the word 'Orient' has lost all deictic potential.

Although the great oscillation of the term 'Orient' remains inscribed in the contemporary construct of the Orient, in its everyday usage the term has undergone a decisive geo-discursive shift in meaning. Today, the Orient has become nearly synonymous with the Greater Middle East or the Islamicate Middle East and North Africa region.[51] Linguistically, this shift, which occurred mainly in the second half of the twentieth century, manifests as a tendency to denominate what used to be called the 'Near East' as the 'Middle East':

> What is now the Middle East, had, until the early twentieth century, been known to the West as the Near East, and before that, for much of the nineteenth century, it is probably true to say that the cities of Istanbul (Constantinople), Jerusalem and Cairo seemed more familiar to the British [and Western] public than they do today.[52]

As a result of limiting the mental map of the Orient to Islamicate societies in the Middle East and North Africa region, the former has come to be almost completely identified with Islam, the most rapidly growing religion worldwide.[53] At the same time, the Islamicate world is often conflated with the so-called Arab world. As a consequence of this conflation, the difference between the signifiers 'Muslim' and 'Arab' is unbeknownst to many in the West, and the great diversity of Islamicate communities all around the globe is drastically reduced and homogenised.[54]

Securitisation and Othering

Bin Laden, beards, bombs and burkas, the so-called refugee crisis, the rise of the self-proclaimed Islamic State and terrorism – in the last two decades, the Islamicate world has been presented mainly in terms of gender inequality, backwardness, fanaticism, threat and terrorism. With bestsellers such as Bernard Lewis' *What Went Wrong? The Clash between Islam and Modernity in the Middle East* (2002)[55] or *The Crisis of Islam: Holy War and Unholy Terror* (2004),[56] their author's '(in)famous exhortation that Islam is a failed civilization'[57] and a threat to the rest of the world is endlessly reiterated – not least in the form of Samuel Huntington's argument of a 'clash of civilizations'.[58] At the institutional level, this discourse of fear finds expression in the rise of right-wing extremist organisations and political parties in numerous Western countries.

In view of such developments, stating that Islam has become a politicised issue is an understatement. Rather, it is a case of instrumentalised fear – or securitisation, as this process is called in international relations and security studies. Securitisation is an extreme form of politicisation which is used to justify extraordinary measures in the name of security.[59] As a constructivist concept, securitisation – instead of focusing on material givens or the allegedly objective existence of imminent danger – describes the ways in which issues are successfully declared as existential threats.[60] First developed by the Copenhagen School around Barry Buzan, Ole Wæver and Jaap de Wilde, the concept of securitisation attracted great attention when it was introduced in 1998. Especially since the end of the Cold War and the start of the so-called War on Terror, 'interest in how political elites and other actors construct security threats and justify coercive measures abroad and at home'[61] has grown substantially, and the concept of securitisation has continued to provide the theoretical underpinnings to many of these discussions up to today.

Despite this strong interest in matters of security, however, most Western discussions of security remain limited to hegemonic and ahistorical analyses of a defence against terrorism and immigration.[62] As a consequence, the creation of difference and processes of Othering on which securitisation relies as well as their deleterious effects on those who are securitised mostly remain unmentioned. In fact, although receiving considerably less attention than terrorist attacks in Western cities, examples such as the curtailment of rights for Muslims in Western Europe,[63] the torture in Abu Ghraib and anti-Muslim attacks in numerous Western cities critically illustrate that '[t]he securitised subject is, of course, anything but secure …'[64]

Neo-Orientalism and the Economy of Insecurity

Without the ongoing profound changes in the economy of insecurity, the functions of securitisation are hard to fathom. Since the beginning of the twenty-first century, 'an era that has been marked by the US-led war on terror and the emergence of security as the *raison d'état*',[65] security has become the dominant political principle. According to Giorgio Agamben, it has become so established in Western political discourse that security reasons have replaced reasons of State.[66] Nonetheless, security nowadays features mainly as a visible absence: in the modern-day security state, the relationship between fear and the state, as described by Thomas Hobbes in his social contract theory, has been reversed. Hobbes designates the state as the instance which ends what he calls the state of nature, that is, a situation allegedly characterised by fear and the war of all against all.[67] According to this view, the state is the only option with which to achieve security. In the present day, however, because fear functions as their prime legitimation, many neo-liberal states have a vital interest in upholding a permanent sense of insecurity. They do so, for instance, by means of declaring a state of emergency or by redirecting fears stemming from the disintegration of social security through the securitisation of certain collective identities. The aim of these measures is not to increase security but, in contrast, to instrumentalise fear in a way which benefits the government.[68]

Thus, harnessing fear, the security state does not only instrumentalise insecurity, but it also exacerbates insecurity. Although paradoxical at first sight, the security state's reaction to perceived external threats to so-called Western values in fact often consists of a progressive internal erosion and self-restriction of the very democratic liberties purportedly endangered by the perilous Other. While full-body scanners, video surveillance or telecommunications data retention are examples of how the logic of the security state operates at the cost of civil liberties and rights, the case of France illustrates how considerable elements of its emergency measures – such as the 'near absence of the judiciary and the lack of tangible evidence required in police decision-making'[69] – have been transformed into ordinary law. In the name of security, the security state thus endangers civil liberties such as the presumption of innocence. At the same time, it neglects other, less readily instrumentalised and less easily solvable potential risks such as climate change or the risk of a nuclear disaster.⁷⁰ In short, infringing on civil rights while ignoring other potential risks, the security state does the opposite of what it promises to do – and capitalises on it.⁷¹

In this economy of insecurity, securitisation functions as a

> conjurer's trick, calculated to be just that; it consists in shifting anxiety from problems that governments are incapable of handling (or are not keen on trying to handle) to problems that governments can be seen – daily and on thousands of screens – to be eagerly and (sometimes) successfully tackling.⁷²

In particular, securitisation often serves to project fears stemming from internal systemic problems onto the allegedly problematic and dangerous Other. During the so-called refugee crisis in 2015, this translation of fear became particularly visible. According to Zygmunt Bauman,

> [c]apitalizing on the anxiety caused by the influx of strangers – who, it is feared, will push down further the wages and the salaries that already refuse to grow, and lengthen yet more the already abominably long queues of people lining up (to no effect) for the stubbornly scarce jobs – is a temptation which very few politicians already in office, or aspiring to an office, would be able to resist.⁷³

Transforming the fear of social decline into figurations of the securitised Other, the securitisation of refugees illustrates how an economy of insecurity is created in which the framing of Islamicate alterity as threatening the population both from without and from within fulfils a biopolitical function: securitised figurations of potential sexual offenders, terrorists or high-birthrate immigrant families said to endanger the so-called natural population facilitate 'the production of a biopolitical body …'⁷⁴ While neglecting the extreme distress of those whom it excludes from the realm of security, the production of this biopolitical body can then be instrumentalised in culturalised discourse about the alleged clash of civilisations.

As a means of delineating alleged 'core cultures' against the foil of the Other, such culturalised discourse serves to create appearances of social cohesion in what in fact are societies inwardly torn by inequality. Especially in societies without much socio-economic justice and security in its wider – social – sense,⁷⁵ one deprived group can easily be played off against the other.

Due to the ongoing deregulation of increasingly globalised labour markets, the '"flexibilization" of work' and the resulting 'growing fragility of social positions and instability of socially recognized identities', as well as because of the 'unstoppable expansion of the ranks of the precariat', '[t]he widespread sense of existential insecurity is a hard fact …'[76] This, in turn, facilitates the mistrust against potential rivals for increasingly scarce social standing and security.[77] Ambalavaner Sivanandan calls this entanglement 'xenoracism', a kind of racism which is no longer merely 'colour-coded', so that it

> is not just directed at those with darker skins, from the former colonial territories, but at the newer categories of the displaced, the dispossessed and the uprooted, who are beating at western Europe's doors, the Europe that helped to displace them in the first place.[78]

It is against this backdrop of downward mobility and xenoracism that the securitisation and racialisation of the Islamicate Other have become so influential.

While issues such as the unemployment or poverty of refugees or immigrants from Islamicate countries are often read exclusively through the cultural lens,[79] the connections between racism, discrimination and exploitation in the capitalist system are, in contrast, discounted in many explanations of social problems. As, however, '[r]acism has always been an instrument of discrimination … [a]nd discrimination has always been a tool of exploitation',[80] the culturalisation and securitisation of Muslims must be considered in the context of the capitalist system:

> Racism, in that sense, has always been rooted in the economic compulsions of the capitalist system. But it manifests itself, first and foremost, as a cultural phenomenon, susceptible to cultural solutions such as multicultural education and the promotion of ethnic identities. Redressing the problem of cultural inequality, however, does not by itself redress the problem of economic inequality. Racism needs to be tackled at both levels – the cultural and the economic – at once, remembering that the one provides the rationale for the other. Racism, in sum, is conditioned by economic imperatives, but negotiated through cultural agency: religion, literature, art, science, the media and so on.[81]

In the greater context of the neo-liberal system, securitisation thus is not only attendant on a pronounced emphasis on identity politics, which activates diversity as an economic resource while obfuscating inequality,[82] but it also relies on a pronounced culturalised Othering. Projected onto the Other, the reasons for well-founded fears of social decline are consequently left unchanged. As a result, the insecurity of those most affected by social inequality is exacerbated, and – what is more and as the rise in anti-Muslim racism illustrates – the processes of Othering and racialisation on which securitisation relies also endanger those who are construed as a threat.

Neo-Orientalism and Anti-Muslim Racism

To state that 'Islamophobia' has become a buzzword is hardly an exaggeration. Not only does it (or related terms such as anti-Muslim racism, Muslimophobia, anti-Muslim prejudice, anti-Islamism, anti-Muslimism and so forth) continually reappear in public discourse, but research on the topic and discussions about the appropriateness of its terminology abound as well. Coined in 1922 by Orientalist Etienne Dinet in *L'Orient vu de l'Occident*,[83] Islamophobia, probably the term most frequently used in the English-speaking world to denote the phenomenon, gained momentum at the end of the 1980s and the beginning of the 1990s. In its modern political context, it was first employed in the American magazine *Insight* in 1991. From there, it found its way into the international debate.[84] In 1997, the Runnymede Trust Commission on British Muslims and Islamophobia provided the first – albeit controversial – definition of the term.[85] The report argues that, although not ideal, the word Islamophobia

> is a useful shorthand way of referring to dread or hatred of Islam – and, therefore, to fear or dislike of all or most Muslims. Such dread and dislike have existed in western countries and cultures for several centuries. In the last twenty years, however, the dislike has become more explicit, more extreme and more dangerous.[86]

This initial attempt at a definition has decisively influenced a debate on the nomenclature which is still raging today. While the *Oxford English Dictionary* defines Islamophobia as the '[i]ntense dislike or fear of Islam, esp. as a political force; hostility or prejudice towards Muslims',[87] Jocelyne Cesari describes it as denoting 'a modern and secular anti-Islamic discourse and practice appearing in the public sphere with the integration of Muslim immigrant communities and intensifying after 9/11'.[88]

Whereas Islamophobia is a widespread phenomenon, the term itself thus remains highly contested. Conflating Muslims and Islam, the first component of the word, 'Islam(o)', triggers debate because it presents the religion (and not its followers) as the object of fear and discrimination.[89] Due to its Greek component stem 'phobia' (denoting 'fear'), Islamophobia is, moreover, reminiscent both of social phenomena such as homophobia or xenophobia and of psychological anxiety disorders.[90] However, the implication of irrational fear which is carried by the component 'phobia'[91] is often criticised or dismissed altogether:[92]

> Islamophobia is also not a phobia in the clinical psychology sense of an individual anxiety disorder, but rather, the suffix [sic] 'phobia' is used in the same way as xenophobia and homophobia 'to connote socially, culturally and politically produced prejudice, aversions and discrimination against specific [socially constructed] categories of humans, in this case Muslims'.[93]

Without achieving complete congruence, phenomena identified as Islamophobia often significantly overlap with general racism. In fact, they are so intricately interwoven with other forms of racism that sometimes resentment against people who appear to be Muslim seems to have become a racist proxy discourse,[94] a form of socially accepted racism in times when other forms of racism have become more latent. In Edward Said's words,

> [t]here also seems to have been a strange revival of canonical, though previously discredited, Orientalist ideas about Muslim, generally non-white, people – ideas which have achieved a startling prominence at a time when racial or religious misrepresentations of every other cultural group are no longer circulated with such impunity. Malicious generalizations about Islam have become the last acceptable form of denigration of foreign culture in the West …[95]

In empirical studies designed to gather reliable data on discrimination specifically against Muslims, the conflation of general racism and resentment against Muslims poses a considerable problem.[96] It is difficult to extrapolate what kinds of prejudice are directed at somebody for simply being a follower of Islam, and what discrimination stems from the association of Islam as a presumably non-white religion: while a so-called white convert is likely to be treated differently from a (supposed) so-called non-white Muslim, a non-white Christian might experience similar resentment as a non-white Muslim.[97]

As a consequence, although it is often argued that – as Islam is not a race, but a religion – discrimination against Muslims cannot be categorised as racism, Islam and mostly non-white traits remain conflated. Muslims or people considered to be Muslim are thus often racialised to an extent which makes it difficult to substantiate the assertion 'that being Muslim is a voluntary choice and therefore not deserving of the same protection as involuntary identities'.[98] Examples such as the death of Brazilian Jean Charles de Menezes, killed on 22 July 2005 by London police after being misidentified as one of the fugitives responsible for the failed 21 July 2005 London bombings,[99] tragically illustrate this associative conflation of outward appearance, assumed Muslim faith and – in this case – terrorism.

Moreover, such a distinction between voluntary and involuntary identities neglects the fact that construction of difference is always based on arbitrary markers which are charged with social relevance. As the distinction between voluntary versus involuntary identities is often said to have become obsolete in the second half of the twentieth century,[100] nowadays, there is a 'common demarcation between so-called "old" biological and "new" cultural racism',[101] in which 'cultural characteristics tend to *replace* biological features and operate in the same essentialised way'.[102] According to this distinction, racism is no longer seen as discrimination based on supposed racial attribution, but as the construction of socially relevant characteristics as markers of difference. As opposed to earlier forms of racism resting on allegedly biological features, these characteristics are often linked with the alleged cultural shortcomings of those who are Othered. While the focus on racial versus cultural markers of difference on which this distinction relies might indeed be pertinent, what such a differentiation underemphasises is the fact that forms of biological racism also always rely on racialisation, that is, the construction of difference along arbitrary markers.[103]

Because of the intersection between general racism and discrimination against Muslims, because of the difficulties inherent in the term 'Islamophobia' and in order to highlight the process of racialisation, the term 'anti-Muslim racism' will be used in this book to denote discrimination against people who come from or are considered to have a Muslim background.[104] Following research on cultural racism in the tradition of Frantz Fanon and Stuart Hall, the term 'anti-Muslim racism' places special emphasis on the *process* of how a Muslim is constructed as the Other, that is, on the process of racialisation.[105] By underlining the process of racialisation, the term 'anti-Muslim racism' helps to clarify that both 'old' and 'new' forms of racism are not directed against a group already given: it is only through the process of racialisation that racism constructs its object and that these constructions become social reality.[106] Instead of focusing on the fear of something assumed to be a given (as implied by the terms 'Islamophobia' and 'Muslimophobia'), the term thus helps to analyse how Muslims or people considered to be Muslim become the Other, and, as such, a potential object of fear.

Framing Islam

Discussions about anti-Muslim racism often become particularly fierce once they become self-reflective. According to Floris Biskamp, controversies about how to speak about Islam are marked by such stridency because they are frequently characterised by both anti-democratic interpretations of Islam and anti-democratic ways of speaking about Islam.[107] As a consequence, it is often difficult to identify where a legitimate critique of anti-egalitarian religious positions in some interpretations of Islam ends and where both the immunisation of a necessary religious critique and an anti-democratic stigmatisation of Islam and Muslims begins.[108] When addressing the question of *how to talk about* Islam, discussions about anti-Muslim racism thus frequently end in a quandary with two irreconcilable positions: while one camp accuses the other of racism disguised as religious criticism, the second camp denounces the first as naïve apologists of religious fanaticism and as traitors to democracy and Enlightenment values who wrongly accuse them of racism. Accordingly, what the first camp calls anti-Muslim racism or Islamophobia, the second declares to be justified criticism of Islam.[109]

The debate around homonationalism,[110] that is, the co-optation of originally liberal (in this case pro-LGBTIQ) arguments now instrumentalised for illiberal causes, serves as a case in point here. Arguments initially employed in the name of inclusion and equality are now used to foster a new binary which plays off a more liberal stance towards LGBTIQ subjectivities against an allegedly homophobic Islamicate stance. A similar co-optation of liberal arguments for illiberal causes can be observed in the case of women's rights, when traditionally conservative politicians with little to no interest in questions of gender equality opportunistically present themselves as a bastion against allegedly misogynist Arabs and Muslims.[111] Not only do such ambivalent positions help to spread anti-Muslim or nationalist thinking in circles previously rather averse to exclusive reasoning, but they also stand in the way of a more differentiated assessment of possible gender injustice on both sides of the divide.

As these examples illustrate, the dilemma of speaking about anti-Muslim racism often lies in the reductionist and opportunistic framing of certain topics as specifically Muslim issues.[112] This holds true not only for derogatory or hostile depictions of Muslims. As a social interaction, anti-Muslim racism begins much earlier: if a range of topics is increasingly discussed in a Muslim context and through a culturalised lens whereas other explanatory social factors are ignored, the division between Muslim and non-Muslim gains more and more importance. In fact, the problems of anti-Muslim racism do not just begin when explicitly hostile and deprecating positions against Muslims are voiced, but they are already present if different issues are increasingly discussed as 'Islamic' issues, if the differentiation between Muslim and non-Muslim gains more and more social relevance, if being Muslim becomes a decisive marker of difference, and when – in the process of full identification[113] – (supposed) Muslims are addressed primarily as Muslims.[114]

Besides the manifest denigration and securitisation of the Islamicate Other, it is thus also this process of full identification which determines the homogenising epistemic violence of Neo-Orientalist frames. In order to explore the intricacies of *how* – in what frames and through what narrative and aesthetic means – these complementary forms of epistemic violence are transported and rendered more socially acceptable, this book sets out to analyse the poetics of one form of Neo-Orientalism with both a high symbolic capital and great imaginative power – literary Neo-Orientalism.

Literary Neo-Orientalism

Conflating beards, bombs, burkas and belly dancing as well as oscillating between securitisation and exoticism, Western fiction continues to allot an uneasy, multilayered and often fallacious position to the Islamicate Other. Reductionist literary figurations such as the bearded bomber, the burka'ed woman,[115] the jihadi bride, the sexually aggressive Muslim refugee, the radicalised Islamist criminal or the Islamist Rage Boy do not only break down sociopolitical and socio-economic complexities,[116] but they also follow a decidedly Western-centric and ahistorical logic. As narrative figurations, they embody and simplify numerous superimposed elements of broader societal discourses – such as classical Orientalism, the Huntingtonian theory of the alleged clash of civilisations, post-9/11 Neo-Orientalism and securitisation. If, at least on the surface, these processes become more fathomable when projected onto such generalised figurations of the Arab and Muslim, he or she – in a process developing its own momentum – is turned into the combined hotspot and principal bearer of a growing social angst.

If especially in eighteenth- and nineteenth-century Orientalism, danger was often aestheticised, in Neo-Orientalist fiction, the dangerous Other is both aestheticised and securitised. As a result, literary Neo-Orientalism oscillates between the poles of insecurity and security as well as between the dangerous and the exotic-escapist. Thus, modulating the scales of security, Neo-Orientalist fiction ties in with the logic of the security state: in order to be effective, a Neo-Orientalist poetics of insecurity depends on the representation of alarming images.[117] At the same time, Neo-Orientalist texts rely on the recognition value of well-known representational structures of the Orientalised and securitised Other. Many narrative texts thus depict and address insecurity but, in their function of a domesticating form such as the novel or novella, they also provide a deceptive sense of security. Thus, like the security state which in fact also often brings forth the insecurity it alleges to alleviate, literary Neo-Orientalism promises security and reassurance in an economy of insecurity which it itself creates.

In this economy of insecurity, Neo-Orientalist fiction does not only create an affective distance from which the reader can safely process insecurity and fear through an aestheticised Othering, but through its aestheticised securitisation of the Islamicate Other, Neo-Orientalist texts also contribute to a proxy discourse which thwarts the broader contextualisation and differentiation of social fears and instead coalesces them in figurations of the Other. On the surface, this projection of fears onto the Other by means of naturalised tropes provides some reassurance. However, this circular corroboration of certain clichés hinders the solution of the actual conflicts informing the stereotypes. In fact, when feeding on or transforming existing social problems such as social inequality and the widespread fear of social decline into a socially acceptable Orientalising poetics, Neo-Orientalist fiction works along the logic of the state of exception as a permanent mechanism of government in the security state. Instead of creating order, disorder is managed,[118] and – in the case of Neo-Orientalist fiction – brought into a marketable form: through an often-voyeuristic exhibition of sex and violence, literary Neo-Orientalism caters to the dominant sales logic of the Western literary market, and it interacts with social preferences for stressing culturalised differences. Despite the opportunity of polyphony which especially the form of the novel offers, Neo-Orientalist fiction thus stylises the Islamicate Other mainly as a danger to the so-called Western way of life – while it leaves the existential insecurity from which those who are securitised suffer mostly unmentioned.

Literary Neo-Orientalism and the Arab Uprisings

When critically examining literary Neo-Orientalism, fiction about the Arab uprisings is promising in several regards. This pertains, firstly, to the level of content. Because of the tension between the initially optimistic reception and the ensuing Neo-Orientalist appropriation of the so-called Arab Spring, fiction about the uprisings is more likely to include differentiated or subversive forms of representation than, for instance, portrayals of Islamist terrorism. While the aesthetics, reception and marketing of novels such as Michel Houellebecq's *Soumission* (2015; *Submission*)[119] also constitute interesting cases in the analysis of the relationship between literature, Orientalism and securitisation, because of the greater probability of also finding examples of literary desecuritisation in depictions of the Arab uprisings, these are more expedient to explore the aesthetic bounds of Neo-Orientalism. Secondly, in their aesthetic dimension, literary adaptations of the uprisings could be a realm where Neo-Orientalist dichotomies are transcended. As fiction does not only reflect, interact with and shape social reality, but can also conjure up possible worlds, it has the potential of creating a new, post-Orientalist imaginary which overcomes binary distinctions between the West and the Middle East and North Africa region.

This transformative potential of literature, however, is confronted with the immense pressure of the literary market and its dominant sales logic. The following chapters will show that while the demands of the literary market indicate an interest in books which can be marketed as open-minded cosmopolitan literature, below the surface Neo-Orientalism takes a subtle but pernicious form even in books published by respected Western presses. In fact, in the guise of seemingly tolerant literature, literary Neo-Orientalism reiterates and provides an imaginary which purports to overcome itself, but which instead further inscribes itself in two complementary strands. In the first strand, depictions of the so-called Arab Spring – even if in an often ironised form – continue to draw on a repertoire of Orientalist narrative strategies. Following the trodden path of convention, these strategies project the Islamicate Other as allegedly affect-driven, prone to violence, lust and passivity, backward as well as incapable of establishing democracy or rule of law. The second strand is based on the first but has a stronger focus on issues of insecurity. This strand feeds on the spread of anti-Muslim racism and on the securitisation of people from an Islamicate background, that is, on their representation as an existential threat to the West. Thus, fuelled by a perceived threat of terrorism or of an alleged cultural alienation due to immigration, Neo-Orientalism translates insecurity into a poetics which oscillates between marketability, convention and affect. Even in representations of the Arab uprisings, Neo-Orientalist writing thus constitutes an ambivalent and profitable gamble with fear.

Against this backdrop, this book presents an analysis of English, French and German language fiction about the so-called Arab Spring, and an examination of the role which the literary market plays in constructing, aestheticising and marketing mental boundaries between the Islamicate world and the West. Through a transnational reading of a wide range of authors from different backgrounds, both non-diasporic and diasporic, the following chapters investigate the commercialisation of Neo-Orientalist and securitised elements in short fiction and novels aimed at the Western literary market

(2011–15). In a comparatist fashion, three analytical chapters juxtapose two texts each. Emerging from the corpus itself, three influential facets of Western securitisation – precarity, affective masculinity and terror – are at the core of these chapters. Their common focus on precarity notwithstanding, Tahar Ben Jelloun's *Par le feu* (2011) and Jonas Lüscher's *Frühling der Barbaren* (2013) feature diametrically opposed approaches of representing the Arab uprisings. While *Par le feu* relies on a frame of distance and difference which reductively portrays Tunisia as a representative of the countries involved in the Arab uprisings, *Frühling der Barbaren* depicts Tunisia as an interdependent part of the global capitalist world. Thereby, the novella does not only dissolve Orientalist synecdoche into glocal metonymy, but it also deconstructs the notion of the Orient as a separate geographical entity. Both Adam Thirlwell's *Kapow!* (2012) and Jochen Beyse's *Rebellion: Zwischenbericht* (2013) foreground the aspect of affective masculinity. Not only do they demonstrate how it is Orientalised, but by means of irony, intertextuality and a pronounced metafictional level, both books try to deconstruct the Western fixation with the allegedly affect-driven and violent Muslim man. As their irony of reversal, however, provides little more than a mirror image of what they try to overcome, it does not suffice to transcend the very epistemic dichotomies which it tries to subvert. *Book of Sands* (2015) by Karim Alrawi and *Rue des voleurs* (2012) by Mathias Énard share marked similarities in their constellation of characters to negotiate the Arab uprisings and the danger of Islamist radicalisation. Both books establish a pronounced antithesis which invites understanding for the protagonists but leaves unexplored the motives of their strikingly similar deuteragonists. These Islamist Rage Boys are presented in frames of difference, distance and danger which rely on animal and fire imagery and on the use of increasing use of words in Arabic from the semantic fields of danger and violence.

By complementing the close readings with approaches from the social sciences, the following chapters engage in an analysis of both the poetics and the sociopolitical functions of Neo-Orientalism. Not only do they thus carve out recurring tropes, frames and figurations which are complicit in rendering Neo-Orientalist and anti-Muslim imagery more socially acceptable, but they also demonstrate how influential frames of insecurity – precarity, affective masculinity and terror – refract the adverse psychosocial consequences of the neo-liberal project into a securitisation of the Other. Retracing how economic and political problems are culturalised into questions of race and gender, this study consequently offers a reversal of perspectives which raises awareness for the insecurity of the securitised.

Despite the relatively high number of English, French and German language novels about the Arab uprisings, there is little secondary literature on the individual texts and no comparative study on them yet. This book not only contributes to discussions of the role of security in literary studies, but it also seeks to close a gap regarding the critical reception of fictionalisations of the Arab uprisings on the Western literary market. My perspective is governed by an expertise in these literatures, English, French and German. I do reflect on literary representations of the Arab uprisings from the respective countries themselves, while recognising my scholarly limitations: this offers an opportunity also to consider my own limited and Eurocentric perspective, a particular vantage point from which to offer a critical view on authors who are often marketed as area experts on the Middle East and North Africa region.

Notes

1. Salman Rushdie [2015]. *Two Years Eight Months & Twenty-Eight Nights*. London: Vintage, 2016. 213–14. Italics in the original.
2. The term 'Islamicate' was introduced by Marshall G. S. Hodgson in his *The Venture of Islam* (1974) to differentiate between the spheres of the religious and the non-religious. While Hodgson uses the term 'Islamic' to designate the former, he coined the term 'Islamicate' to refer 'not directly to the religion, Islam, itself, but to the social and cultural complex historically associated with Islam and the Muslims, both among Muslims themselves and even when found among non-Muslims' (Marshall G. S. Hodgson. *The Venture of Islam: Conscience and History in a World Civilization Vol. 1: The Classical Age of Islam*. Chicago: University of Chicago Press, 1974. 59). Following broader and more recent understandings of the term, this study uses the term 'Islamicate' to refer to both associations with and hybrid spaces in Muslim-majority societies and diasporic Muslim communities, that is, to signal 'the hybrid trace rather than pure presence or absence of Islam' (Srinivas Aravamudan. 'East-West Fiction as World Literature: The *Hayy* Problem Reconfigured'. *Eighteenth-Century Studies* 47.2 (2014): 195–231. 198). See also Siavash Saffari et al., eds. *Unsettling Colonial Modernity in Islamicate Contexts*. Newcastle upon Tyne: Cambridge

Scholars Publishing, 2017. 1–2; Markus Dressler et al. 'Islamicate Secularities: New Perspectives on a Contested Concept'. *Historical Social Research* 44.3 (2019): 7–34. 12–13.

3. Hamid Dabashi. *The Arab Spring: The End of Postcolonialism?* London and New York: Zed Books, 2012. 65.
4. El-Sayed el-Aswad. 'Images of Muslims in Western Scholarship and Media after 9/11'. *Digest of Middle East Studies* 22.1 (2013): 39–56. 39.
5. Peter Morey and Amina Yaqin. *Framing Muslims: Stereotyping and Representation after 9/11*. Cambridge, MA: Harvard University Press, 2011. 1.
6. For other definitions of Neo-Orientalism which appeared prior to this one or have been published after the time of writing, see, for instance, Ali Behdad and Juliet Williams. 'Neo-Orientalism'. *Globalizing American Studies*. Eds Brian T. Edwards and Gaonkar Dilip Parameshwar. Chicago: University of Chicago Press, 2010. 283–99, and Peter Morey. 'Applications of Neo-Orientalism and Islamophobia in Recent Writing'. *Orientalism and Literature*. Ed. Geoffrey P. Nash. Cambridge: Cambridge University Press, 2019. 269–85. 270.
7. Peter Morey and Amina Yaqin. 2011. 1.
8. See, for instance, Rana Kabbani. *Imperial Fictions: Europe's Myths of Orient*. London, San Francisco and Beirut: SAQI, 2008. 35–40.
9. For one of many discussions of the securitisation of Islam in Western Europe, see, for instance, June Edmunds. 'The "New" Barbarians: Governmentality, Securitization and Islam in Western Europe'. *Contemporary Islam* 6.1 (2012): 67–84.
10. Mahmut Mutman. 'From Orientalism to Islamophobia'. *Orientalism and Literature*. Ed. Geoffrey P. Nash. Cambridge: Cambridge University Press, 2019. 255–68. 256; Mohammed Samiei. 'Neo-Orientalism? The Relationship Between the West and Islam in Our Globalised World'. *Third World Quarterly* 31.7 (2010): 1145–60. 1152.
11. Sama Maani. 'Warum wir Linken über den Islam nicht reden können'. *Der Standard*. 10 January 2017 (website – last accessed 3 January 2020); Floris Biskamp. *Orientalismus und demokratische Öffentlichkeit: Antimuslimischer Rassismus aus Sicht postkolonialer und neuerer kritischer Theorie*. Bielefeld: Transcript, 2016. 63.
12. Mubarak Altwaiji. 'Neo-Orientalism and the Neo-Imperialism Thesis: Post-9/11 US and Arab World Relationship'. *Arab Studies Quarterly* 36.4 (2014): 313–23. 313.

13. Ali Behdad and Juliet Williams. 2010. 284–5. Lisa Lau calls this form of Orientalism 'Re-Orientalism'. Lisa Lau. 'Re-Orientalism: The Perpetration and Development of Orientalism by Orientals'. *Modern Asian Studies* 43.2 (2009): 571–90.
14. For the role of securitisation for those securitised, see, for instance, Marc Botha. 'Toward a Critical Poetics of Securitization: A Response to Anker, Castronovo, Harkins, Masterson, and Williams'. *American Literary History* 28.4 (2016): 779–86. 783.
15. Mustapha Marrouchi. 'Willed from the Bottom Up: The Postcolonial Turned Revolutionary'. *The Journal of North African Studies* 18.3 (2013): 387–401. 390.
16. Oliver Nachtwey. 'Transnationale Protestbewegungen in der Abstiegsgesellschaft – die Occupy-Proteste in Deutschland'. *Working Paper der DFG-KollegforscherInnengruppe Postwachstumsgesellschaften* 4 (2014): 1.
17. Mustapha Marrouchi. 2013. 394.
18. Joseph E. Stiglitz. 'The 99 Percent Wakes Up'. *The Daily Beast*. 5 February 2012 (website – last accessed 2 February 2015). Excerpt originally published in *From Cairo to Wall Street: Voices from the Global Spring*. New York: The New Press, 2012.
19. Hamid Dabashi. 2012; Slavoj Žižek. *The Year of Dreaming Dangerously*. London and New York: Verso, 2012.
20. Slavoj Žižek. 2012.
21. Hamid Dabashi. 2012. 252.
22. Ibid. 15.
23. Lorella Ventura. 'The "Arab Spring" and Orientalist Stereotypes: The Role of Orientalism in the Narration of the Revolts in the Arab World'. *Interventions* 19.2 (2017): 282–97; Stefan Borg. 'The Arab Uprisings, the Liberal Civilizing Narrative and the Problem of Orientalism'. *Middle East Critique* 25.3 (2016): 211–27.
24. Julia Gerlach. *Der verpasste Frühling: Woran die Arabellion gescheitert ist*. Bonn: Bundeszentrale für politische Bildung, 2016. 14.
25. Corinna Mullin and Brahim Rouabah. 'Requiem for Tunisia's Revolution?' *Jadaliyya*. 22 December 2014 (website – last accessed 2 February 2015).
26. Marc Botha. 2016. 783.
27. Edward W. Said. *Orientalism* [1978]. Ed. with new Afterword and Preface. London: Penguin, 2003. 2.
28. Ibid. 6.

29. See, for instance, Peter Morey and Amina Yaqin. 2011. 1–3; Lorella Ventura. 2017. 282–97; Stefan Borg. 2016. 211–27; el-Sayed el-Aswad. 2013. 39; Hamid Dabashi. *Post-Orientalism: Knowledge and Power in Time of Terror*. New Brunswick, NJ and London: Transaction, 2009. 21.
30. Although this mention has become almost commonplace, Said's critique of Orientalism ranks among the most cited pieces of literary criticism and is frequently considered as the founding document of postcolonial studies. At the same time, there have been massive attacks on *Orientalism*'s methodological soundness, especially on its oscillation between humanist and poststructuralist readings and their contradictory notions of truth, on its limited or false understanding of the Foucauldian notion of discourse, or on its narrow focus on the established literary canons of the late eighteenth and nineteenth century. The main criticism levelled at *Orientalism*, however, is that although it might be right in identifying the Orient as a construction imagined by the West, the study reduces the Oriental to his or her role within the framework of Orientalist discourse (Daniel Martin Varisco. *Reading Orientalism: Said and the Unsaid*. Seattle and London: University of Washington Press, 2007. 3–28, xii). As Orientalism could consequently also be said to perpetuate the dichotomy it criticises by sketching a simplified unidirectional exchange between Orient and Occident, the lack of agential space for those Orientalised is another point of criticism (Birte Heidemann. '"We Are the Glue Keeping the Civilization Together": Post-Orientalism and Counter-Orientalism in H. M. Naqvi's *Home Boy*'. *Journal of Postcolonial Writing* 48.3 (2012): 289–98. 297).
31. Deepa Kumar. 'Framing Islam: The Resurgence of Orientalism during the Bush II Era'. *Journal of Communication Inquiry* 34.3 (2010): 254–77. 267.
32. Ibid. 267.
33. Ibid. 254.
34. Tariq Amin-Khan. 'New Orientalism, Securitisation and the Western Media's Incendiary Racism'. *Third World Quarterly* 33.9 (2012): 1595–610. 1597.
35. Ibid. 1596. In North American contributions about current forms of Orientalism, it has become common to speak of 'New Orientalism' rather than 'Neo-Orientalism'. This book uses the latter term: firstly, it expresses the continuities between Orientalism today and classical Orientalism – which are of great significance for the poetics in fictional texts – much better than 'New Orientalism', which is often associated with too smooth a 'transition between (old, literary) Orientalism and new Orientalism since 9/11'.

(Kenichi Yamaguchi. 'Rationalization and Concealment of Violence in American Responses to 9/11: Orientalism(s) in a State of Exception'. *Journal of Postcolonial Writing* 48.3 (2012): 241–51. 242.) Secondly, the term 'Neo-Orientalism' paradigmatically aligns this resurgence of an old discourse in its updated version into its greater social context, which is determined by other 'neo-isms', such as neo-liberalism and all its repercussions.

36. The following line of thought is taken from Andrea Polaschegg. *Der andere Orientalismus: Regeln deutsch-morgenländischer Imagination im 19. Jahrhundert.* Berlin and New York: Walter de Gruyter, 2005. 63–101.
37. Edward W. Said. 2003. 4.
38. Ibid. 17.
39. J. A. Cuddon. 'Orientalism'. *Dictionary of Literary Terms & Literary Theory.* 3rd edn. London et al.: Penguin, 1999. 618–22. 619.
40. Andrea Polaschegg. 2005. 97.
41. Ibid. 82.
42. Ibid. 73.
43. Heinz Hiebler. *Hugo von Hofmannsthal und die Medienkultur der Moderne.* Würzburg: Königshausen & Neumann, 2003. 168.
44. Andrea Polaschegg. 2005. 74.
45. Ibid. 74.
46. Ibid. 79–80.
47. Ibid. 88.
48. J. A. Cuddon. 'Orientalism'. 1999. 620.
49. See Andrea Polaschegg. 2005. 63–101.
50. Ibid. 66.
51. El-Sayed el-Aswad. 2013. 40.
52. Nicholas Tromans. 'Introduction'. *The Lure of the East: British Orientalist Painting.* Ed. Nicholas Tromans. New Haven: Yale University Press, 2008. 10–21. 10.
53. Mubarak Altwaiji. 2014. 316.
54. For one attempt at explaining this difference, see for instance Haroon Moghul. 'Why Arab and Muslim Are Not Synonymous'. *The Huffington Post.* 10 November 2010 (website – last accessed 13 February 2017). The widely used expression 'Arab and Muslim world' does not only contain broad over-generalisations, but it is also ambiguous as to whether it designates the whole of the Arab world plus the whole of the Muslim world (both homogenisations by themselves), or whether only the area where both intersect is meant. In the first

case, the area referred to would again significantly exceed the Greater Middle Eastern associations of the word 'Orient', while in the second case, important countries also tightly connected with the construct of the Orient, for instance Iran, would be excluded.

55. Bernard Lewis. *What Went Wrong? The Clash between Islam and Modernity in the Middle East*. New York: Harper Perennial, 2002. Quoted in el-Sayed el-Aswad. 2013. 41.
56. Bernard Lewis. *The Crisis of Islam: Holy War and Unholy Terror*. London: Phoenix, 2004. Quoted in Mubarak Altwaiji. 2014. 318.
57. Pavan Kumar Malreddy. 'Introduction: Orientalism(s) after 9/11'. *Journal of Postcolonial Writing* 3 (2012): 233–40. 237.
58. For Bernard Lewis' mention of cultural 'clash', see Bernard Lewis. 'The Roots of Muslim Rage: Why So Many Muslims Deeply Resent the West, and Why Their Bitterness Will Not Easily Be Mollified'. *The Atlantic*. 1 September 1990 (website – last accessed 18 February 2015). Huntington adopted this idea from Bernard Lewis and propounded it in an even more acrid form in *The Clash of Civilizations and the Remaking of World Order*. New York: Simon & Schuster, 1996.
59. Barry Buzan, Ole Wæver and Jaap de Wilde: *Security: A New Framework for Analysis*. Boulder: Lynne Rienner, 1998.
60. Ibid. 32.
61. Scott D. Watson. '"Framing" the Copenhagen School: Integrating the Literature on Threat Construction'. *Millenium: Journal of International Studies* 40.2 (2012): 279–301. 279.
62. Tarak Barkawi and Mark Laffey. 'The Postcolonial Moment in Security Studies'. *Review of International Studies* 32 (2006): 329–52. 329. For further critiques of the hegemonic bias and blind spots in the process of securitisation, see also Sarah Bertrand. 'Can the Subaltern Securitize? Postcolonial Perspectives on Securitization Theory and Its Critics'. *European Journal of International Security* 3.3 (2018): 281–99; Lene Hansen. 'The Little Mermaid's Silent Security Dilemma and the Absence of Gender in the Copenhagen School'. *Millenium: Journal of International Studies* 29.2 (2000): 285–306; Mark Laffey and Suthaharan Nadarajah. 'Postcolonialism'. *Contemporary Security Studies*. Ed. Alan Collins. Oxford: Oxford University Press, 2016. 122–38.
63. June Edmunds. 2011. 67.
64. Marc Botha. 2016. 783.

65. Stephen Morton and Stephen Bygrave. 'Introduction'. *Foucault in an Age of Terror: Essays on Biopolitics and the Defence of Society*. Eds Stephen Morton and Stephen Bygrave. Basingstoke and New York: Palgrave Macmillan, 2008. 1–13. 1.
66. Giorgio Agamben. 'De l'État de droit à l'État de sécurité'. *Le Monde*. 23 December 2015 (website – last accessed 22 September 2017). The following line of thought is also by Agamben.
67. For a critique of the concept of the 'state of nature' and its colonialist implications, see Oliver Eberl. *Naturzustand und Barbarei: Begründung und Kritik staatlicher Ordnung im Zeichen des Kolonialismus*. Hamburg: Hamburger Edition, 2021.
68. Zygmunt Bauman. *Strangers at Our Door*. Cambridge: Polity Press, 2016. 17–18.
69. Anne-Sylvaine Chassany. 'France: The Permanent State of Emergency'. *Financial Times*. 2 October 2017 (website – last accessed 4 October 2017); 'Frankreich macht den Ausnahmezustand zum Gesetz'. *Deutsche Welle*. 3 October 2017 (website – last accessed 4 October 2017).
70. Ulrich Beck. *Risikogesellschaft: Auf dem Weg in eine andere Moderne*. Frankfurt: Suhrkamp, 1986. 9.
71. Giorgio Agamben. 2015.
72. Zygmunt Bauman. 2016. 30.
73. Ibid. 17–18.
74. Giorgio Agamben. *Homo Sacer: Sovereign Power and Bare Life*. Trans. Daniel Heller-Roazen. Stanford: Stanford University Press, 1998. 6.
75. For the relationship between fear and social status, see, for instance, Heinz Bude. *Gesellschaft der Angst*. Hamburg: Hamburger Edition, 2015; Oliver Nachtwey. *Die Abstiegsgesellschaft – Über das Aufbegehren in der regressiven Moderne*. Berlin: Suhrkamp, 2016.
76. Zygmunt Bauman. 2016. 29.
77. Ambalavaner Sivanandan. 'Poverty Is the New Black'. *Race & Class* 43.2 (2001): 1–5. 1.
78. Quoted in Kenichi Yamaguchi. 2012. 248.
79. Wolfgang Aschauer. 'Die Wahrnehmung von Umbrüchen, Ungleichheiten und Unsicherheiten als neue Erklärungsfaktoren der Fremden- und Islamfeindlichkeit in Europa'. *Identität und Inklusion im europäischen Sozialraum*. Eds Elisabeth Klaus et al. Wiesbaden: VS Verlag, 2010. 87–112. 104.
80. Ambalavaner Sivanandan. 2001. 1.

81. Ibid. 1.
82. Walter Benn Michaels. 'Let Them Eat Diversity: On the Politics of Identity'. Interview by Bhaskar Sunkara. *Jacobin*. 1 January 2011 (website – last accesssed 5 January 2021).
83. Jocelyne Cesari. *Securitization and Religious Divides in Europe: Muslims in Western Europe after 9/11: Why the Term Islamophobia is More a Predicament than an Explanation*. Submission to the Changing Landscape of Citizenship and Security – 6th PCRD of European Commission. Paris, 2006. 5.
84. Luzie H. Kahlweiß and Samuel Salzborn. '"Islamophobie" als politischer Kampfbegriff: Zur konzeptionellen und empirischen Kritik des Islamophobiebegriffs'. *Jahrbuch für Extremismus- und Terrorismusforschung 2011/2012* (II). Ed. Armin Pfahl-Traughber. Brühl: Fachhochschule des Bundes für öffentliche Verwaltung, 2012. 248–63. 253; Michail Loginov. 'Islamophobie, Islam- und Muslimfeindlichkeit: Versuch einer konsensfähigen Definition'. *forum kriminalprävention*. January 2016. 52.
85. Runnymede Trust. *Islamophobia: A Challenge for Us All*. London, 1997. The report bases its definition on the problematic binary distinction between eight 'closed' versus 'open views of Islam', such as, for instance, 1. 'Islam seen as a single monolithic bloc, static and unresponsive to new realities' versus 'Islam seen as diverse and progressive, with internal differences, debates and development', or 5. 'Islam seen as a political ideology, used for political or military advantage' versus 'Islam seen as a genuine religious faith, practised sincerely by its adherents' [quoted in the summary pdf of the report]. For a more detailed discussion of the report, see Floris Biskamp, 2016. 33–7.
86. Runnymede Trust. 1997. 1.
87. 'Islamophobia'. *Oxford English Dictionary*. No date (website – last accessed 28 August 2017).
88. Jocelyne Cesari. 2006. 5.
89. Sama Maani. 'Der Begriff Islamophobie. Interview mit Sama Maani'. Interview by Nikolai Schreiter and Nikola Staritz. *Malmoe*. 12 May 2015 (website – last accessed 25 November 2016); Jennifer E. Cheng. 'Islamophobia, Muslimophobia or Racism? Parliamentary Discourses on Islam and Muslims in Debates on the Minaret Ban in Switzerland'. *Discourse and Society* 26.5 (2015): 562–86. Accessed in web format with page numbers 1–15. 1–2.
90. Luzie H. Kahlweiß and Samuel Salzborn. 2012. 252.
91. Jocelyne Cesari. 2006. 6.
92. For instance, Sama Maani. 2015.

93. Jennifer E. Cheng. 2015. 3.
94. Sama Maani. 2015.
95. Edward W. Said [1981]. *Covering Islam: How the Media and the Experts Determine How We See the Rest of the World*. New York: Vintage, 1997. xi–xii.
96. Luzie H. Kahlweiß and Samuel Salzborn. 2012. 249; Floris Biskamp. 2016. 33–56.
97. Jennifer E. Cheng. 2015. 2; Sama Maani. 2015.
98. Jennifer E. Cheng, 2015. 2. Cheng simply points out this argument but argues against it; Sama Maani. 2015.
99. For an interesting short documentary on the death of Jean Charles de Menezes, see Kays Khalil's short film montage *Hit the Floor*. Fachhochschule Düsseldorf, 2006.
100. Floris Biskamp. 2016. 59.
101. Jennifer E. Cheng. 2015. 4.
102. Ibid. 4. Italics in the original.
103. Floris Biskamp, 2016. 58. Although mostly an extremely helpful figure of thought, this view can be criticised for negating the possible (pre-)existence of cultural differences altogether.
104. Floris Biskamp. 2016. Due to its broad perspective and theoretically founded approach, this study extensively contextualises the phenomenon of anti-Muslim racism and thus offers a great degree of differentiation. Further influential research on 'Islamophobia' includes the *Islamophobia Studies Yearbook*, edited by Farid Hafez, the project *Gruppenbezogene Menschenfeindlichkeit* led by Wilhelm Heitmeyer at the University of Bielefeld in Germany, the 'Mitte-Studien' conducted at the University of Leipzig, for instance by Oliver Decker, Johannes Kiess and Elmar Brähler. *Die enthemmte Mitte: Autoritäre und rechtsextreme Einstellung in Deutschland*. Psychosozial-Verlag: Gießen, 2016; and, with a more distinct positioning, the Islamophobia Research and Documentation Project (IRDP) housed at UC Berkeley's Center for Race and Gender: https://irdproject.com/about/. Last accessed 28 August 2017.
105. Floris Biskamp. 2016. 58–61.
106. Ibid. 58–61.
107. Ibid. 20.
108. Ibid. 20.
109. Ibid. 12–13. The following line of thought is also by Biskamp.
110. Jasbir K. Puar. *Terrorist Assemblages: Homonationalism in Queer Times*. Durham, NC and London: Duke University Press, 2007.

111. See Sara R. Farris. *In the Name of Women's Rights: The Rise of Femonationalism.* Durham, NC: Duke University Press, 2017.
112. In this context, one might ask how much sense it makes, for instance, to pose the question whether Islam, the religion (of course another broad overgeneralisation), needs a sexual revolution (as Seyran Ateş does in her book *Der Islam braucht eine sexuelle Revolution: Eine Streitschrift.* Berlin: Ullstein, 2009). Rather, it seems that the onus of such tasks lies with the respective societies at large, and not with religion, an institution which, more generally and transcending the individual example of Islam, often functions as a conservative player in society anyway. If, additionally, one takes into consideration that in questions such as this one, culture and religion are conflated, putting the emphasis on the social instead of on the religious is the more promising approach.
113. Sana Maani. 2017.
114. Floris Biskamp, 2016. 63.
115. Peter Morey and Amina Yaqin. 2011. 2–3.
116. When using expressions such as Islamist Rage Boy, jihadi bride and burka'ed women, I do not refer to any real groups of people, but to representational structures and figurations. For reasons of better readability, however, I do not use scare quotes.
117. In his eponymous study, Johannes Voelz also uses the expression 'poetics of insecurity'. However, while his work tries to foreground agency by following a narrative of the empowerment of the individual in conceptualising uncertainty as a 'resource for gain' and 'a generative force' (15), this book focuses on how a poetics of insecurity is complicit in processes of structural discrimination. Johannes Voelz. *The Poetics of Insecurity: American Fiction and the Uses of Threat.* Cambridge: Cambridge University Press, 2018.
118. Giorgio Agamben. 'On Security and Terror'. Trans. Soenke Zehle. *Libcom. org.* 24 September 2006 (website – last accessed 28 August 2017). Originally published in *Frankfurter Allgemeine Zeitung.* 20 September 2001.
119. Michel Houellebecq. *Soumission.* Paris: Flammarion, 2015.

2

THE ARAB UPRISINGS AND THE WESTERN LITERARY MARKET

The Midan has been our Holy Grail for forty years. Since 1972, when (then-president) Sadat's forces dragged the student protestors at dawn from around the empty plinth at its center and into jail, demonstrations and marches have tried and failed to get into Tahrir. Two years ago we managed to hold a corner of a traffic island in front of the Mugamma3 building for an hour. We were fewer than fifty people, and the government surrounded us with maybe two thousand Central Security soldiers, the chests and shoulders of their officers heavy with brass …

[A]s well as housing the symbols of military and political power, Tahrir is home to the civic spirit of Egypt. The Egyptian Antiquities Museum (1902) marks the northern end of the Midan, and when in 1908 the Egyptian national movement founded – through public donations – the first secular Egyptian University, they rented the palace of Khawaga Gianaclus – now the old campus of the American University in Cairo – at the other end … And early in the 1952 revolution, the small mosque near the Mugamma3 was enlarged and dedicated to Sheikh Omar Makram, the popular leader against Napoleon's French Expedition in 1798, against the British 'Fraser' Expedition of 1807, and later against Muhammed Ali himself when Sheikh Omar felt the ruler was taxing the people unfairly. Omar Makram died in exile, but his statue is part of our revolution; a meeting place, an inspiration, a bearer of flags and microphones and balloons.[1]

In *Cairo: Memoir of a City Transformed*, Ahdaf Soueif – activist, commentator and one of Egypt's internationally most well-known authors – takes the reader through the first year of the Egyptian revolution. Unlike most Western representations of the Arab uprisings, Soueif's memoir does not portray the Egyptian uprisings as an unprecedented upsurge of a hitherto unknown revolutionary energy which was suddenly sparked by Mohamed Bouazizi's self-immolation in Tunisia. Instead, passages such as the one quoted above provide historical depth to the uprisings. Thereby, they do not only give the reader an idea of the long history of dissidence,[2] but they also allow for the fact that '[f]or many Egyptians, 2011 was a continuation of the 1977 "Bread Riots" that were a continuation of the 1952 revolution that was a continuation of the 1919 revolution.'[3]

In contrast – and as the following chapters will show – many Western texts revert to Western revolutionary models to explain the so-called 'Arab Spring', or they present the Arab uprisings in ahistorical terms. As a consequence of this widespread Eurocentric and ahistorical perspective in Western representations, even well-meaning analyses of the uprisings are often misrepresentations.[4] In fact, most Western representations declare the uprisings as 'failed', except in Tunisia. As the situation in some countries, most notably Syria, is indeed worse than before the uprisings, such an assessment might seem obvious. However, by neglecting both precursors and future effects of the uprisings, this evaluation does not only disregard the fact that the uprisings have revived and reinforced a revolutionary dynamic,[5] but it also stifles the idea that the uprisings could have less foreseeable outcomes in the future.[6] These outcomes, Saleem Haddad suggests, might take decades to manifest – especially as they are often obscured by a predominantly negative framing of the aftermath of the uprisings in the media:

> I don't think enough time has gone by for us to really assess what they've accomplished. I think we were all naive (we both in the Arab world and in the West) about how long revolutions take. I remain optimistic. We are in a dark period, but there is hope. I just got back from southern Turkey,

where I was interviewing Syrian activists who remain committed to the idea of a Syrian democracy, and are doing amazing work on the ground in Syria, under terrible conditions, to achieve a better future for the country. These voices are rarely heard in the global media, which tends to focus on the boogeymen of ISIS and Assad. I think these revolutions will produce a better future, but I'm less certain of whether we will see this future in our lifetime.[7]

In Western representations, the historicity and the continuing potential of the uprisings thus remain largely neglected, whereas both can be found in many Arab literary narratives written prior to and following the uprisings.[8] In fact, as Lindsey Moore shows for the case of Egypt, 'Egyptian literary narratives produce prequels to and sequels of official revolutions (in 1919, 1952, in a sense 1970, and 2011) and expose the co-optation of revolutionary discourse by a state that fails to deliver on its promises.'[9] In addition to Ahdaf Soueif's memoir quoted at the beginning, Khaled Al Khamissi's 2006 bestseller *Taxi* serves as another example which vividly demonstrates the continuity of dissidence.[10] Published in 2006 and translated into English in 2008, *Taxi* is a collection of short stories which illustrates how openly dissident many in the population were even before the beginning of the Arab uprisings. In this, *Taxi* is often seen as a literary anticipation of the Arab uprisings.[11]

In addition to this greater historical depth in Arab literature from before and after the uprisings, there is an underlying temporal continuity which is particularly noticeable in the future-oriented dystopias currently on the rise in Arabic-speaking countries.[12] One of these dystopias is *The Queue* (2013/2016).[13] Published in Arabic in 2013 and translated into English, German and Italian, *The Queue* is the debut novel of Basma Abdel Aziz – an Egyptian journalist and psychiatrist nicknamed 'The Rebel' because of her criticism of and activism against oppression, corruption and torture in Egypt.[14] Set in an unnamed country based on Egypt, *The Queue* deals with the aftermath of the Arab uprisings, which are called the 'Disgraceful Events' in the novel.[15] The text features numerous characters, most of whom are waiting in the increasingly longer queue in front of the 'Gate'. This 'Gate' is a government institution allegedly granting citizens permission for basic daily affairs – but which in fact never opens. Although *The Queue* is set in an indeterminate future, the novel evokes a dystopian vision of the authoritarian present in post-revolutionary Egypt. At the same time, however, *The Queue* resists closure and foregrounds 'the possibility of dissident representation'[16] even in the face of what appears to be complete oppression. In this ambivalence of its dystopian vision, *The Queue* can be read as an important counterpoint to the tenor of allegedly finished and failed revolutions dominant in Western coverage, and the author's forthcoming second novel, *Here Is a Body*, appears to be continuing this commitment.[17]

Besides *The Queue*, Alaa Al Aswani's novel *The Republic of False Truths* (2018/2021) is another Arabic novel in translation which depicts the Arab uprisings and which is widely circulated on the Western market. Internationally known for his bestselling ironic portrayal of Egyptian society in *The Yacoubian Building* (2002/2004),[18] Alaa Al Aswani is an Egyptian writer, dentist and spokesperson of Kefaya, a political protest movement against Hosni Mubarak founded in 2004.[19] Not only was Al Aswani's work an important inspiration for many protestors in the Egyptian uprisings, but he also chronicled the uprisings in numerous newspaper articles. These articles also appeared in book form in 2011.[20] Forbidden in Egypt and yet to appear in English translation,[21] *The Republic of False Truths* is Al Aswani's fictionalisation of the uprisings. In its Arabic original, it was first released in Lebanon, followed by translations into Italian and French. The novel was released in its German translation on the tenth anniversary of the beginning of the uprisings in Egypt.[22]

While *The Republic of False Truths* itself is marked by a fine irony directed against the self-righteousness of those in power, by an insightful critique of the pernicious effects of globalised capitalism on Egypt's economy as well as by great sociological polyphony giving voice to a wide cast of characters from different backgrounds,[23] the marketing of the German translation of the novel constitutes an interesting case of paratextual Neo-Orientalism. Although praising the novel as an 'unforgettable portrait of modern Egyptian society',[24] the dust cover blurb produced by Hanser – one of the most renowned publishing houses in Germany – turns the novel's complexity into marketable clichés:

Cairo, 25 January 2011, 25,000 people demonstrate against Mubarak. They dream of massive change, but while love relationships flourish in the enthusiastic mass, civil rights activist Khaled is murdered in plain view.

> His girlfriend Dania refuses to give up resistance – even against her own father, the bigoted chief of the secret service who preaches Islamic values but secretly watches porn.[25]

Highlighting a daughter fighting against her oppressive father as the central conflict, the blurb draws on the common Orientalist stereotype of tyrannical men who oppress their wives and daughters. By prioritising this narrative over the sociopolitical depth of the novel, the blurb follows a marketing logic also underlying the success of so-called female 'Muslim Misery Memoirs'.[26] In this, it runs counter to the text itself, which provides a more differentiated picture of the role of gender and sexualised violence during the Egyptian uprisings: especially by giving a voice to victims of the notorious virginity tests,[27] the novel presents sexualised violence not as a cultural phenomenon but as a practice used by the Egyptian state to systematically undermine the protests.[28] While the novel thus dedicates much representational space to the role of sexualised violence in the Egyptian security state as well as to the protest not just by young users of social media, but also by workers, trade unions and the population at large,[29] the German translation is marketed according to culturalised expectations about a conflict between the young and the old, between so-called modernity, tradition and Islam, and between highly gendered individuals. What this example amply illustrates is how heavily the marketing of translations from Arabic depends on gendered and culturalised clichés. Even if dust cover blurbs often feature a condensation of kitsch and clichés, the great discrepancy between the culturalised paratext of the German translation and the text itself indicates how even prestigious publishers instrumentalise Neo-Orientalist parameters to cater to the demands of the literary market.

As the cases of *The Queue* and *The Republic of False Truths* illustrate, it is often literary writing in the form of the novel which is chosen for translation. According to Lindsey Moore, '[p]articularly where there is weak publishing infrastructure and / or limited reading public, literary fiction is increasingly oriented toward an international market.'[30] In such contexts, it is 'the novel, in particular, [which] tends to be legitimized through translation'.[31] While literary writing consequently still often remains reserved for the literate and affluent,[32] the Arab uprisings have brought forth a plethora of other popular cultural forms, ranging from graffiti and graphic novels to short films, plays and poetry. Bringing in marginalised perspectives,[33] these popular cultural forms are a crucial element of revolutionary activism.[34]

This revolutionary potential of popular culture is discussed in several collections of essays and short stories designed to represent different Arab perspectives and modes of cultural expression.[35] *Writing Revolution: From Tunis to Damascus* (2013) brings together testimonies, mostly translated from Arabic, by witnesses and participants of the uprisings from a wide range of countries.[36] Accounting for the importance of both the historicity and the continuing potential of the uprisings, the dust cover blurb of this collection highlights that

> [s]ituated between past, present and future – in a space where the personal and the political collide – these voices are part of an ongoing process, one that is at once hopeful and heartbreaking. Unique amongst material emanating from and about the convulsions in the Arab Middle East, these creative and original writers speak of history, determination and struggle, as well as of political and poetic engagement with questions of identity and activism. This book gives a moving and inspiring insight into the Arab revolutions and uprisings: why they are happening and what might come next.[37]

What is implicit but performative in *Writing Revolution* is actively spelled out in *Translating Dissent: Voices from and with the Egyptian Revolution* (2016) edited by Mona Baker[38] and *Translating Egypt's Revolution: The Language of Tahrir* (2012) edited by Samia Mehrez.[39] Analysing sources ranging 'from documentary film and subtitling to oral narratives, webcomics and street art',[40] and from 'translated chants, banners, jokes, poems, and interviews, as well as presidential speeches and military communiqués',[41] these collections analyse a wide range of forms – written, oral and visual – to explore the role of translation, both interlingual and intersemiotic, in the Egyptian uprisings and beyond. By also including contributions about the relationship between the Arab uprisings and other global protest movements in 2011, both collections, moreover, highlight how not just representations of, but also the political inspiration of the so-called Arab Spring were translated in other countries and contexts.

While these collections explore the role of translation in reaching both local and global audiences, few of the cultural forms which they analyse have reached the Western market. Apart from the Arabic novels in translation already discussed, notable exceptions are Magdy El Shafee's graphic novel *Metro* (2008/2012),[42] a collection of plays compiled by the University of Chicago Press with the title *Tahrir Tales: Plays from the Egyptian Revolution* (2016),[43] and two works by Samar Yazbek, that is, the prose poem 'Waiting for Death: I Will Not Carry Flowers to My Grave' (2011) and a memoir, *A Woman in the Crossfire: Diaries of the Syrian Revolution* (2011/2012).[44] For the latter, Samar Yazbek won the PEN/Pinter International Writer of Courage Award in 2012. Having had to flee from Syria because she was on the regime's death list, Yazbek secretly returned to Syria several times and published her experiences in *The Crossing: My Journey to the Shattered Heart of Syria* (2015).[45] In addition to Yazbek's memoir, Mona Prince's memoir *Revolution Is My Name* (2012/2014), an eyewitness account of the first eighteen days of protests on Tahrir Square, has been translated into English (by Samia Mehrez, editor of *Translating Egypt's Revolution: The Language of Tahrir*).[46] Emphasising the continuities of the protests against Mubarak's regime in Egypt, *Tahrir Tales* also includes plays written prior to 2011. Moreover, this collection of plays aims at providing an insight into a vast array of issues ranging from 'government corruption, class inequalities, police brutality, the treatment of migrants and refugees'.[47] Not coincidentally, the first of the collection's five sections is entitled 'Disparity and Corruption', and – as with the other works in translation – the plays also feature female perspectives.

In addition to these works in translation, the Western literary market has produced a body of representations of the Arab uprisings in English and French by diasporic writers, and a range of representations by Western writers in English, French and German. Besides the texts by diasporic writers discussed in more detail in the following close readings, that is, Tahar Ben Jelloun's *Par le feu* (2011; 'By Fire') and Karim Alrawi's *Book of Sands: A Novel of the Arab Uprisings* (2015), there are English language memoirs by diasporic authors such as Ahdaf Soueif and semi-autobiographical or biographical novels by, for instance, Omar Robert Hamilton and Hisham Matar. While Soueif's memoir takes the reader both through the first eighteen days of the uprisings in Cairo and through the first year after the revolution (and has, moreover, in its new edition been updated with a postscript reflecting on the developments up until 2013), her son Omar

Robert Hamilton's debut novel *The City Always Wins* (2017) turns the author's own engagement in the 2011 and 2013 Egyptian uprisings into fiction.[48] Emphasising the proleptic impulses of the uprisings, the novel consists of three parts. While Part I, which is set between October 2011 and February 2012, is entitled 'Tomorrow', Part II, 'Today', depicts the time span from November 2012 and August 2013. Part III, 'Yesterday', is set during the al-Sisi era. Although this temporal composition, with its inversion of 'tomorrow' and 'yesterday', implies a regression, the text is still centred on the present – and this present is, as suggested by the novel's title, a present of continuing revolutionary potential.[49] Offering a Libyan perspective on the repercussions of the uprisings is Hisham Matar's memoir *The Return: Fathers, Sons and the Land in Between* (2016).[50] *The Return* has won numerous prizes, including the 2017 Pulitzer Prize and the PEN/Jean Stein Award,[51] and illustrates Matar's return to Libya after the fall of Gaddafi, in the hope of finding his father, a political dissident who had been kidnapped twenty-two years earlier. In addition to these English language memoirs by diasporic writers, there is one French language memoir by Franco-American writer Jonathan Littell, *Carnets de Homs* (2012; *Syrian Notebooks: Inside the Homs Uprising*, 2015),[52] which has received wider attention, despite the author's warning at the beginning of the book that his text is more of a documentation than literary writing.[53] As the title indicates, this memoir consists of the notebooks which Littell used when, from 16 January to 2 February 2012, he did research on the uprisings in Syria for articles commissioned by the French daily *Le Monde*. Published as an e-book soon after Littell's sojourn in Syria, *Carnets de Homs* has now also been published in paperback by Gallimard in France and was released in the English translation by Verso and in the German translation by Hanser.[54]

With Saleem Haddad's *Guapa* (2016) and Rachid Boudjedra's *Printemps* (2014; 'Spring'),[55] two novels explore the role of queerness in the Arab uprisings. Also containing autobiographical elements, Saleem Haddad's debut novel *Guapa* follows Rasa, the homosexual first-person narrator, through the queer underground of an unnamed Islamicate city for one day. Asked about the unnamed country in which his novel is set, Haddad, writer, aid worker and filmmaker born to an Iraqi-German mother and a Lebanese-Palestinian father,[56] answered:

Politically, I didn't want to present an 'anthropological' or 'political' study of one country. There was something appealing about confusing readers that I enjoyed, and I wanted to, as much as is possible, make it difficult for someone who wanted to take my text and use it as a 'study' of gay or queer societies in a specific country.[57]

In its awareness of the increased post-9/11 demand for 'representative' texts about Islamicate countries on the Western literary market,[58] this answer can, firstly, be read as a direct response to the 'tendency to view non-Western literatures as essentially anthropological in nature – affording the assumed Western reader an insight into exotically different lives …'[59] Secondly, and as Nadia Atia proffers, Haddad – both in his novel and in public statements – actively resists a potential homonational co-optation of his critique of the treatment of queer people in the Middle East by rejecting oversimplifying narratives which victimise queer Arabs.[60] Further underlining its resistance to unilateral appropriation, *Guapa* employs numerous heterolingual elements in Arabic without always translating them.[61] Instead of using Arabic words and phrases to emphasise problems, gender issues and danger only, the novel features a wide range of transliterated Arabic words and phrases and gradually unfolds their meaning. In this, the use of these heterolingual elements does not only function as an act of cultural translation,[62] but it also subverts the Neo-Orientalist literary strategy of employing heterolingual Arabic elements as a means of exoticisation and securitisation discussed in Chapter Five of this book.

Also negotiating queerness against the backdrop of the Arab uprisings, *Printemps*, a novel by the prolific Algerian writer Rachid Boudjedra, follows thirty-year-old Teldj, a former Olympic medal winner and homosexual university teacher of erotic Arabic literature. Traumatised by the murder of her mother by the Islamists in the Algerian Civil War, Teldj draws a parallel between the aftermath of the Arab uprisings and the Algerian Civil War. Despite the novel's title and unlike *Guapa*, *Printemps* thus sets its protagonist's homosexuality against a thoroughly pessimistic evaluation of the uprisings as an Islamist winter.[63] Both in its perspective and in its more conventional stylistics, *Printemps* greatly differs from *Guapa*. While Haddad's debut is driven by a proleptic impulse and the attempt to find the linguistic means to overcome the taboo of homosexuality,[64] *Printemps* explores its protagonist's queerness mainly by processing the taboos of the past.

With Mohammed Moulessehoul, better known under his pen name Yasmina Khadra, another Algerian writer fictionalised the Arab uprisings – although with a completely different approach. His novel *La Dernière Nuit du Raïs* (2015),[65] more explicitly translated into English as *The Dictator's Last Night* and into German as *Die letzte Nacht des Muammar al-Gaddafi*,[66] merges fact and fiction to narrate the last hours in the life of Gaddafi before he was killed by rebel forces on 20 October 2011. Alternating between the present tense of the first-person narrator's account of his last night in his home town of Sirte and between flashbacks to his poor Bedouin childhood, the novel portrays Gaddafi as a megalomaniac but nonetheless charismatic dictator, thus taking a completely different perspective from Hisham Matar's *The Return*, which illustrates the fate of one of the numerous victims of the Gaddafi regime – and its support by the West.

Western Fictionalisations of the Arab Uprisings

Ten years after the so-called Arab Spring, the body of Western fictionalisations of the uprisings can be classified into several groups. Firstly, there is a group of short prose fiction, mostly in German. Published soon after the Arab uprisings, this group contains Jochen Beyse's *Rebellion: Zwischenbericht* (2013; 'Rebellion: Status Report'), Jonas Lüscher's *Frühling der Barbaren* (2013; *Barbarian Spring*), Hans Platzgumer's *Trans-Maghreb: Novelle vom Bauträger Anton Corwald* (2012; 'Trans-Maghreb: A Novella about Anton Corwald, Building Constructor') and Adam Thirlwell's *Kapow!* (2012).[67] Not only are all of these texts written by men, but they also feature male Western first-person narrators who, as will become clear in the following chapters, voice their difficulties in understanding and representing the Arab uprisings.

While the short texts previously mentioned were written by authors with a background in the arts and humanities, a second group comprises works by so-called area experts. For instance, Marc Trévidic's debut novel *Ahlam* (2016) received widespread attention due to its author's status as France's former chief anti-terrorism judge.[68] Not only did Trévidic warn of the imminent danger of a terrorist attack in France before the November 2015 Paris attacks,[69] he was also involved in interrogating one of the terrorists in the aftermath of the attacks on the Bataclan.⁷⁰ Published soon after the Paris attacks, Trévidic's novel *Ahlam* is set in Tunisia before and during the Jasmine Revolution. Permeated by Orientalist clichés and following a civilising narrative, the novel casts the Arab uprisings as the coming of age of two siblings, Ahlam and her brother Issam, who – educated in the arts by Paul, a Frenchman – are portrayed as growing up in harmony. When the Jasmine Revolution begins, however, the siblings – epitomising the different factions in their country – become estranged. While Issam increasingly radicalises himself and turns into an Islamist Rage Boy,⁷¹ his sister joins the uprisings and begins a relationship with Paul. While it is unimaginable that – due to its immense stylistic and conceptual weaknesses – *Ahlam* would have received any, let alone any favourable reviews in the more serious media, Trévidic, who had previously published works of non-fiction about his work as an anti-terrorism judge,⁷² has been successful with this book. The novel has been translated into German, Spanish and Italian, and its author was, among others, invited to the prestigious 2016 International Literature Festival in Berlin.⁷³ Both the text itself and its reception thus constitute a perhaps well-meaning but nonetheless blatant case of literary Neo-Orientalism. In this, *Ahlam* represents the second group of literary representations of the Arab uprisings on the Western market: like Mathias Énard's *Rue des voleurs* (2012; *Street of Thieves*),⁷⁴ whose author is marketed as a humanistic area expert, and Tahar Ben Jelloun's *Par le feu* (2011; 'By Fire') and *L'Étincelle: Révoltes dans les pays arabes* (2011; 'The Spark'),⁷⁵ the circulation and reception of *Ahlam* vividly illustrates 'the post-9/11 craving of the general public … for "authentic" and "expert" information about Islam and the Middle East …'⁷⁶

As this previous list of authors exemplifies, the third group of Western fiction about the Arab uprisings is almost visibly absent: namely the voice of women. Perhaps surprisingly, both in works translated from Arabic and in the works of diasporic writers in English and French, the female perspective is more present than in works by Western writers. Not only is this gender imbalance remarkable in itself, but it further corroborates the argument advanced in Chapter Four that the allegation of sexism in Islamicate countries in fact often serves as a prism through which Western gender inequalities can be refracted. Moreover, and as the case of the now well-known Franco-Moroccan author Leïla Slimani reveals, this gender inequality also heavily influences the Western literary market. In fact, it still appears to be much more difficult for a woman to launch a book fictionalising political events than for a man, and it seems to be more difficult for a woman to have a book with a political topic accepted than one with a private and individual story: while Slimani's first novel about the Arab uprisings was rejected by several publishers, she became famous with a novel about a nymphomaniac woman (which she published with the most prestigious publisher in France); later on, she won the Prix Goncourt for a novel about a nanny who kills two children.[77]

In this male-dominated section of the literary market, G. Willow Wilson's novel *Alif the Unseen* (2012) is therefore the exception rather than the rule.[78] The fact that this novel by a female writer was actually published might, firstly, be due to Wilson's prior positioning on the literary market. Her graphic novel *Cairo* (2007) enjoyed popular success[79] and Wilson also wrote a memoir, entitled *The Butterfly Mosque: A Young American Woman's Journey to Love and Islam* (2010),[80] which deals with the author's experiences in Egypt during the Mubarak regime. Not only does Wilson thus meet the demands for authentic and expert insight into the uprisings, but as *Alif the Unseen* is also in line with widely successful magic realist writing, this mode might have served as another selling point of Wilson's book.

In its adoption of the magic realist mode, *Alif the Unseen* represents a fourth group of fiction about the Arab uprisings published on the Western literary market. As will be further explored in the close reading of *Book of Sands* in Chapter Five, the use of magic realism in writing on the Arab uprisings serves as a mode of exploring phenomena which are hard to fathom. In addition to this structural reason, the magic realist mode used in both these novels is also in line with a common trend in postcolonial literature. This mode does not only fulfil the exoticising expectations towards literature marketed as 'postcolonial'.[81] As Elleke Boehmer observes, the magic realist mode is also intricately linked with one of the two dominant inflections of postcolonial literature, that is, the 'globalized hybridizing inflection'.[82] Through the choice of magic realism, these two novels thus interweave Neo-Orientalist tendencies with a highly marketable strand of postcolonial literature – a strategy which is also ironically used in Salman Rushdie's *Two Years Eight Months & Twenty-Eight Nights* (2015).[83]

As the following close readings will illustrate in more detail, in contrast to the more proleptic and subversive representations in many of the originally Arabic and diasporic works, most of the Western literary depictions of the Arab uprisings have little revolutionary impetus. Instead, most of these texts refract different facets of insecurity into a pronounced and securitised Othering, and the Neo-Orientalist undertow on the Western literary market is so strong that it also affects the writing of diasporic authors such as Tahar Ben Jelloun and Karim Alrawi.

Devised as a critique of this strong Neo-Orientalist undertow on the Western literary market, the following chapters focus on English, French and German language perspectives marketed as open-minded cosmopolitan literature published by influential Western presses, but which, below the surface, often perpetuate the very stereotypes which they try to deconstruct. By comparing English, French and German language fiction written by authors from different backgrounds and countries, this book covers a substantial part of the Western literary market; additionally, the countries of the publishing houses represent influential Western players. Both to avoid the impression of homogeneity and so as not to perpetuate binaries drawn along national lines which no longer hold on the globalised market, this book brings together close readings of works by diasporic authors and Western authors in one analytical frame. Through this transnational reading of a wide range of authors from different backgrounds, this study analyses the commercialisation of Neo-Orientalist and securitised elements in short fiction and novels aimed at the Western literary market. In addition to revealing striking transnational similarities of narrative structures and configurations which transcend the literary traditions of individual countries,[84] the comparative approach of this study is consequently not only designed to transcend the Anglophone bias in postcolonial studies,[85] but also to do justice to the transnational dimensions of Neo-Orientalism in the literary field.

In order to show how securitisation begins and functions at the micro level, this book presents the particular poetics of Neo-Orientalism in close readings of texts with a similar positioning in the literary field. All of the texts selected for close reading have won literary prizes, or they were written by authors who had previously received prestigious prizes. In addition to the fact that the texts chosen for close reading were originally published in languages which are dominant on the global literary market, that is, English, French and German, three of the four non-English language books have also been translated into English and other European languages. With regard to production, all of these texts were published by major Western presses, that is, by cultural players who are often complicit in maintaining the unequal opportunities of writers from the Global North and Global South to participate in the global literary market.[86] Such presses include renowned long-standing and traditional presses, such as Gallimard in France, multinational publishers such as HarperCollins, but also smaller independent publishers who try to manage the balancing act between literary quality and profitability. As the following chapters will reveal, the high demand for Neo-Orientalist texts and the pressure of the literary market in general do not only determine the book selection of mega-conglomerate publishers, but they also influence the selection processes of the more renowned as well as smaller presses. In the case of Visual Editions, the publisher of *Kapow!*, the latter becomes most visible: originally committed to publishing experimental literature,[87] Visual Editions now specialises in commercial storytelling for the global campaigns of international corporations.[88]

Prioritising the criteria of the language of publication as well as the positioning in the literary field over the country of origin of the authors thus also accounts for the capitalist exploitation of Orientalised and securitised forms of representation. In their function as cultural capital and in their aestheticising and imaginative-utopian dimensions, especially those texts positioned in the higher segment of the literary market help to diffuse securitised discourse into mainstream society. Although I would like to distance myself from problematic categories such as 'high-brow' and 'low-brow' literature and their inherent elitism, when it comes to the social function of literature, I argue that the positioning with regard to production, circulation and reception are instrumental in granting not only visibility, but also authority and prestige to certain books. In a discussion of how more subtle forms of representing the Islamicate Other help to render securitisation more socially acceptable, this is particularly pertinent. Even though some argue that 'Orientalism in a pejorative sense comes bubbling up from below'[89] and advocate the analysis of exactly this kind of 'Pulp Orientalism' which is '"dumbed down" for mass consumption',[90] this study pursues a different aim: while an assessment of the ways in which Neo-Orientalist narrative practices render the uprisings attractive as a backdrop to pulp fiction would also be of interest, this study analyses whether, in literature which does *not* ostentatiously use Orientalisation and securitisation as its selling points, the reverse holds true: namely that Orientalism also quietly trickles 'down from above'.

In this conception, *Literary Neo-Orientalism and the Arab Uprisings* complements the existing literature on Arab postcolonial literature in two ways, that is, with regard to time and gaze. Although I began working on this book well before the publication of Lindsey Moore's *Narrating Postcolonial Arab Nations* in 2018,[91] my critique of the Occidentalist view of the Arab uprisings can in many ways be read as a complementation and continuation of Moore's study: while '*Narrating Postcolonial Arab Nations* explores the *longue durée* of postcoloniality in Arab creative narratives from the last half-century that both represent and enact revolt (*al-thawrah*) against (post)colonial regimes', it does 'not focus on literatures of the so-called Arab Spring, but rather on literary representations of conditions that made the recent Arab uprisings necessary and possible, perhaps inevitable'.[92] Where the temporal scope of Moore's work ends, this book thus continues, and while Moore's book explores the postcolonial potential of Arab literary narratives, this book critiques the Neo-Orientalist tendencies which often obliterate this potential.

Notes

1. Ahdaf Soueif. *Cairo: Memoir of a City Transformed*. London: Bloomsbury, 2012. 7–9.
2. Lindsey Moore. *Narrating Postcolonial Arab Nations: Egypt, Algeria, Lebanon, Palestine*. New York and Abingdon: Routledge, 2018. 3.
3. Caroline Rooney. 'Popular Culture and the Arab Spring'. *The Edinburgh Companion to the Postcolonial Middle East*. Eds Anna Ball and Karim Mattar. Edinburgh: Edinburgh University Press, 2018. 407–26. 414.
4. Ibid. 420.
5. Lindsey Moore. *Narrating Postcolonial Arab Nations*. 2018. 3.
6. Ibid. 22.
7. Saleem Haddad. 'On the Arab Spring and Writing About the Queer Arab Experience'. Interview by Stuart Waterman. *Lambda Literary*. 21 May 2016 (website – last accessed 15 January 2021).

8. For more on the revolutionary impulses in Egyptian, Algerian, Lebanese and Palestinian literature published before the Arab uprisings, see Lindsey Moore, *Narrating Postcolonial Arab Nations*. 2018; for a discussion of Egyptian literature from both before and during the uprisings, see Susanne Schanda. *Literatur der Rebellion: Ägyptens Schriftsteller erzählen vom Umbruch*. Zurich: Rotpunktverlag, 2013.
9. Lindsey Moore. *Narrating Postcolonial Arab Nations*. 2018. 14.
10. Khaled Al Khamissi [2006]. *Taxi*. Trans. Jonathan Wright. London: Aflame Books, 2008.
11. Khaled Al Khamissi and Stefan Weidner. 'Arabischer Frühling'. Trans. Günther Orth. *Qantara.de*. 19 May 2011 (website – last accessed 10 January 2020); Werner Bloch. 'Egypt's Culture on Four Wheels'. *Qantara.de*. 13 March 2011 (website – last accessed 10 January 2020); Caroline Rooney. 2018. 421.
12. Lindsey Moore. '"What Happens After Saying No?" Egyptian Uprisings and Afterwords in Basma Adel Aziz's *The Queue* and Omar Robert Hamilton's *The City Always Wins*'. *CounterText* 4.2 (2018): 192–211. 195.
13. Basma Abdel Aziz [2013]. *The Queue*. Trans. Elisabeth Jaquette. New York: Melville House, 2016.
14. Ibid. Back cover.
15. Ibid. 6.
16. Lindsey Moore. 'What Happens After Saying No?' 2018. 192, 201.
17. Basma Abdel Aziz. *Here Is a Body*. Trans. Jonathan Wright. Cairo: Hoopoe, 2021.
18. Alaa Al Aswani [2002]. *The Yacoubian Building*. Trans. Humphrey T. Davies. Cairo: The American University in Cairo Press, 2004.
19. Susanne Schanda. 2013. 48.
20. Alaa Al Aswani. *On the State of Egypt: What Caused the Revolution*. Trans. Jonathan Wright. Edinburgh: Canongate, 2011.
21. Alaa Al Aswani [2018]. *The Republic of False Truths*. Trans. S. R. Fellowes. London: Faber & Faber, 2021.
22. Alaa Al Aswani [2018]. *Die Republik der Träumer*. Trans. Markus Lemke. Munich: Hanser, 2021.
23. Ibid. 66–7.
24. Dust cover blurb. My translation.
25. Ibid.

26. Peter Morey. 'Applications of Neo-Orientalism and Islamophobia in Recent Writing'. *Orientalism and Literature*. Ed. Geoffrey P. Nash. Cambridge: Cambridge University Press, 2019. 269–85. 270.
27. Alaa Al Aswani [2018]. *Die Republik der Träumer*. 2021. 281–9, 316.
28. Paul Amar. 'Turning the Gendered Politics of the Security State Inside Out? Charging the Police with Sexual Harassment in Egypt'. *International Feminist Journal of Politics* 13.3 (2011): 299–328. 310.
29. Alaa Al Aswani [2018]. *Die Republik der Träumer*. 2021. 148, 159, 211. For the role of the workers' movement in the Egyptian revolution, see also Anne Alexander and Mostafa Bassiouny. *Bread, Freedom, Social Justice: Workers and the Egyptian Revolution*. London: Zed Books, 2014.
30. Lindsey Moore. *Narrating Postcolonial Arab Nations*. 2018. 17.
31. Ibid. 17.
32. Ibid. 17.
33. Ibid. 17.
34. Caroline Rooney. 2018. 407–26.
35. Ibid. 421.
36. Layla Al-Zubaidi et al., eds. *Writing Revolution: The Voices from Tunis to Damascus*. London: I. B. Tauris, 2013.
37. Ibid. Dust cover blurb.
38. Mona Baker, ed. *Translating Dissent: Voices from and with the Egyptian Revolution*. New York and Abingdon: Routledge, 2016.
39. Samia Mehrez, ed. *Translating Egypt's Revolution: The Language of Tahrir*. Cairo: The American University in Cairo Press, 2012.
40. Mona Baker. 2016. Dust cover blurb.
41. Samia Mehrez. 2012. Dust cover blurb.
42. Magdy El Shafee [2008]. *Metro*. Trans. Chip Rossetti. New York: Macmillan, 2012.
43. Mohammed Albakry and Rebekah Maggor, eds. *Tahrir Plays: Plays From the Egyptian Revolution*. Chicago: University of Chicago Press, 2016.
44. Samar Yazbek. 'Waiting for Death: I Will Not Carry Flowers to My Grave'. Trans. Anne-Marie McManus. *Jadaliyya*. 2 April 2011 (website – last accessed 15 January 2021); Samar Yazbek [2011]. *A Woman in the Crossfire: Diaries of the Syrian Revolution*. Trans. Max Weiss. London: Haus, 2012.
45. Samar Yazbek. *The Crossing: My Journey to the Shattered Heart of Syria*. Trans. Nashwa Gowanlock and Ruth Ahmedzai Kemp. London: Rider, 2015.

46. Mona Prince [2012]. *Revolution Is My Name*. Trans. Samia Mehrez. Cairo: The American University in Cairo Press, 2014.
47. Marcia Lynx Qualey. 'The Drama of Protest'. *Qantara*. 20 December 2016 (website – last accessed 15 January 2021).
48. Omar Robert Hamilton. *The City Always Wins*. London: Faber & Faber, 2017; Lindsey Moore. 'What Happens After Saying No?' 2018. 202.
49. Ibid. 202, 205.
50. Hisham Matar. *The Return: Fathers, Sons and the Land in Between*. New York: Viking, 2016.
51. 'The Return'. *HishamMatar.com*. No date (website – last accessed 17 January 2021).
52. Jonathan Littell. *Carnets de Homs*. Paris: Gallimard, 2012.
53. First sentence. Quoted in the French Kindle edition.
54. Jonathan Littell [2012]. *Syrian Notebooks: Inside the Homs Uprising*. Trans. Charlotte Mandell. London: Verso, 2015; Jonathan Littell. *Notizen aus Homs*. Trans. Dorit Gesa Engelhardt. Munich: Hanser, 2012.
55. Saleem Haddad. *Guapa*. London: Europa Editions, 2016; Rachid Boudjedra. *Printemps*. Paris: Grasset, 2014.
56. Bibliographical information quoted in Saleem Haddad. 2016. Front matter.
57. Saleem Haddad. 'On the Arab Spring and Writing About the Queer Arab Experience'. 2016.
58. Peter Morey. *Islamophobia and the Novel*. New York: Columbia University Press, 2018. 6; Ali Behdad and Juliet Williams. 'Neo-Orientalism'. *Globalizing American Studies*. Eds Brian T. Edwards and Gaonkar Dilip Parameshwar. Chicago: University of Chicago Press, 2010. 283–99. 289.
59. Peter Morey. 2018. 6; see also Graham Huggan. 'African Literature and the Anthropological Exotic'. *The Postcolonial Exotic: Marketing the Margins*. London: Routledge, 2001. 34–57.
60. Nadia Atia. 'Queering the Arab Spring: Belonging in Saleem Haddad's *Guapa*'. *Wasafiri* 34.2 (2019): 54–60. 54.
61. Ibid. 54.
62. Ibid. 57. Atia quotes Waïl Hassan's concept here. Waïl S. Hassan. *Immigrant Narratives: Orientalism and Cultural Translation in Arab American and Arab British Literature*. Oxford: Oxford University Press, 2011.
63. Renaud de Rochebrune. 'Et il est comment le dernier Rachid Boudjedra'. *JeuneAfrique*. 29 June 2014 (website – last accessed 17 January 2021).
64. Nadia Atia. 2019. 56–7.

65. Yasmina Khadra. *La dernière nuit du Raïs*. Paris: Julliard, 2015.
66. Yasmina Khadra. *The Dictator's Last Night*. Trans. Julian Evans. London: Gallic, 2015; Yasmina Khadra. *Die letzte Nache des Muammar al-Gaddafi*. Trans. Regina Keil-Sagawe. Hamburg: Osburg, 2015.
67. Jochen Beyse. *Rebellion: Zwischenbericht*. Zurich: Diaphanes, 2013; Jonas Lüscher [2013]. *Frühling der Barbaren*. Munich: btb, 2015; Hans Platzgumer. *Trans-Maghreb: Novelle vom Bauträger Anton Corwald*. Innsbruck: Limbus, 2012; Adam Thirlwell. *Kapow!* London: Visual Editions, 2012.
68. Marc Trévidic. *Ahlam*. Paris: J. C. Lattès, 2016.
69. Marc Trévidic. 'On manque d'hommes pour neutraliser les terroristes'. Interview by Frédéric Helbert. *Paris Match*. 30 September 2015 (website – last accessed 19 January 2021).
70. 'Marc Trévidic'. *Rowohlt*. No date (website – last accessed 19 January 2021).
71. For more on this figuration and its role in depictions of the Arab uprisings, see Chapter Five.
72. Marc Trévidic. *Au coeur de l'anti-terrorisme*. Paris: J. C. Lattès, 2011; Marc Trévidic. *Terroristes: Les 7 pilliers de la déraison*. Paris: J. C. Lattès, 2013.
73. 'Marc Trévidic'. *Internationales Literaturfestival Berlin*. No date (website – last accessed 30 March 2019).
74. Mathias Énard. *Rue des voleurs*. Arles: Actes Sud, 2012.
75. In English, both of these pieces have been jointly published in Tahar Ben Jelloun. *By Fire: Writings on the Arab Spring*. Trans. Rita S. Nezami. Evanston: Curbstone/Northwestern University Press, 2016. Tahar Ben Jelloun. *Par le feu: Récit*. Paris: Gallimard, 2011; Tahar Ben Jelloun. *L'Étincelle: Révoltes dans les pays arabes*. Paris: Gallimard, 2011.
76. Ali Behdad and Juliet Williams. 2010. 289.
77. Leïla Slimani. 'Gegen die Angst'. Interview by Khuê Phạm. *Zeit Magazin*. 23 August 2018. 14–20. 18.
78. G. Willow Wilson. *Alif the Unseen*. London: Corvus, 2012.
79. G. Willow Wilson. *Cairo*. New York: Vertigo, 2007.
80. G. Willow Wilson. *The Butterfly Mosque: A Young American Woman's Journey to Love and Islam*. New York: Grove, 2010.
81. Graham Huggan. 2001. 25.
82. Elleke Boehmer. *Postcolonial Poetics: 21st-Century Critical Readings*. Basingstoke: Palgrave Macmillan, 2018. 69.
83. Salman Rushdie [2015]. *Two Years Eight Nights & Twenty-Eight Nights*. London, Vintage, 2016.

84. For a detailed study on the historical peculiarities of German Orientalism, see Andrea Polaschegg. *Der andere Orientalismus: Regeln deutsch-morgenländischer Imagination im 19. Jahrhundert*. Berlin and New York: Walter de Gruyter, 2005.
85. Karim Mattar. 'Edward Said and the Institution of Postcolonial Studies'. *The Edinburgh Companion to the Postcolonial Middle East*. Eds Anna Ball and Karim Mattar. Edinburgh: Edinburgh University Press, 2018. 23–42. 23.
86. For forms of literary domination on the global literary market, see Pascale Casanova. *The World Republic of Letters*. Cambridge, MA: Harvard University Press, 2004.
87. 'Der Leser spielt mit'. *Neue Zürcher Zeitung*. 9 October 2015 (website – last accessed 15 January 2021).
88. 'About'. *Visual Editions*. No date (website – last accessed 15 January 2021).
89. Robert Irwin. 'How and Why the West Misrepresents the East'. *The Times Literary Supplement*. 19 August 2011 (website – last accessed 18 February 2015).
90. Pavan Kumar Malreddy. 'Introduction: Orientalism(s) after 9/11'. *Journal of Postcolonial Writing* 3 (2012): 236.
91. Lindsey Moore. *Narrating Postcolonial Arab Nations*. 2018.
92. Ibid. 3.

3

PRECARITY FAR AND NEAR: THE ARAB UPRISINGS IN TAHAR BEN JELLOUN'S *PAR LE FEU* AND JONAS LÜSCHER'S *FRÜHLING DER BARBAREN*

The *THOUSAND AND ONE NIGHTS RESORT* in the oasis at Tschub was modelled on a nomadic Berber settlement – or, to be more precise, on what market researchers thought a first-class tourist to Tunisia might imagine when he pictured a typical Berber settlement. Assuming, that is, he could picture such a thing at all and wasn't, impartial as a blank sheet of paper and receptive as an empty vessel, simply being spoon-fed ideas by a world-renowned resort designer from Magdeburg …

The camel-driver was leading the beast by its reins. Jenny had made him swap his Rooney football shirt for a costume that she'd got an intern from the trading floor – who'd vainly hoped to get an invitation to the wedding in return – to copy from pictures of Tuareg horsemen in a travel brochure. She was pleased with the outcome; Kelly's white dress was set off wonderfully by the man's indigo-coloured robes, exactly the effect she'd intended. It also confirmed that she'd been right to pooh-pooh the intern's objections that there weren't actually any Tuareg in Tunisia.

But as he attempted to lead the camel up the two steps onto the stage, the fake desert warrior, his vision obscured by the unfamiliar headdress, stumbled and tripped over the over-long hem of his indigo-blue robes. This so alarmed the camel that it refused point-blank to go any further. Nor could it be persuaded to kneel down in the usual way to allow the bride to dismount with dignity. The camel-driver tried cajoling the beast, then resorted to tugging it ever more impatiently by the reins, as Quicky began kicking the back of its knees.[1]

Palm trees, exotic lighting, mysterious music, stunning colours, a scared camel, a stumbling camel-driver and a choleric ex-soldier: one of the key scenes in Jonas Lüscher's *Barbarian Spring*, the wedding of two London City traders at a Tunisian desert luxury resort, ironically amasses Orientalist fantasies and juxtaposes them with the reality of their exploitative and uncompromising commodification. In the stylised setting of the resort, a camel-driver is paid to perform an Otherness which fulfils the exoticising expectations of the Western customers. In order to satisfy the tourists' desire for difference, he is forced to swap his Rooney shirt, which indicates how globalisation has already changed the region,[2] for a costume modelled on a travel catalogue's depiction of an ethnic group not even existent in Tunisia. Dependent on this Orientalist charade to earn his living, he is forced to wear robes which physically hinder him from doing his job. The systemic injustices inherent in this scene are reified by Quicky, one of the wedding guests and the master of ceremonies. An ex-soldier in Iraq turned mercenary turned banker, he epitomises the considerable overlap between military and economic forms of globalised capitalism. Both at the literal and the figurative level, his aggressive behaviour – kicking the camel so as to bring it to its knees – visualises how violence and oppression function as the predominant principles of the capitalist system, and how the wealth of the few comes at the expense of the precarity of the many.

In contrast to most other Western fiction as well as media coverage about the Arab uprisings, *Barbarian Spring* highlights the role which global interdependencies play with regard to the desolate living conditions of economically disadvantaged people in general – and their role in the Arab uprisings in particular. While the 2011 revolts in cities such as New York, Barcelona, London and Athens were mainly read against the backdrop of the financial crisis of 2007/8, the perspective of global economic issues rarely framed Western explanations for the 'Arab Spring'.[3] So if in discussions about the Indignados and the Occupy and Blockupy Movements, systemic aspects came to the fore, they featured only marginally in Western media coverage of the Arab uprisings. Instead, these uprisings were – in a 'convenient mystification' – almost exclusively presented as 'a product of corruption unique to politics in the Arab world'.[4] This portrayal results, on the one hand, from the fact that corruption and state injustice were indeed grounds for the revolts in the respective countries. On the other hand, however, it results from a strong representational bias.[5] Not only did most Western political and media discourse neglect long-standing co-operations of Western states with dictators such as Ben Ali or Gaddafi, but it also ignored the systemic link between the global financial crisis in 2007/8 and the massive rise in food prices in several Arab countries. As a consequence, the negative impact of neo-liberal competition on the socio-economically disadvantaged demographic groups in the respective countries was mostly left unmentioned, and the precarious living conditions of the populations were often dismissed as a result of local problems only.[6]

By means of a contrastive close reading of Tahar Ben Jelloun's *Par le feu* ('By Fire') and Jonas Lüscher's *Frühling der Barbaren* (*Barbarian Spring*), this chapter sets out to illustrate what role precarity plays in representations of the Arab uprisings – and how in Neo-Orientalist discourse more generally it serves to Other Western fears of social decline. In contrast to precariousness, a human condition which is shared by all because everyone is vulnerable to injury, suffering and death,[7] precarity is unequally distributed: while some are more protected, the poor and marginalised are endangered by economic insecurity, violence, war and natural catastrophes and are thus particularly vulnerable.[8]

Par le feu (2011),[9] the first imaginative rendering of the revolts to be published on the Western literary market, adopts a similar perspective as most Western political and media discourse. It presents precarity mainly as an endemic problem of Arab countries. In contrast, *Frühling der Barbaren* (2013) focuses on the nexus between Orientalism as a form of cultural capitalism and the precarity of the Other. By ironising its protagonist's attempts at ethical distancation from the devastating effects of predatory capitalism, it can be said to fictionalise what Judith Butler theorises:

> We can be alive or dead to the sufferings of others – they can be dead or alive to us. But it is only when we understand that what happens there also happens here, and that 'here' is already an elsewhere, and necessarily so, that

we stand a chance of grasping the difficult and shifting global connections in ways that let us know the transport and the constraint of what we might still call ethics.[10]

Especially as both *Par le feu* and *Frühling der Barbaren* have been turned into school editions, a comparison of the poetics by which they translate the precarity of others into the question of global ethics is particularly interesting. Not only does it illustrate how an exclusionary framing forgoes the 'limited but necessary reversibility of proximity and distance' on which the emergence of ethical demands depends,[11] but it also shows how a Neo-Orientalist poetics of distance and difference allows the reader to feel ethical – without feeling responsible:

> For now, I want only to suggest in a fairly elementary way that if I am only bound to those who are close to me, already familiar, then my ethics are invariably parochial, communitarian, and exclusionary … If I am only bound to those who suffer at a distance, but never those who are close to me, then I evacuate my situation in an effort to secure the distance that allows me to entertain ethical feeling and even feel myself to be ethical.[12]

Tahar Ben Jelloun: *Par le feu*

Tahar Ben Jelloun was born in Fez in 1944. Since 1971 and following a five-year imprisonment for political activism in Morocco, he has mostly been living in Paris.[13] He received the prestigious Prix Goncourt for his novel *La Nuit sacrée* (1987; *The Sacred Night*) and in the meantime has become a member of the Goncourt Academy himself. Since the publication of his book *L'Enfant de sable* (1985; *The Sand Child*), he has been marketed as one of the most important contemporary literary and intellectual voices from the Maghreb writing in French.[14] His categorisation as an Arab writer and intellectual is, however, too unidimensional. Despite his Moroccan origin, his activity as a Goncourt Academy member as well as his long-standing and prolific publishing history with Gallimard,[15] one of France's most renowned presses, suggest that the author is not only part of the French literary establishment,[16] but that his main target audience is the French literary market.[17] In fact, Ben Jelloun's books are first and foremost geared to the tastes and demands of the Western literary market, and in his role as an intellectual and go-to for anything related to Islam, he is marketed as an area expert explaining the Islamicate world to the West.[18]

To what great degree Ben Jelloun's perception and self-fashioning as an engaged writer and intellectual affected his treatment of the Arab uprisings becomes apparent in his opening speech at the 2011 International Literature Festival in Berlin.[19] In this speech, Ben Jelloun lays out his ideals of committed literature and how they influenced his writing on the 'Arab Spring'. According to Ben Jelloun's essentialising ideals, the writer is the one who is able to see 'the truth, even if everything is done so as to drown it in noise, fog, and appearances'.[20] After writing articles on Mohamed Bouazizi's self-immolation, Ben Jelloun decided to fictionalise this unusual act to explore the motives for a deed without tradition in Arab-speaking countries.[21] Released in June 2011, *Par le feu*, a short text of fifty-six pages, weaves a narration around the weeks leading up to Bouazizi's self-immolation on 17 December 2010 – the act by which Bouazizi is said to have set into motion the Jasmine Revolution in Tunisia, and, by extension, the so-called Arab Spring. The text's ambiguous subtitle 'récit' – which could simply mean 'account' but also 'story' – underlines Ben Jelloun's conception of the role of the author as the one who translates the invisible through the means of literature and thereby transcends bearing witness in search of some kind of greater truth.[22] This 'greater truth' is mediated to the reader through the strong presence of a heterodiegetic narrator – that is, through a third-person narrator who is not a character in the story-world, but who explains, with a claim to authority, 'the hidden truth' about Bouazizi's fate to the Western reader.

Whereas the blurb of the book explicitly mentions Bouazizi's name, in the text itself the protagonist's surname is left out. This increases the story's exemplarity: proceeding from the tragic story of an individual turned iconic, the text aims at synecdochially representing the fates of many other young men in similar situations.[23] Thus turning its protagonist into the representative of a whole generation, *Par le feu* can be read as an endeavour to create a committed piece of writing which complies with Ben Jelloun's declared responsibilities of the author. So although Bouazizi is easily discernible in *Par le feu*, Ben Jelloun has – in accordance with his idea about the role of the writer and to reinforce the book's message – also made use of his creative leeway in introducing considerable changes to Bouazizi's life. The kind of changes as well as the focus, framing and form in fictionalising Mohamed's story, however, illustrate the problematic role which essentialist claims to truth in writing – marketed as area expertise – continue to play in Neo-Orientalist discourse.

Time and the Orient

In present-day Neo-Orientalist discourse, the Middle East and North Africa region is still frequently depicted as lagging behind in civilisation.[24] In the realm of fiction, the trope of backwardness often relegates the respective countries to a stereotypical realm in which the sun allegedly burns so relentlessly that all activity is muted to passivity and never-ending stasis. Outmoded though they might at first appear, clichés such as these – dating back to Montesquieu's climate theory and beyond[25] – have been reiterated to this day.[26] This is, of course, not to say that more nuanced writing does not exist. However, the success on the literary market and the positive reception of novels such as Martin Mosebach's *Mogador* (2016) or Marc Trévidic's *Ahlam* (2016) as well as the great media attention they received illustrate the extent to which Orientalist stereotypes of backwardness are still accepted, even in institutions with a high cultural capital.[27]

Due to this discourse of backwardness and because of widespread associations of Islam with anti-modernist tendencies, time is often presented as obeying different rules in the Islamicate world. Although representations which portray languor and passivity as common obstacles to progress in the Middle East and North Africa region can rather be expected in pulp-Orientalist texts '"dumbed down" for mass consumption',[28] there is a more general tendency in Western discourse to anchor the region in an indefinite past.[29] In fact,

> [the] mention of Islam becomes a time-distancing device in and of itself. It connotes the absence of reforms, and thus pushes the Orient back into the sorry state attributed to it by the time-honoured tradition of Orientalism, always behind, never to achieve equal footing with the European powers.[30]

Discourses of reform – which frequently imply the backwardness of Islamicate societies – function in a similar way. Negotiations of reform in the Middle East and North Africa region – of which literature on the Arab uprisings can be seen as a prime example – often reverberate with echoes of a different temporal continuum linked to that specific geographical space. In Johannes Fabian's terms, this framing can be called 'allochronic'.[31] It presents the object of analysis in a time different from the temporality of the observer, so that it denies those who are represented access to a temporal space in which they can actively forge their own history.[32] Especially as the so-called Arab Spring was often depicted less as a propulsive movement, but rather as a catching up to Western standards of modernity and democracy by allegedly underdeveloped societies,[33] the notion of time in representations of the Arab uprisings consequently constitutes an important Neo-Orientalist feature.

In *Par le feu*, it is the form and framing which evoke the impression of an indefinite past. Like Camus' *L'Étranger* (1942), *Par le feu* begins and ends with incidents of death;[34] in the few pages in between, prolepses furthermore uphold death as a lingering presence. At the beginning of the story, the protagonist just returns home from his father's funeral and, in an act of desperation which foreshadows his own death at the end of the story, he burns his university degree in history. Roughly in the middle of the *récit*, Mohamed proleptically dreams that his father – clad all in white like his son during his self-immolation (*Feu*: 44) – asks him to join him in death (*Feu*: 33). Additionally, Mohamed witnesses the cortege for a young internet activist which foreshadows his own death and the reactions it triggers (*Feu*: 39).

The death of Mohamed's father and the university degree which the protagonist burns are elements which have been added; they create a circular frame of death and fire for the story. Within this frame, *Par le feu* opens up the necropolitical dimension of Mohamed's act: by showing how Mohamed is treated as bare life,[35] spat at and slapped by the corrupt local officials of government institutions, the text visualises how power is used to dictate how some people may live and how others must die – physically, but also socially.[36] In *Par le feu*, Mohamed feels like a socially dead person walking; in the end, he has nothing with which to counter the repression but his body:

> Mohamed avait la bouche sèche, sa salive devint amère. Il respirait avec difficulté. Il se dit : 'Si j'avais une arme, je viderais tout le chargeur sur ces salauds. Je n'ai pas d'arme, mais j'ai encore mon corps, ma vie, ma foutue vie, c'est ça mon arme …' (*Feu*: 45)[37]

As, however, the text presents the protagonist in a mentally fragile state after the death of his father, it foregrounds psychological reasons at the expense of structural explanations and thus tones down the important necropolitical dimension upon which it touches. Moreover, by turning the protagonist into a representative of rather well-educated adolescents, *Par le feu* aligns his story with a Western media narrative which stylised mostly young protesters who used social media as the force behind the uprisings.[38] If *Par le feu* thus starts exploring the issue of necropolitics, its frame of death and fire at the same time domesticates it by confining its wider implications to the narrow limits of this particular narrative.

In addition, the text evokes Mohamed's self-immolation from a temporal distance only. Next to the two instances of death which mark the *récit*'s beginning and end, the forty-one pages in between leave little room for developments in the present time. For less than half a sentence, the temporal space stays dialogic. Then, it yields to the pressure of the *passé simple*, a literary form of the past tense, which – in the context of poverty-inducing despotism evoked in *Par le feu* – confines Mohamed's story to a past which has little to do with the temporality of the reader: 'En rentrant du cimetière où il venait d'enterrer son père, Mohamed sentit que le fardeau qu'il portait s'était alourdi' (*Feu*: 9).[39] At the very end of the text, after a thoroughly allochronic depiction of Mohamed's country and after his self-immolation, the tense switches to the present. Suggesting that only now that Mohamed has performed this act, and that the Arab uprisings are about to begin, can he and his country enter the realm of the present, this change from the *passé simple* into the present tense uneasily reverberates with the narrative of the alleged backwardness of the Middle East and North Africa region.

The fact that the *récit* is written in a monologic, hermetically sealed mode – which is so heavily burdened by its moral that every attempt to let the action speak for itself in more mimetic scenes is crushed – further reinforces the allochronic impression in *Par le feu*. Although its twenty-four short scenes and their different settings are dispersed across the home town of the protagonist and might thus convey the impression of a broader interest in the sociopolitical context that ultimately motivated the protagonist's suicide, his interlocutors' role as mere programmatic mouthpieces quickly becomes clear. In one scene, for instance, two plain-clothes policemen spy on and then harass Mohamed. After they have slapped him and have thrown over his cart of produce, bystanders begin to assemble around him and comment on the incident in a theatrical fashion:

> – C'est dégueulasse ! Quelle honte ! S'en prendre à un malheureux vendeur …
> – Ils se comportent comme dans les films sur la Mafia … Ils veulent leur pourcentage, les salauds !
> – Ça ne peut plus durer ! Un jour ou l'autre, Dieu fera briller la vérité. (*Feu*: 32–3)[40]

Aside from the unlikeliness of such overt support for an alleged dissident in the police state portrayed in *Par le feu*, hackneyed phrases such as 'malheureux vendeur' and 'comme dans les films sur la Mafia' create the impression of an indignant speaking chorus airing the book's moral interpretation of the events. Thus, neither the mimetic scenes nor the descriptive sections grasp the opening offered by the present tense of the dialogues – namely the opportunity to break away from the allochronic time frame evoked by the closed circular frame of the narration. Instead, dialogue is reduced to a formal monotone in the guise of polyphony.

Scenes with a decidedly backward flavour further amplify this effect of a faraway time clearly sealed off. When, for instance, Mohamed's brother Yassine talks about the futility of attempts to try to escape the circle of poverty ('tu t'as bossé comme un fou et après : pas de boulot, tu reprends la charrette de papa' *Feu*: 30),[41] his resignation is cast against the background of the fate of a former caretaker, who loses his job, thus resorts to stealing a chicken and is beaten by the police for his theft. On the one hand, this incident further visualises the extreme precarity of the population. On the other hand, however, by introducing a 'c'était bizarre' (*Feu*: 31) and by levelling man and chicken by means of the simile 'la poule criait comme lui', this scene trivialises the severity of the man's situation and reduces it to a distant cliché of injustice in a despotic system:

> Je l'ai reconnu, c'est le concierge de l'immeuble en verre, tu vois, celui à l'autre bout de notre quartier, celui qu'ils ont renvoyé, on ne sait pas trop

pourquoi ; là, il avait volé une poule, c'était bizarre, la poule criait comme lui car il ne voulait pas la lâcher. Il en a reçu des coups ... (*Feu*: 31)[42]

More subtle changes to Mohamed Bouazizi's story, which depend on the regional knowledge of the reader, also function as time-distancing devices. Apart from the modification of Ben Ali's twenty-four years in office into the fictional president's thirty years as head of state, a deviation which further highlights the undemocratic and stagnant nature of the regime, the currency is changed in *Par le feu*. Instead of the Tunisian dinar, the rial, which served as Tunisia's currency until 1891,[43] is (re-)introduced. At first glance, opting against the dinar, with which the reader might be familiar from *The Arabian Nights*, appears to be a move into the temporality of the observer. At second glance, however, this change – although it might suppress the allochronic association with *The Arabian Nights* – not only re-establishes a link with Tunisia's pre-1891 past, but at the same time undergirds the discourse of poverty-inducing despotism. By aligning the setting with states such as Iran, Oman, Yemen, Qatar and Saudi Arabia, all of which share the currency rial/riyal, the story fosters associations of backwardness, social injustice, despotism and religious fundamentalism, and invokes an allochronic time frame in which reform and change seem highly unlikely.

Because of this enclosed temporal framing of the story, what is implied to be Tunisia in 2010/11 is not only inextricably linked with anti-modern tendencies but is presented as so far removed from the influence of current affairs that all modernising impulses seem to either become lost on the long way into the narrative past of the book or to bounce off its firm delimitations. The choice of intertextual references in *Par le feu*, most notably *Spartacus* (1960), complements this impression of a civilisation which is lagging behind. While Mohamed witnesses how 'notamment le film *Spartacus* joué par Kirk Douglas' (*Feu*: 27) is destroyed by the wheels of a National Security van and even tells Zineb that 'La police a vaincu Spartacus !' (*Feu*: 28),[44] this allusion to the slave uprising against the Roman oligarchy is implied to foreshadow the revolution which is about to begin. Not only does it thus suggest that highly commercialised Western role models serve as guidance on how to achieve democracy and rule of law, but it also aligns the country with a point in Western history more than 2,000 years ago.

Despotism and the Orientalist Synecdoche

Within its allochronic framing, *Par le feu* tries to paint a comprehensive picture of precarity as the result of a corrupt and abusive police state and of a despotic regime. To foreground the ordinariness of repression, the *récit* presents a great number of scenes. In fact, as the leitmotif in the story, state violence and corruption feature on most of the pages of the text. After Mohamed – who is now the breadwinner of the family – decides to take up his father's business as a street fruit vendor, he is continually confronted with aggressive police officers: twelve of the book's twenty-four short chapters contain scenes in which the protagonist is routinely checked by agents, who, both in uniform and in plain-clothes, verbally and physically harass and humiliate him.[45] Rendering Mohamed increasingly desperate, they repeatedly demand bribes, blackmail him or chase him from his selling spot (for instance, *Feu*: 18, 22–3, 24, 38). This abusive behaviour culminates in a scene in which police officers throw Mohamed to the ground, kick him violently and confiscate his cart of produce (*Feu*: 40). Introduced by 'Ce fut violent' (*Feu*: 40),[46] this scene draws a stark contrast between the police and their victims: while Mohamed is described as 'impuissant' (*Feu*: 41; 'powerless') and lies helplessly on the ground while being physically attacked, the police officers are depicted as invariably violent and callously opportunistic.

To intensify this contrast, the text complements its direct portrayal of corruption and state violence from which the protagonist suffers with incidents of police transgressions which Mohamed witnesses indirectly. For instance, when he comes across a funeral procession, Mohamed hears about the case of an alleged internet activist. While plain-clothes policemen take pictures of the cortege, Mohamed learns that the deceased was arrested and that, a week later, his dead body was deposited on his parents' doorstep (*Feu*: 39). In this way, the scenes assemble different scenarios of injustice into a broader picture. As, however, they only enumerate the transgressions by the police without providing the characters with psychological depth, this combination of showing and telling does not result in a more rounded portrayal of the precarious state in which the characters involved find themselves; instead, as characters, they remain flat and fleeting – and their suffering distant.

Despite Tahar Ben Jelloun's declared goal of creating a 'sober and direct'[47] piece of literature on the so-called Arab Spring, the accumulation of short scenes and flat characters – in combination with the often-indignant tone of the commenting narrator – creates a unidimensional and melodramatic impression. This also holds true for the depiction of the despotic ruler in *Par le feu*, a president who is highly evocative of Ben Ali. In addition to the fear instilled by the transgressions of the police, the story offers the corrupt and despotic behaviour of the president's family and the concomitant precarity of the population as the reasons for Mohamed's self-immolation. If the protagonist's family illustrates that the citizens live at or below the poverty level, chapter 14 portrays the president as vain and surrounded by luxury.

Although the historic Ben Ali, his wife Leila and her family – having withheld a third of Tunisia's public funds[48] – are indeed notorious for their extreme corruption and self-enrichment, the framing and form of the text create a contrived impression. *Par le feu* presents the despotic, self-enriching rulers, who count and capitalise on their subjects' devoutness and child-like nature so as to exploit and oppress them (*Feu*: 27), in a highly stereotypical fashion. Describing how the president 'fit un signe de la main comme s'il saluait un enfant' and 'musique sirupeuse' (*Feu*: 30) is played,[49] the text reduces its representation of politics to a charade played for immature citizens, who can be fooled by theatrical enactments of their head of state. With the aid of make-up, empty rhetoric and music on the one hand, and intimidation and nepotism on the other, so the text suggests, the president has been able to control the fate of the country for the last thirty years. The comments of the narrator additionally underscore this marked contrast and simplistic mode of representation:

> À la maison, la vieille télé était allumée. Une émission célébrait les trente ans de règne du président de la République. On le voyait en compagnie de sa femme qui avait pris beaucoup de poids. Ils étaient maquillés, bien habillés, trop bien habillés, trop propres, pas un cheveu ne dépassait, le sourire gras et satisfait. (*Feu*: 29)[50]

In an allusion to the nepotic nature of the regime, the president's wife is shown addressing the nation (*Feu*: 29–30). Having gained weight (both literally and symbolically), she claims that it is due to God's good will and especially to her husband's hard and indefatigable work that the country is prospering – while in fact the *récit* goes to great lengths to refute this assertion. So even though the president's wife avers that 'Dieu merci, le pays marche bien, les citoyens sont reconnaissants ; ils nous expriment tous les jours leur soutien, car ils se rendent compte que le pays avance et que la prospérité est là !' (*Feu*: 30),[51] scenes in which the people voice their disgust with the corrupt system belie her.[52] In order to demonstrate this contradiction and thus to undermine the empty rhetoric of the speech, *Par le feu* contrasts her statements with scenes which illustrate the widespread precarity of the population: for instance, before her speech, Mohamed and his girlfriend observe street children lighting a fire in order to keep warm (*Feu*: 28); at the end of the chapter, Yassine tells Mohamed about the precarious situation of the former caretaker (*Feu*: 30–1).

The modulation between the two extremes of the social spectrum sketched in this chapter – that is, between the depiction of the corrupt presidential couple and the depiction of the street children and the caretaker – is revealing in itself. It is achieved via the Orientalist trope of the allegedly passive Easterner,[53] embodied by Mohamed's mother. While the president justifies his lifestyle and his wife claims that he works incredibly hard, Mohamed's mother is presented as slumbering. In this state of half-awareness, she might or might not realise the charade on television. What is striking about this juxtaposition is that whereas the president's wife is given a voice by means of direct speech, Mohamed's mother – already restricted by the precarious living conditions of her family – is muted. Albeit critically, *Par le feu* thus reiterates the words of the powerful while not granting any representational space to the thoughts of Mohamed's mother. By reducing her portrayal to a brief description of her slumbering (*Feu*: 30), the text both represents but also further marginalises her precarity. If at the level of content, it does portray Mohamed's mother as living in precarious conditions, the level of form consequently reduplicates this deprivation: here, the subaltern cannot speak.[54]

Relying on a clear-cut dichotomy of roles, *Par le feu* thus casts the actively self-enriching presidential couple as grotesque despots, who, by means of the police state, control a population whom the text presents as not having any choice in the face of the injustices from which they suffer. If the text depicts the president as proactive, it paints his citizens as either passive or as deploring the conditions, but not, however, in active protest. Only briefly does *Par le feu* differentiate its binary representation of repression and precarity by showing how the regime expertly understands how to play its poverty-stricken population off against each other. This is illustrated in the following explanation, which Mohamed gives his mother after the police came to their house:

> Ces gens-là [the police agents] sont payés pour nous créer des problèmes ; si tu cherches un peu, tu découvriras que le flic est issu d'une famille aussi pauvre que la nôtre. Mais, comme tu sais, les pauvres ne s'aiment pas entre eux ... (*Feu*: 21)[55]

However, instead of further exploring the constraints which the precarious living conditions impose on the population and its agency, *Par le feu* reduces any alternative civil practices to mere mentions. Although it presents Mohamed as a former member of the 'diplômés chômeurs' (*Feu*: 20), a group of young graduates protesting against the high unemployment rate among people with a university degree,[56] this group's campaigns or those of any comparable movements are not shown. Instead, the text focuses on the harassment Mohamed has to endure due to his former membership. *Par le feu* consequently presents state violence at the expense of representational space for developments in civil society – a civil society which it portrays consisting of stock characters only and whose reactions it reduces to a generic lament or resignation in the face of repression. By doing so in a co-textual framework which includes – without marking them as ironic – sentences such as 'Il ne manquait que les charmeurs de serpents, les voyantes, les sorciers et autres charlatans' (*Feu*: 27),[57] the text, moreover, Orientalises its characters.

As a result of this Orientalisation of repression and especially with the international dimension of a Western political elite backing Ben Ali[58] – for, among others, economic and trade reasons – remaining completely unmentioned, *Par le feu* casts the political stasis and concomitant precarity of the population as a local problem. So, while with its focus on precarity, *Par le feu* does depict serious existing problems, it nonetheless reduces the issue to the binary opposition of the self-enriching despot and citizens which it portrays as resigned and passive. Thus presenting despotism and poverty as going hand in hand, the *récit* foregrounds microeconomic and allegedly home-made problems. As opposed to this, it leaves the important macroeconomic dimension of the uprisings out of consideration. Even though Tunisia was an exception during the 2007/8 financial crisis in that its 'financial sector remained fairly robust',[59] exports did go down massively, negatively affecting the export and labour markets.[60] In *Par le feu*, however, foreign influences are reduced to one single passing mention: Mohamed briefly considers applying for a microcredit but decides against it due to reasons of impracticality (*Feu*: 11–12). So apart from this short criticism of Western development aid, *Par le feu* presents Mohamed's country as without any connections with the globalised economy. If this limited view might be linked to the perspective of the focaliser, the heterodiegetic narrator comments so frequently in the text that the absence of global contextualisation seems worth noting. Mohamed's self-immolation, by contrast, features as an isolated act leading to the implosion of what is presented as the vacuum of self-inflicted political stasis in a despotic country devoid of any noteworthy civil society. As a consequence, and even while decrying the regime, the *récit* presents Mohamed's act and its repercussions as an isolated spasmodic thrust of a society allegedly lagging behind the West – and which it marks by its sudden transition from the *passé simple* to the present tense.

Ending on the word 'death', the book's concluding sentence alludes to the question of appropriating Mohamed Bouazizi's story: 'Jamais personne ne lui [Mohamed] volera sa mort' (*Feu*: 50).[61] When a cinema producer approaches Mohamed's family to obtain the exclusive film rights to Mohamed's tragic story, the protagonist's sisters indignantly spurn the offer:

> Mais ses deux filles, elles, avaient bien saisi : ce type achète la mort de notre frère pour se faire du fric ! Quelle horreur, quelle horreur absolue ! L'histoire de Mohamed n'appartient à personne ; c'est l'histoire d'un homme simple, comme il y en a des millions, qui, à force d'être écrasé, humilié, nié dans sa vie, fini par devenir l'étincelle qui embrase le monde. Jamais personne ne lui volera sa mort. (*Feu*: 50)[62]

Due to the fact that the sisters' indirect discourse is rendered without quotation marks, the remainder of the paragraph cannot clearly be attributed either to them or to the narrator.[63] Nevertheless, the wording as well as the reference to Mohamed's supra-individual relevance suggest at least a strong narratorial presence which mediates his sisters' opinion and condemns the film producer's offer.[64] If the last paragraph can be read as a critique of the appropriation of a tragic event by the entertainment industry, the concluding sentence raises the unsettling question whether, to a certain degree, exploiting the story is what the *récit* itself might have done.[65] Mary Anne Lewis argues that in order to avoid this very accusation – which echoes the criticism Ben Jelloun faced after Les Éditions du Seuil released his 2001 novel *Cette aveuglante absence de lumière* (*The Blinding Absence of Light*),[66] the author did not wait long but published his book in the midst of the political upheavals and used a third-person narrator instead of a first-person narrator.[67] This commenting heterodiegetic narrator, however, does not only reduce the beginning of the Arab uprisings to an unequivocal narrative marketed under the name of a so-called area expert, but he also confines Mohamed's story to the realm of allochronic time.

How naturalised this allochronic impression of the text seems to be is illustrated by the often uncritical reception of the text – most prominently so by another writer–intellectual often quoted in discourse about the Islamicate world. On the back cover of the English translation of *Par le feu*, Salman Rushdie provides the following quote: 'Tahar Ben Jelloun's response, in both fiction and nonfiction, to the death by self-immolation of Mohamed Bouazizi in Tunisia – the "spark" that lit the "fire" of the Arab Spring – is both a valuable political document and a powerful artistic act.'[68] Moreover, in an academic article on the text, Sara Izzo does not shy away from interpreting the *récit* by means of a comparison of Mohamed Bouazizi's story and the *Arabian Nights*. To corroborate her own argument that Ben Jelloun's fictionalisation of Bouazizi's self-immolation constitutes a literary intervention, Izzo quotes a paragraph by Marianne Gozlan. Claiming that Bouazizi's story would not scar the *Arabian Nights*, Gozlan briefly retraces Bouazizi's act and its effects in a series of clichés.[69] Without challenging Gozlan's Orientalist undertones and without reflecting on the reception history of the *Arabian Nights*, Izzo cites her to underline that Bouazizi's act constitutes a historical moment – as if this text were the only point of reference against which the Arab world can be measured:

> L'histoire de Mohamed Bouazizi se calligraphiera désormais tel un conte immortel dans l'histoire arabe. Elle s'est déroulée à la fin de la première

décennie du XXIᵉ siècle, mais ne déparerait pas dans un récit de *Mille et Une Nuits*. Un marchand de fruits d'une province inconnue a défait le tyran qui vivait dans le velours, l'or et la prosternation de ses vizirs au cœur de son palais. Et cela, qui tissera la légende, n'est pas une légende mais une réalité, jaillie des jours de la Tunisie profonde et que l'intégralité des imaginaires arabes a reconnue immédiatement pour sienne.[70]

While this reflects that – in the intellectual, journalistic and scholarly work on the Arab uprisings – allochronic frames are still recurrent, in *Par le feu* itself, they cast the narrative in a backward-looking frame. As a consequence, the story's focus on corruption and state injustice as the reasons for Mohamed's precarious living conditions presents Mohamed's fate as a result of decidedly localised, Orientalised problems which are far removed from the Western reader: questions of vulnerability and precarity are mainly portrayed as the results of a corrupt despotic ruler and his police state.

Jonas Lüscher: *Frühling der Barbaren*

Born in Zurich in 1976, Jonas Lüscher is a Swiss-German writer. Before studying philosophy, he trained as a primary school teacher and also worked as a freelance editor and screenwriter in Munich.[71] In 2011, he started working on a doctoral thesis which – building on Richard Rorty's theory of neopragmatism – deals with the role of narration in describing social complexity. In 2014, he left the Swiss Federal Institute of Technology in Zurich without completing his PhD. His first published work of fiction, *Frühling der Barbaren*, was nominated for both the Swiss Book Prize and the German Book Prize and won the Franz Hessel Prize for Contemporary Literature in 2013 as well as the Hans Fallada Prize in 2016. As of spring 2020, it has been translated into twenty languages. In 2017, Jonas Lüscher received the Swiss Book Prize for his second novel *Kraft* (2016). Both *Frühling der Barbaren* and *Kraft* have received great critical acclaim. Lüscher has been living in Munich since 2001.

Translated into English as *Barbarian Spring*,[72] *Frühling der Barbaren* imagines how, on the globalised capitalist market, precariousness can turn into precarity overnight. As indicated by the pun in the title, *Frühling der Barbaren* stirs up notions of alleged progress and its Others against the backdrop of the so-called Arab Spring ('Arabischer Frühling'): while the mask of Western civilisation falls, the uprisings gain new momentum. The novella's protagonist, Preising, is a Swiss industrial heir. He performs exclusively representative functions for his company, Prixxing, the global market leader in Wolfram CBC circuits, an invention necessary for every mobile phone mast in the world (*Frühling*: 8). On a business trip to Tunisia, where child workers produce circuits for Prixxing under inhumane working conditions, Preising witnesses how a group of young London city traders celebrates a luxury wedding at a desert resort. When the British pound crashes and the former elite find themselves penniless, this celebration of excess abruptly turns into massacre. Physically unscathed, Preising escapes from the inferno of the burning resort, but is afterwards committed to a mental hospital by the CEO of his company. There, he relates his story to a fellow patient.

Similar to *Par le feu*, *Frühling der Barbaren* connects questions of precarity with the Arab uprisings. However, while *Par le feu* presents precarity mainly as an endemic problem of an Arab country, *Frühling der Barbaren* explores its systemic dimensions. In Lüscher's novella, it is the financial crisis which facilitates a second wave of the uprisings. Thereby reminding the reader of the repercussions of the financial crisis of 2007/8 for the so-called Arab Spring, *Frühling der Barbaren* focuses on the implications of globalisation and thwarts unidirectional narratives of putative Western progress and an allegedly anti-modern Islamicate world.[73] Whereas *Par le feu* can be read as an attempt to explain the precarious living conditions of a young man from the Middle East and North Africa region to a Western audience, *Frühling der Barbaren* – situated between the Tunisian desert and the psychiatric hospital – thus defies uniform claims to truth and opts for the edges of so-called civilisation.

Truth and the Other

Following the epigraph – a definition of barbarism by sociologist Franz Borkenau – *Frühling der Barbaren* begins with the sentence '"Nein," sagte Preising, "du stellst die falschen Fragen"…' (*Frühling*: 7).[74] Repeated almost verbatim but rendered even more absolute in the singular at the end of the book ('"Du stellst schon wieder die falsche Frage," sagte Preising' (*Frühling*: 125)),[75] this sentence creates a spiral-shaped frame for the narrations in between. In combination with the friction between the frame and embedded stories of the novella, it calls narrative reliability into question and makes the protagonist's attempt to re-install his order of discourse appear futile. While implicitly, the 'du' ('you') used in the opening and closing sentences also addresses the reader, at the diegetic level of the story-world, Preising directs these words to a fellow patient. The latter is staying at the same psychiatric hospital in Switzerland, has started the habit of joining Preising during his walks along the high yellow walls of the hospital garden (*Frühling*: 7–8) and functions as the narrator of the novella's frame story.

As patients at a mental institution, both the frame narrator and Preising inhabit ambiguous narrative positions.[76] According to the logic of a society which uses the mental hospital to discard its deviant Others – those threatening its rationalist logic[77] – both Preising and his fellow patient could be considered unreliable narrators. And indeed, the frame narrator openly voices doubts as to the credibility of the protagonist's stories. He thereby creates additional distance to Preising's embedded story: 'Ob Preisings Geschichten wahr waren oder nicht, wusste man nie so genau, aber darum ging es nicht. Preising ging es um die Moral' (*Frühling*: 15).[78] Although there is a third – omniscient – narrator who first appears on the second page and fills some of the narrative gaps between the frame narrator and Preising's two narratives, the ironic tone he uses further undermines narrative reliability (see, for instance, *Frühling*: 8–10). Doubts about what information is reliable are consequently not only aroused by the friction between the different diegetic levels, but also by the narrative tone and the fact that two of the three narrators are in a mental institution.

Playing with expectations of reliability and hegemonic discourse, the novella presents the psychiatric institution as a space of counter-rationality which challenges common notions of rationality, mental illness, difference and so-called civilisation. It can be read, as Jonas Lüscher indicates, less as an 'Irrenhaus' ('madhouse') and more as an 'Ort des Rückzugs in irren Zeiten' (a 'safe haven in mad times').[79] As such, the mental hospital functions as a heterotopia, as 'a sort of counter arrangement, of effectively realized utopia, in which all the real arrangements, all the other real arrangements that can be found within society, are at one and the same time represented, challenged, and overturned …'[80] At the level of form, this challenging and overturning of norms is reflected by the text's transcendence of its own novella form. Typically, a novella is 'restricted to a single event, situation and conflict, which produces an element of suspense and leads to an unexpected turning point (*Wendepunkt*) so that the conclusion surprises even while it is a logical outcome'.[81] *Frühling der Barbaren*, however, does not only introduce many subplots, but by highlighting Preising and the frame narrator's isolation behind the high yellow walls of the hospital garden, it also deconstructs the social dimension of the frame narrative which the novella often contains.[82]

Through its juxtaposition of civilisation and its Others by means of the heterotopia, *Frühling der Barbaren* provides a critique of the constructedness of such notions. Excluded from the so-called realm of reason, Preising and the frame narrator embody a critique of the conditions on the outside of the mental institution. Not appearing more unreasonable than the ruling financial elite depicted in the novella, they subvert the distinction between rationality and mental illness. Though not in conflict with the law, the kind of calculating rationale which the ruthless British traders represent appears inherently violent even before the crash of the British pound. When Great Britain goes bankrupt, the former financial elite's implicit but conformist brutality becomes explicit and physical.

Simultaneously, the text uses this juxtaposition to criticise the construct of reason in a society which ostracises the Other and comes up with institutions which regard healing as teaching the Other how to act in a conformist way.[83] In a truly biopolitical manner, dominant dictums based on performance logic and success have inscribed themselves in the mind and psyche of the frame narrator. Probably due to the loss of his child (*Frühling*: 36), he suffers from depression, an ailment almost prototypical of those considering themselves non-achievers in neo-liberal societies.[84] The frame narrator judges himself as dysfunctional and debases himself as someone – 'einer wie ich' – who performs poorly (*Frühling*: 8). Expressing his internalised self-contempt, he self-deprecatorily states that his condition is a 'common depression' (*Frühling*: 15).

In contrast, Preising's ailment – a kind of detached inertia bordering on the pathological – defies standard categorisation. While Preising himself hails it as sober-mindedness, his psychiatrist deems him to be in need of treatment.

She is, however, at a loss as to what psychopathological causes are at the root of her patient's condition:

> Und meist waren seine Geschichten Zeugnis seiner eigenen Besonnenheit, auf die er sich viel einbildete.
>
> Eine Besonnenheit, die Frau Doktor Betschart allerdings für behandlungsbedürftig hielt und für die sie auch drei Wochen nach Preisings Einlieferung immer noch nach der richtigen psychopathologischen Bezeichnung suchte. Die Diagnose schien schwierig, die Symptomatik unscharf, und auch die Uneinsichtigkeit des Patienten, die abwechslungsweise charmant und liebenswürdig, dann aber auch wieder mit ermüdender Starrköpfigkeit daherkam, vereinfachte die Sache nicht. (*Frühling*: 15)[85]

Preising's condition could best be read as a form of escapism from an interconnected world in which he, as the owner of a global company, refuses to assume responsibility – both for himself and for others.[86] If Preising cannot be diagnosed according to standard clinical categories, it is because his refusal to assume responsibility epitomises a systemic wrong, not an individual psychopathology – a wrong which is at the root of the neo-liberal system, not the individual psyche. The fact that Preising, who expresses this systemic condition, is referred to the mental hospital serves as a critique of how, by treating systemic problems at the individual level, conventional psychology often stabilises the very structures whose pernicious effects it tries to lessen.

As a young man, Preising already makes a half-hearted attempt to elude his father's business world and to escape into the world of fine arts. He interrupts his business studies and starts attending a private vocal school in Paris. Before his father dies, however, Preising completes his business degree, and then – at least officially – follows in his father's footsteps (*Frühling*: 8–9). In his company, now a globalised company with the anglicised name Prixxing and operating on five continents, he, however, retreats to merely representational functions and cedes command to his CEO Prodanovic and a 'Riege entschlussfreudiger Leistungsträger und Wertschöpfer' (*Frühling*: 9).[87] Both Preising's stay in Tunisia and at the mental institution can be seen as further attempts to either escape into spaces marked as irrational by Western society or into counter-worlds to Western rationality. Ironically, it is Prodanovic, the son of a Bosnian waiter, who arranges both Preising's trip to Tunisia and his referral to the psychiatric ward. Carrying the capitalist logic of commercialisation in his name,[88] Prodanovic turned Preising's family business – at that time at the brink of bankruptcy – into a global player (*Frühling*: 9). Preising thankfully hands over responsibility to his CEO and uses Prodanovic as an excuse for his own escapisms: "'Vielleicht," begann er endlich seine Geschichte, "wäre das alles nicht geschehen, hätte mich Prodanovic nicht in den Urlaub geschickt."' (*Frühling*: 8)[89] Just as in this sentence, Preising turns Prodanovic into the subject and himself into the object, Preising generally avoids fulfilling the role of the acting subject. Not only does this allow him to comment on what happens around him from a safe distance, but he also uses this tactic to relativise his own ethics. As the head of a company responsible for precarious working conditions and even child labour in its ancillary industries, the protagonist thus embodies how those with the necessary symbolic and financial means shirk their responsibility by distancing themselves from the suffering of others – in his case through an Orientalised form of cultural relativism.

Orientalism, Cultural Capitalism and Precarity

Although Preising tries to find refuge in the supposed counter-worlds of the fine arts, Orientalist exoticism and the mental institution, he keeps imbuing these heterotopias with his cultural capitalist attitude. As the ambiguity of his name indicates – the German *Preis* translates both as 'price' and 'cost' – Preising can uphold this position because he has the necessary monetary means: he can pay for goods and services of cultural capitalism in line with his liking while causing others high costs. When Preising finds himself in a globalised Tunisia which contradicts his Orientalist fantasies, he Orientalises and exoticises everything he sees around him. In his rendering of the happenings in Tunisia (or, to complicate things further, in the frame narrator's rendering of what Preising said), the protagonist thus perpetuates the myth of a timeless and unchanging Orient which he knows mainly from books – and which has nothing to do with the precarity he witnesses and his company's activities therein.

Preising's Orientalist stereotypes serve him, firstly, to find easy – localised – explanations for complex – globalised – situations. Secondly, they help Preising spice up his stories. For instance, consciously raising Orientalist expectations in his fellow patient, he begins his story with the words: 'Eine Geschichte ... aus der sich etwas lernen lässt. Eine Geschichte voller *unglaublicher* Wendungen, *abenteuerlicher* Gefahren und *exotischer* Versuchungen' (*Frühling*: 7; my italics).[90] After this enumeration of mystifying clichés, Preising tells the frame narrator how Moncef Daghfous, a Tunisian businessman, offered him his six daughters (and even considered promising him his sons) in order to become his business partner (*Frühling*: 13). When Daghfous is called away as one of his phosphate factories has started burning, his daughters serve Preising tea and regional sweets under the auspices of an old woman. However, as soon as they hear that their father died in the fire, they break with Preising's Orientalist expectations. Without further ado, they throw him out, and the laconic fashion in which they dash Preising's Orientalist narration style creates comicality:

> Als derselbe Hausangestellte die traurige Nachricht überbrachte, rechnete ich mit einem folkloristischen Trauerritual. Lautes Wehklagen, Haareraufen, expressives Zerkratzen der vom Schmerz verzerrten Gesichter, Schwächeanfall und dergleichen mehr. Stattdessen sahen sich die sechs Töchter schweigend an, räumten die Teegläser und die silberne Kanne weg und stellten mich mit einem angebissenen Baklava in der Hand auf die Straße. (*Frühling*: 15)[91]

Given the hyperbolic enumeration of clichés in this quotation, it remains unclear to what extent Preising himself – or possibly even the frame narrator – intensifies the contrast between the protagonist's expectations and his actual experience so as to make the story more entertaining. In fact, the novella uses this ambiguity to not only parody the Orientalist stereotypes themselves, but also to criticise their bourgeois and seemingly inveterate use as a form of entertainment – a form of entertainment which Preising cannot resist. Although Preising in his stories for instance wants to (or at least pretends to) skip his experiences with his business partners, the Malouchs, his Orientalist exoticism gains the upper hand. Interspersing his renderings with stereotypes, he indulges both in his infatuation with the odours and colours of the souk and his enthusiasm for having discovered these clichés:

> 'Ich überspringe,' sagte Preising, 'das Dinner in Malouchs Haus, köstlich, elegant, exotisch. Seine Frau, très charmante, überraschend modern. Das Haus, ein Palast, ganz traditionell, aber viele Fernsehapparate. Alles sehr nett. Aber doch ein Geschäftsessen. Wiewohl wir übers Geschäft kaum sprachen. Ich überspringe, es tut nichts zur eigentlichen Sache. Genauso wenig wie der Besuch des Souk am nächsten Morgen, den ich in Begleitung Saidas unternahm. Abenteuerlich überwältigend. Die Gerüche. Aber das ist eine andere Geschichte. Die Farben übrigens auch, überwältigend.' (*Frühling*: 19–20)[92]

Preising's interest in 'foreign cultures' (*Frühling*: 59) thus constitutes a form of exoticism which he likes to delve into as long as it is offered to him in a consumable form. In his complacently erudite and bourgeois exoticism, other places serve Preising mainly as a foil for his exoticist knowledge. When, for instance, he comes to the Hôtel d'Elisha, he insists on calling it by Elisha's Roman name 'Dido', thereby appropriating it into his knowledge of the Western canon:

> Er ließ sich also, die ersten Takte von Purcells Dido-Oper pfeifend, von der Geschäftsführerin Saida Malouch ins *Hôtel d'Elisha* führen, welches er konsequent als l'Hôtel Dido bezeichnete, dies sei schließlich der Name, unter dem die geliebte Königin ihrem Volk bekannt gewesen sei. (*Frühling*: 18)[93]

Full of enthusiasm, he tells the frame narrator about the ruse which Dido uses to abuse the hospitality of Berber king Iarbas: asking for a small strip of land which could be encompassed by an oxhide, Dido tricks Iarbas by cutting the oxhide into fine strips. She encircles a hill with these and is thus able to colonise a considerable piece of land on the coast of North Africa.[94] As this example illustrates, Preising does not question the moral implications of any kind of story as long as it comes with the nimbus of erudition. Instead, he displays a light-hearted approach to exoticism verging on the dangerous – as the impact of the story of the Berber wedding meal illustrates later on in the novella.

At least once in the novella, however, Preising displays a degree of narrative self-reflection which raises doubts as to whether his use of Orientalist tropes really is as ingenuous as he pretends it to be. After a digression on the surprising number of sweat glands which camels have, he metafictionally remarks that 'immerhin seien Kamele doch in seiner Geschichte so etwas wie ein Leitmotiv' (*Frühling*: 77).[95] This shows that at least to a certain extent, the protagonist consciously instrumentalises his culturally relativist and Orientalist views. As illustrated by his self-examination in a mirror with an Oriental décor, these views provide him with an exoticised frame for his own passivity and incapability of making even basic decisions:

> Dann stellte er sich vor den Spiegel mit dem orientalischen Rahmen, öffnete und schloss fünfmal den zweitobersten Hemdknopf, wobei er sich immer wieder prüfend betrachtete, bis er sich mit geschlossenen Augen zu einer komplizierten Bewegung der linken Hand durchrang, bei der es gänzlich dem Zufall überlassen war, ob der Knopf am Ende offen oder geschlossen blieb. (*Frühling*: 43)[96]

A superficially educated and entertaining tool, Preising's stereotypes consequently do not only help him reduce complexity in the world around him, but they go hand in hand with a more general, opportunistic cultural relativism which provides him with excuses for his irresponsible behaviour. For instance, in order to avoid taking a clear stance with regard to the issue of child labour, Preising seizes on threadbare platitudes. Moncef Daghfous, wanting to become the protagonist's business partner, offers to assemble Preising's CBC circuits on the outskirts of Tunis, in a sweatshop exploiting under-age Dinka refugees from Darfur. Not only does Preising not decline the offer, but he purports to accept it because, at a dinner party organised by Prodanovic's liberal business club, another businessman told him that 'the child labour thing was not as clear-cut as it seemed':[97]

> Preising hätte nur zu gerne abgelehnt, aber die Geschichte mit der Kinderarbeit war so einfach nicht. Er erinnerte sich an ein Abendessen mit Prodanovics liberalem Unternehmerclub, anlässlich dessen ihm sein Tischnachbar erklärt hatte, wie schwierig das mit der Kinderarbeit sei. Viel schwieriger, als dies gemeinhin der Gutmensch gerne hätte, aber so einfach sei es eben nicht, und unter gewissen Umständen sei es vielleicht dann doch das kleinere Übel. (*Frühling*: 12–13)[98]

While the businessman at Preising's table masks his pursuit of profit into an excuse for child labour, Moncef Daghfous openly praises the child workers as '[g]eschickte kleine Kerle' (*Frühling*: 12).[99] Both, however, accept child labour if it helps to maximise profits, and Preising uses exotisation and cultural relativism to mask and create a distance from the precarity for which he and his company are responsible. His cultural relativism is thus quickly debunked as a neo-liberal mask which allows the protagonist to feel ethical without feeling responsible – a phenomenon which causes the frame narrator to describe Preising as an

> erklärter Kulturrelativist, und zwar von einer gänzlich unchauvinistischen Sorte. Sein Liberalismus war ein Relativismus von der handwarmen Art eines Kinderbeckens. Gleichwohl war er auf unseren Spaziergängen immer bereit, die Tugendethik wie eine Monstranz vor sich herzutragen. (*Frühling*: 13)[100]

In only a little less blatant form, this kind of cultural relativism is also displayed by Sanford, a sociology professor and the father of the groom. When Sanford wants to take Preising to visit the ruins of a Berber settlement, Saida insists they take Rachid, the pool attendant, with them. Annoyed by Saida's insistence and taken aback by her brusque behaviour, Sanford quickly leaves all differentiation aside and 'verstieg sich aus lauter Ärger zur chauvinistischen These, die traditionelle Rolle der Frau in der muslimischen Gesellschaft müsse vielleicht aus westlicher Perspektive doch neu überdacht werden' (*Frühling*: 47).[101] Slightly hindered in his pride of discovery, the sociology professor thus voices overgeneralising culturalist hypotheses to express his anger and come to terms with the fact that he has just been overruled by a Tunisian woman. Not unexpectedly, Preising seizes this opportunity to chime in and – completely off topic – lecture 'about native peoples' (*Barbarian Spring*: 53).

At the level of form, the text highlights this opportunistic mix of cultural relativism, Orientalism and the refusal to assume responsibility both by turning this mix into the *unerhörte Begebenheit*, the 'event without precedent',[102] which is so constitutive of the novella form,[103] and by undermining it through the subversive use of intertextual references. In *Frühling der Barbaren*, it is this dangerous mix – and not the crash of the British pound – which constitutes the actual catastrophe. This catastrophe is instigated by three key moments in the text, all of which feature camels,[104] an animal emblematic not just of

Asia,[105] but also constitutive of the construct of the Orient.[106] Illustrating the different shapes of Preising's Orientalism and cultural relativism, the camel functions as the concrete symbol, the *Dingsymbol*.[107]

The protagonist first encounters camels on his way to the desert resort. When the jeep has to stop, he is jolted out of his daydreams and witnesses a gory spectacle on the road in front of him. A coach full of foreign tourists crashed into a herd of camels, ten or fifteen of which now lie dead and distorted on the road, while their owner has a heated argument with the coach driver under the supervision of armed soldiers. Whereas his business partner Saida Malouch enters the discussion, Preising stays in the car. To the frame narrator, he justifies his behaviour in the following way:

> 'Es war *laut*, es war *hektisch*, und es entbehrte nicht einer gewissen *Aggressivität*,' berichtete Preising mit sichtbarer Missbilligung. 'Und es zog sich dahin, ohne dass man sich auch nur im Geringsten zu einigen schien. In diesen Teilen der Welt, da hat der Disput einen ganz anderen Stellenwert … Versuche niemals, dich einzumischen.' (*Frühling*: 23; my italics)[108]

Instead of discerning the situation at hand, Preising explains it by means of a string of negative and essentialist clichés. Although his company produces circuits in exactly 'diesen Teilen der Welt', both his wording and his position show how Preising dissociates himself from his responsibility in a globalised world. His watching the scene from behind the window of a climatised car physically illustrates how he, a representative of the global North, coldly distances himself from the suffering of those who he presents as separate from himself. Unable to empathise, he becomes bored ('es zog sich dahin') and starts reading the newspapers – a behaviour which further highlights the duplicity of the protagonist's ethics. Confronted with great suffering right in front of him, he again decides not to act but resorts to reading about what is going on at a distance.

As Preising learns from the driver of the jeep, this accident destroys the camel driver's entire means of existence. As the roads are reserved for those with modern capital emblematised by jeeps or tourist coaches, the man does not elicit any empathy from Saida or the driver. Instead, concrete economic interests dominate their estimation of the situation. Not only will the passengers of the coach now miss their flights home, but other guests in the resort will miss out on a camel ride, as those camels were to be used for that purpose. A capitalist semantics also informs Preising's reactions. For a moment, he is moved by how the camel driver closes his dead animals' eyes. Having consumed this strong image, the protagonist is, however, unable to feel for the man, and his emotions are mainly structured in economic terms: 'Preising stockte der Atem, und eine große Traurigkeit *nahm von ihm Besitz*', and '... die Trauer und der Schmerz des Karawanenführers hatten derart *von mir Besitz ergriffen* ...' (*Frühling*: 24, 25; my italics).[109] Following this logic, Preising considers giving the camel driver the value of the thirteen camels, namely 1,500 francs, a sum which his shares in Prixxing yield in a single day (*Frühling*: 26–7). In the end, he nevertheless finds many relativising excuses not to help the man and drives off with Saida without having empathised or acted.

The reason why Preising is invited to the wedding of the two London city traders and thus witnesses the second key moment in the novella which features a camel, is that at the resort, he begins reading the German translation of Mahmoud Messadi's *Die Genese des Vergessens* (1945/74). Having found a quiet spot, a secluded canopy bed on a hill, Preising is joined by Pippa, the groom's mother. As two complete strangers sharing a mattress, they experience some awkward moments. However, when they find out that incidentally they are reading the same book, they start a lively conversation:

> Als ich jedoch kurz mein Buch zur Seite legte, um meine Sonnenbrille zu putzen, ertappte ich sie dabei, wie sie einen Seitenblick auf meine Lektüre warf. 'We seem to have the same interests,' sagte sie und hielt den Umschlag ihres Buches hoch. Tatsächlich lasen wir beide Mahmoud Messadis *Die Genese des Vergessens*, sie in englischer Übersetzung, ich in deutscher. Meine Buchhändlerin hatte es mir verkauft, als sie von meiner Tunesienreise erfuhr, es sei, so sagte sie, das wichtigste Werk der modernen tunesischen, ja vielleicht sogar der modernen arabischen Literatur.
>
> Bücher sind ein wundervoller Gesprächseinstieg. (*Frühling*: 32)[110]

While Pippa, whose daughter died on a Hurtigruten cruise ship on which she had been working as a librarian,[111] has a genuine interest in literature (*Frühling*: 40), Preising uses literature as a commodity and as a means of containing the so-called Orient. As reflected by his word choice, his relationship with books is mainly that of a consumer: 'Meine Buchhändlerin hatte es [Messadi's book] mir *verkauft* … es sei, so sagte sie, *das wichtigste Werk …*' Here, the choice of the verb, Preising's passive role as the customer as opposed to the bookseller's function as the agent, as well as the importance of the ranking of Messadi's book as one of the most important works of modern Arabic literature all follow the capitalist logic of commercialisation.

Although Pippa and Preising's conversation about literature appears more refined than the openly materialistic bearing of the young generation at the pool,[112] their encounter nonetheless presents capitalism in its cultural form. The fact that both of them read the same book does not only align with the commodification of world literature on the globalised market, but it also serves as a reminder that in the Orientalist tradition, the Orient was mostly studied as 'a textual universe', and that 'the rapport between an Orientalist and the Orient was textual …'[113] Next to underlining this textual dimension by means of intertexts, *Frühling der Babaren* uses its protagonist to illustrate the importance of literature in the Orientalist tradition. In fact, Preising's approach to Tunisia is a predominantly textual one. He prefers reading books to any real encounter, and his disappointed reaction during his visit to the ruins of a Berber settlement reiterates that of 'some of the early-nineteenth-century German Orientalists [whose] first view of an eight-armed Indian statue cured them completely of their Orientalist taste':[114] 'Du weißt, wie sehr ich mich für fremde Kulturen begeistern kann, aber diese Vielkammerbauten waren in Relation zu den Entbehrungen und der ganzen Aufregung eine Enttäuschung' (*Frühling*: 59).[115]

At the meta-level, this foregrounding of Orientalism as a textual universe can be read as, firstly, a self-referential criticism: despite its attempt to forego a unified image of the so-called Orient and although it undermines Orientalist stereotypes, the novella posits that this very universe serves as its springboard. Secondly, this focus on textuality and its exploitation serves as a critique of the Neo-Orientalist merger of an intertextual path-dependency and a capitalist logic which commodifies narratives. The latter becomes particularly clear in the story of the alleged traditional Berber wedding meal, the novella's third key moment involving a camel. Having intently listened to what Pippa has to say about Arabic literature, Preising hesitantly goes on a desert trip with her husband, Sanford, the next day. When Sanford begins to lecture Preising on the particularities of Berber village societies, however, Preising quickly loses himself in fragmentary platitudes about other peoples and then stops listening altogether. In order to regain Preising's attention, Sanford tells him how a traditional Berber wedding meal is allegedly prepared:

> Sanford bemühte sich, Preisings Aufmerksamkeit wiederzuerlangen und tischte die Geschichte vom traditionellen berberischen Hochzeitsmahl auf, welches im Wesentlichen aus einem gebratenen Kamel mit Couscous bestand. Das am Stück gebratene Kamel allerdings, so dozierte er, sei aufs Raffinierteste in der Art einer russischen Matroschkapuppe gefüllt mit einem ganzen Hammel, welcher mit einer Ziege, die wiederum mit einer Trappe und jene mit einem Dutzend mit Berberitzen und Datteln gefüllten Wachteln gefüllt sei. Preising misstraute der Geschichte. Er hatte das Gefühl, er habe sie oder Varianten davon schon anderswo gehört, und eher in humoristischen Zusammenhängen. (*Frühling*: 54)[116]

Even though Preising doubts the story, he tells it to the other wedding guests in order to impress them:

> Preising versuchte, ein paar der jungen Leute zu beeindrucken, indem er Sanfords Geschichte vom berberischen Kamelbraten zum Besten gab, worauf ihn zwei der Frauen nur noch mit Mister Mungo Park ansprachen. Darauf konnte er sich keinen Reim machen. (*Frühling*: 87)[117]

Unlike Preising, who is at a loss as to why they start addressing him as Mister Mungo Park, two of the wedding guests recognise the story of the recipe as a passage from T. C. Boyle's *Water Music* (1981).[118] *Water Music* fictionalises the explorations of the Niger River carried out by the historical Scottish figure Mungo Park and described in the latter's *Travels in the Interior Districts of Africa* (1799).[119]

When, after the crash of British pound, the brokers are no longer able to pay for the services at the resort, Quicky, who does not realise that the story is an intertextual joke either, promises the others an authentic Berber meal. Having killed Rachid, who tries to protect the animals (*Frühling*: 116–17), Quicky and his followers start putting the recipe into action. Faced with precarity for the first time in their lives, the city traders thus destroy the livelihood of many others:

> Man hatte das tote Kamel an den Hinterbeinen, mit vereinten Kräften an einem Strick ziehend, an den galgenförmigen Ständer eines großen Sonnenschirms gehängt und mit scharfem Hieb den Leib aufgeschnitten, sodass die Gedärme auf die glasierten Fliesen quollen. Eine magere Brünette in knappen Shorts und Bikini wühlte bis zu den Ellenbogen versunken in dem Tier, während andere sich bemühten, dem Kadaver das filzige Fell vom Leib zu ziehen. Quicky brachte mit einem gezielten Hieb die Hündin zum Schweigen, die panisch am Beckenrand stehend ihr leblos treibendes Herrchen [Rachid] angekläfft hatte. Dann nahm er sich die winselnden Welpen vor und schnitt einem nach dem anderen die Kehle durch... [E]inige der Losgelassenen [entfachten] mit den hölzernen Sonnenliegen im Sand unter den Palmen ein großes Feuer ... und andere [weideten] die Hunde aus ... um schließlich in einer grotesken, an Wahnsinn nicht zu überbietenden Umkehrbewegung, [sic] die Welpen in den mageren Mutterleib zurückzustopfen und die tote Hündin, mit ihrem von ihrer gemeuchelten Brut geschwollenen Leib, in die blutrot klaffende Höhlung des Kamels zu verfrachten. (*Frühling*: 118)[120]

A brutal parody of cultural capitalism, this slaughter scene marks the worst excess of Orientalism in the novella. In line with the logic of commercialisation, the brokers unwittingly turn an alleged cultural item, the story, into a commodity.

In this dismantling portrayal, the novella does not only let the action speak for itself, but by means of intertexts, it further subverts the presumed binary of Western progress and Oriental backwardness. Evoking Laura Wade's play *Posh* (2010),[121] the behaviour of the brokers, who all went to 'top universities' (*Frühling*: 98), serves as a critique of the often unscrupulous behaviour of the so-called elite. *Posh* stages a fictionalised version of the notorious Oxford Bullingdon Club – an Oxford society known for bringing forth future leaders. In *Posh*, the members of the club insist on having a ten-bird roast – a bird in a bird in a bird and so forth – before letting go of all alleged civilisation and beginning a massacre. Similarly, in *Frühling der Barbaren*, the bankers lose all social inhibitions and cause a bloodbath at the resort when they start preparing the stuffed camel. An intertextual reference to Ingeborg Bachmann's unfinished novel *Das Buch Franza* (1978; *The Book of Franza*) further fosters the novella's narrative subversion of presenting the Arab uprisings as a closing of an alleged civilisational gap. Not only does Bachmann's book feature a wedding and slaughter scene including a camel as well, but, more importantly, it depicts the crimes of extreme civilisation as far worse than those of so-called barbarism.[122]

By employing the camel in all its stereotypicality while at the same time self-referentially commenting on this clichéd use, *Frühling der Barbaren* consequently creates a bitter parable on the connection between Orientalism, cultural capitalism, precarity and the ethics of global responsibility. Demonstrating the nexus between these different issues, the camel – although not an unequivocal symbol itself – helps to create a textual coherence which illustrates the underlying brutality even before the pound sterling collapses: while in the first instance, the coach (with Western tourists inside photographing and filming the accident to underline their anecdote with gory pictures (*Frühling*: 22)) runs over a herd of camels, in the second instance, a camel delivers the British bride to her groom, in a wedding serving to further concentrate and accumulate capital. In the third instance, then, Westerners slaughter the camel.[123] Symbolised by the slaughter of the camel and the wish to eat it, this third instance marks the complete Western appropriation of the so-called Orient – at the touristic, commercial, literary and eventually even physical level – as well as the danger of literary and touristic Orientalist assumptions.

It is against this backdrop of brutal neo-liberalism and Orientalism that *Frühling der Barbaren* sets the so-called Arab Spring. In the novella, the uprisings happen offstage and are mediated several times. By means of this distribution of representational space, *Frühling der Barbaren* foregrounds questions of global economic dependencies over portrayals of precarity as an exclusively home-made problem. Moreover, the text thus raises awareness for the decisive role of both individual perspective and the media in representations of the Arab uprisings: Preising only sees an announcement on television which he does not understand and which he has Rachid explain.

The latter tells the protagonist that renegade Muslim Brothers and the Marxist–Leninist Fourteenth of January Front have formed an alliance and are now using the crisis of capitalism to provide the uprisings with new impetus:

> Statt Saida traf er [Preising] nur den Bademeister an, der gebannt vor einem Fernseher saß und einem Mann beim Verlesen einer Proklamation zusah. Geduldig wartete Preising, bis der Mann geendet hatte, um sich dann von Rachid erklären zu lassen, dass eine ungewöhnliche Allianz aus abtrünnigen Muslimbrüdern und marxistisch-leninistischer Front des 14. Januar die Gunst der Stunde, also die Krise des Kapitals, genutzt hatte, um dem arabischen Frühling zu einer zweiten Blüte zu verhelfen. Doch diesmal sei man entschlossen, die Sache zu Ende zu führen, mit eisernem Besen zu kehren und die ganzen Geldsäcke, die Günstlinge und Nutznießer des alten Regimes, die den Umsturz unbeschadet überstanden hatten, ja, die im demokratischen Tunesien sogar noch besser dastünden, weil sie die Pfründe des Gestürzten unter sich aufgeteilt hatten, endgültig zu beseitigen und ihr Vermögen wieder dem rechtmäßigen Besitzer, dem tunesischen Volk nämlich, zuzuführen. Die Tage der mächtigen und reichen Familienclans seien gezählt. Preising, der sehr richtig annahm, dass die Malouchs zu jenen zu zählen seien, erschrak und machte sich sowohl um Saida, wie auch um sich selbst, schließlich war er Gast der Familie Malouch, Sorgen, die auch der Bademeister nicht zu entkräften in der Lage war, wiewohl er versicherte, man spreche nur von Enteignung und nicht von Enthauptung, man lebe ja nicht mehr im Tunesien Ben Alis. (*Frühling*: 110–11)[124]

With its focus on the 'crisis of capitalism', this quotation redirects a great share of the responsibility for the precarious situation of great parts of the population from Ben Ali to a number of rich beneficiaries of both the old regime and the neo-liberal system. By demonstrating how the fall of the dictator alone has not solved Tunisia's problems, the novella highlights the systemic dimension of precarity. Through its mention of the Malouch family and its dubious business connections to Preising, *Frühling der Barbaren*, moreover, suggests that on the globalised market, rentier state theory does not suffice as a comprehensive explanation for local precarity.

After the resort starts burning, Saida and Preising flee in a jeep. Ironically, they find refuge in the sweatshop – the place which symbolises the precarity which they inflict and through which they enrich themselves at the cost of others. There, the foreman tries to strike a deal with Preising. In order to do so, he denounces Saida, who is beaten and arrested by four officers:

> Vier Uniformierte holten Saida ab. An den Haaren schleiften sie sie an den langen Tischen vorbei, an denen die Kinder die Köpfe gesenkt hielten und nicht von ihrer Arbeit abließen ... [Preising sah], wie Saida stolperte, wie sie sie mit Stiefeln traten und am Kragen ihres René-Lezard-Anzuges über den heißen Asphalt schleiften, die Bluse aufgerissen, den blassen Bauch, den blauen Büstenhalter freilegend. Es war ihm, als habe er dieses Bild schon einmal gesehen, in einem anderen Zusammenhang, unter anderen Vorzeichen, aber er konnte sich nicht erinnern ... (*Frühling*: 124–5)[125]

With the mention of Saida's blue bra, this scene evokes 'The Girl in the Blue Bra'. When she was attacked by the military during the uprisings on Tahrir Square, her black abaya came undone and her stomach and blue bra were exposed. Images of this went viral on 17 December 2011,[126] and the blue bra has since become a 'visual injustice symbol'.[127] By juxtaposing the violence which the state officials inflict on Saida with the brutality inherent in the child labour depicted, *Frühling der Barbaren* resignifies this symbol to include the issue of precarity in its portrayal of abuse and injustice. Through the contrast between the luxury of Saida's German designer suit and the desolate situation of the child workers, the novella illustrates the extremely unequal distribution of vulnerability and precarity. Thereby, *Frühling der Barbaren* presents the multilayered issues of distributional injustice and its global conditionality as a form of precarity and violence. Preising's role in this as well as his opportunism become clear when he, now in the sweatshop where underage Dinka refugees assemble his circuits, sees on television how 'das tunesische Volk durch eine üppig dekorierte Villa flanierte. Eine Villa wie jene, in der sich Preising noch keine vier Tage zuvor ... hatte bewirten lassen' (*Frühling*: 122).[128] Instead of emphasising an alleged civilisational gap of the country as a whole, the novella consequently focuses on the conditions of precarity on the global capitalist market: by foregrounding the detrimental effects of neo-liberalism on the precarious conditions of a great part of the population in Tunisia, Lüscher's book presents Tunisia as an interdependent part of the globalised market and as a country which also suffers from the systemic problems in a globalised world.

The Ethics and Poetics of Precarity

Their common focus on precarity notwithstanding, Tahar Ben Jelloun's *Par le feu* and Jonas Lüscher's *Frühling der Barbaren* feature diametrically opposed approaches of representing the Arab uprisings. These differences are not limited to the formal features of the texts, but also raise pertinent questions as to the role and responsibility of the writer and intellectual in Neo-Orientalist discourse. Due to its allochronic frame of distance and difference, *Par le feu* presents precarity mainly as an endemic problem of an Arab country which has little to do with the lifeworld or temporality of the supposed Western reader. The story focuses primarily on Tunisian state injustice and despotism and presents these as the reasons for Bouazizi's precarious situation and consequent self-immolation. While precarity is thus Orientalised, global interdependencies remain mostly unmentioned. The result is an exclusionary, localised representation of precarity and its role in the Arab uprisings. Through this process of Orientalisation, *Par le feu* detemporalises and decontextualises the uprisings and thereby perpetuates the myth of the Orient.[129] Furthermore, by generalising Mohamed Bouazizi's story and by presenting Tunisia as a synecdoche of the countries involved in the Arab uprisings, the *récit* recreates the dichotomy between the so-called West and the Middle East and North Africa region not to deconstruct it, but rather so that this entity of difference can be explained to the Western reader: *Par le feu* uses an authoritative heterodiegetic narrator who delineates the protagonist's self-immolation in an unequivocal, unidirectional and monological form which additionally creates distance. If this distance allows the reader to feel ethical without feeling responsible,[130] at the same time it enables the reader to externalise their own fears of social decline into the precarity of the Other.

While *Par le feu*, in line with Ben Jelloun's essentialising claim to truth, conveys its message in a straightforward form and explicatory tone, Lüscher's novella creates a polyphony of voices and a hybrid space of irony which undermine such an authoritative approach. By juxtaposing many subplots, three different narrators and considerable friction between these different diegetic levels, *Frühling der Barbaren* renders uniform narration obsolete. So, if in *Par le feu* the strong presence of the heterodiegetic narrator and his claims of objectivity and reliability reduce the beginning of the Arab uprisings to an unequivocal narrative in a book marketed as written by an area expert, *Frühling der Barbaren* diversifies its diegetic levels to self-referentially put into question any attempt at breaking down open-ended complexity into a unified explanation.

Told from the inside of a psychiatric hospital, the novella rearranges the issues of progress, precarity and the Arab uprisings in a way which does not only eschew aligning them according to categories of Orient and Occident, but which satirises and dilutes these notions themselves. Through its subversive use of intertexts and Orientalist clichés, *Frühling der Barbaren* dismantles the myth of the Orient by illustrating how this construct exists mainly as a bourgeois or capitalist form of art or entertainment. By presenting Tunisia as an interdependent part of the global capitalist world, the novella deconstructs the notion of the Orient as a separate geographical entity. Instead of depicting Tunisia as a representative of the construction of the so-called Orient, *Frühling der Barbaren* highlights the role which global interdependencies play with regard to the desolate living conditions of economically disadvantaged people in general – and which they played in the Arab uprisings in particular. Thereby debunking explanations of backwardness or an alleged civilisational gap often found in Western representations of the so-called Arab Spring, the novella dissolves Orientalist synecdoche into glocal metonymy. Thus, the text does not only show 'the dialectical intertwining of past and present, local and global that might be said to define the post/colonial modernity in the Middle East',[131] but through a subversion of its own novella form and by turning its protagonist's refusal to assume responsibility into its actual *unerhörte Begebenheit*,[132] it also reverses the ideas of proximity and distance which determine the way in which the precarity of others translates into ethical demands.[133]

Notes

1. Jonas Lüscher. *Barbarian Spring*. Trans. Peter Lewis. London: Haus Publishing, 2014. 25, 79–81. For the purposes of close reading, the text is henceforth quoted in the German original and in the main text as *Frühling* + page number. Jonas Lüscher [2013]. *Frühling der Barbaren*. Munich: btb, 2015.
2. Stefan Hofer-Krucker Valderrama. 'Die perpetuierte Katastrophe: Globalisierung und ihre Schattenseiten in Jonas Lüschers *Frühling der Barbaren*. Mit einigen

literaturdidaktischen Anmerkungen'. *Globalisierung – Natur – Zukunft erzählen* (2015): 39–57. 47.
3. David McNally. 'Tunisia and the Global Crisis'. *SocialistWorker.org*. 24 January 2011 (website – last accessed 15 December 2017).
4. Ibid.
5. See for instance Lorella Ventura. 'The "Arab Spring" and Orientalist Stereotypes: The Role of Orientalism in the Narration of the Revolts in the Arab World'. *Interventions* 19.2 (2017): 282–97; Stefan Borg. 'The Arab Uprisings, the Liberal Civilizing Narrative and the Problem of Orientalism'. *Middle East Critique* 25.3 (2016): 211–27.
6. David McNally. 2011.
7. Judith Butler. *Frames of War: When is Life Grievable?* London: Verso, 2009. 22.
8. Ibid. 25–6.
9. Tahar Ben Jelloun. *Par le feu: Récit*. Paris: Gallimard, 2011. Henceforth quoted in the main text as *Feu* + page number.
10. Judith Butler. 'Precarious Life, Vulnerability, and the Ethics of Cohabitation'. *The Journal of Speculative Philosophy* 26.2 (2012): 134–51. 150.
11. Ibid. 137.
12. Ibid. 138.
13. Nina Wardleworth. 'The Roman Maghrébin in the Aftermath of the Arab Spring'. *Contemporary French and Francophone Studies* 20.1 (2016): 141–9. 144.
14. Mary Anne Lewis. 'Between Francophonie and World Literature in French: Tahar Ben Jelloun's Evolving Authority'. *The Journal of North African Studies* 21.2 (2016): 301–9. 301–2.
15. Gallimard is currently offering forty-six titles by Tahar Ben Jelloun. 'Tahar Ben Jelloun'. *Gallimard.fr*. No date (website – last accessed 29 April 2020).
16. Nina Wardleworth. 2016. 142.
17. Mary Anne Lewis also argues that 'since the earliest days of his career, Ben Jelloun, as a francophone writer with national origins outside the Métropole writing in French, has written to a primarily French readership'. Mary Anne Lewis. 2016. 303.
18. For one of the numerous examples, see his *L'Islam expliqué aux enfants* (Paris: Seuil, 2002).
19. Tahar Ben Jelloun. 'Que peut la littérature, le cas du printemps arabe?' English translation of the opening speech at the International Literature Festival Berlin 2011. 10 August 2011 (website – last accessed 22 October 2017).

20. Ibid.
21. Deborah Treisman. 'This Week in Fiction: Tahar Ben Jelloun'. *The New Yorker*. 6 September 2013 (website – last accessed 26 April 2015); Tahar Ben Jelloun. 'Que peut la littérature, le cas du printemps arabe?' 2011. For the significance of the act of immolation in Bouazizi's case, see also Peter Hitchcock. 'Immolation'. *The Routledge Companion to Literature and Human Rights*. Eds Sophia A. McClennen and Alexandra Schultheis Moore. Abingdon and New York: Routledge, 2016. 86–94.
22. Tahar Ben Jelloun. 'Que peut la littérature, le cas du printemps arabe?' 2011.
23. Nina Wardleworth. 2016. 146.
24. Lorella Ventura. 2017. 282–97; Stefan Borg. 2016. 211–27.
25. Published in his 1748 treatise *De l'Esprit des lois*. Inge E. Boer. *Disorienting Vision: Rereading Stereotypes in French Orientalist Texts and Images*. Ed. Mieke Bal. Amsterdam and New York: Rodopi, 2004. 37–46.
26. Thilo Sarrazin's *Deutschland schafft sich ab* (2010) serves as an extreme case in point here. Thilo Sarrazin [2010]. *Deutschland schafft sich ab: Wie wir unser Land aufs Spiel setzen*. Munich: Deutsche Verlags-Anstalt, 2016.
27. Martin Mosebach. *Mogador*. Reinbek: Rowohlt, 2016; Marc Trévidic. *Ahlam*. Paris: J. C. Lattès, 2016.
28. Pavan Kumar Malreddy. 'Introduction: Orientalism(s) after 9/11'. *Journal of Postcolonial Writing* 3 (2012): 236.
29. Lorella Ventura. 2017. 282–97; Stefan Borg. 2016. 211–27.
30. Inge E. Boer. 2004. 164.
31. Johannes Fabian. *Time and the Other: How Anthropology Makes Its Object*. New York: Columbia University Press, 1983. 27, 32.
32. Ibid. 27, 32.
33. Julia Blandfort. 'Die Arabischen Revolutionen aus frankophoner Perspektive: Intellektuelle Interventionen als transkultureller Diskurs? Zur Einleitung'. *HeLix* 9 (2016): 1–21. 1; see also Lorella Ventura. 2017. 282–97; Stefan Borg. 2016. 211–27.
34. Jamal El Qasri. 'Le Degré zéro de l'émotion dans *Par le feu* de Tahar Ben Jelloun'. *HeLix* 9 (2016): 61–8. 62.
35. Giorgio Agamben. *Homo Sacer: Die souveräne Macht und das nackte Leben*. Trans. Hubert Thüring. Frankfurt: Suhrkamp, 2002.
36. Achille Mbembe. 'Necropolitics'. *Public Culture* 15.1 (2003): 11–40. 11–12.
37. 'Mohamed's mouth was dry, his saliva bitter. It was hard for him to breathe. He said to himself, "If I had a gun, I would empty it into these bastards.

I don't have a gun, but I still have my body, my life, my wasted life. This is my weapon.'" Tahar Ben Jelloun. *By Fire: Writings on the Arab Spring*. Trans. Rita S. Nezami. Evanston: Curbstone/Northwestern University Press, 2016. 69.
38. Amy Mitchell et al. 'The Role of Social Media in the Arab Uprisings'. *Pew Research Center*. 28 November 2012 (website – last accessed 28 January 2019).
39. 'Returning home from the cemetery where he just buried his father, Mohamed felt as though the burden he carried had become heavier.' 'By Fire'. 2016. 37.
40. 'This is disgusting! How shameful! Attacking a poor street vendor …' – 'They behave as if they were in mafia movies. These bastards all want their share!' – 'This can't go on! One day or other, God will bring the truth to light.' 'By Fire'. 2016. 57.
41. 'you studied like crazy, and then no job. Now you've taken up Dad's cart.' 'By Fire'. 2016. 55.
42. 'I recognized the man. He's the caretaker of that glass building. You know, the one on the other side of your neighbourhood. The man was fired, but nobody knows why. Today he stole a hen. It was bizarre. The man was screaming, and so was the hen, because he wouldn't let go of it. He really got a beating.' 'By Fire'. 2016. 56.
43. Amel Toumi. 'It Takes But a Spark …' *The Arab Review*. No date (website – last accessed 22 March 2015).
44. 'Among them [the DVDs crushed on the ground] was the movie *Spartacus*, starring Kirk Douglas'; 'The police defeated Spartacus!' Ben Jelloun. 'By Fire'. 2016. 52–3.
45. Chapters 6, 9, 10, 12, 13, 15, 16, 17, 18, 19, 20 and 21. Additionally, in chapter 8, a plain-clothes police agent questions Mohamed's mother at home.
46. 'It was violent.' 'By Fire'. 2016. 64.
47. Tahar Ben Jelloun. 'Que peut la littérature, le cas du printemps arabe?' 2011.
48. Angelique Chrisafis. 'Ben Ali Will Not Attend Tunisia Trial for Theft and Fraud'. *The Guardian*. 17 June 2011 (website – last accessed 15 January 2018).
49. 'The President made a gesture with his hand, as though waving to a child'; 'syrupy background music'. 'By Fire'. 2016. 55.
50. 'At home, the old TV was showing a program celebrating the President's thirty-year reign over the Republic. The President appeared with his wife, who had gained a lot of weight. Both wore makeup, were well-dressed – too well dressed, too tidy, with not a hair out of place, and smug, satisfied smiles.' 'By Fire'. 2016. 54–5.

51. 'Thank God the country is doing well. The people are grateful, and they show us their support every day, because they realize the country is prosperous and moving forward!' 'By Fire'. 2016. 55.
52. See, for instance, *Feu*: 32–3.
53. Inge E Boer. 2004. 93.
54. Gayatri Chakravorty Spivak. 'Can the Subaltern Speak?' *Colonial Discourse and Post-Colonial Theory: A Reader*. Eds Patrick Williams and Laura Chrisman. New York: Columbia University Press, 1994. 66–111.
55. 'These people are paid to create problems for us. In all likelihood, that cop comes from a family as poor as ours. But, as you know, the poor don't like one another.' 'By Fire'. 2016. 47.
56. One could of course argue that Ben Jelloun does include the 'diplômés chômeurs' even before they evolved as a group in Tunisia. Izzo remarks that, while in Morocco a structured movement of 'diplômés chômeurs' has been active since 1990, the first demonstration organised by the Union des diplômés chômeurs in Tunisia only happened in September 2012. Nonetheless, *Par le feu* does not portray the group itself or its activities but only its persecution by the police. Sara Izzo. '*Témoin actif* und *traducteur de l'invisible*: Tahar Ben Jellouns Konzept der literarischen Intervention im "Arabischen Frühling"'. *HeLix* 9 (2016): 69–83. 69–70.
57. 'Only snake charmers, fortune-tellers, sorcerers, and other swindlers were missing.' 'By Fire'. 2016. 52.
58. Michael J. Willis. *Politics and Power in the Maghreb: Algeria, Tunisia and Morocco from Independence to the Arab Spring*. Oxford: Oxford University Press, 2014. 333–4; Mahdi Darius Nazemroaya. 'Dictatorship and Neo-Liberalism: The Tunisian People's Uprising'. *GlobalResearch*. 19 January 2011 (website – last accessed 18 January 2018).
59. *Economic Diversification in Africa: A Review of Selected Countries*. OECD/United Nations. OECD Publishing, 2011. 50.
60. Sami Mouley. 'The Effects of the Global Financial Crisis and Combined Transition Factors Associated with the Post-Revolutionary Period: The Case of Tunisia'. *Mediterranean Yearbook* 2013. Barcelona: European Institute of the Mediterranean, 2013. 230–4. 230.
61. 'No one can ever steal his death.' 'By Fire'. 2016. 73.
62. 'But her two daughters understood very well: "This guy wants to buy our brother's death and profit from it! How horrible! What an utter nightmare!" Mohamed's story doesn't belong to anyone. It's the story of a simple man, like

millions of others, who, from being crushed, humiliated, and denied in life, became the spark that set the world ablaze. No one can ever steal his death.' 'By Fire'. 2016. 73.
63. The English translation resolves this ambiguity by means of quotation marks, see n. 62 above.
64. Nina Wardleworth even goes so far as to attribute these words to the author himself. 2016. 146.
65. In his article on immolation, Peter Hitchcock also mentions this irony. Peter Hitchcock. 2016. 91.
66. Tahar Ben Jelloun. *Cette aveuglante absence de lumière*. Paris: Seuil, 2001.
67. Mary Anne Lewis. 2016. 306.
68. Tahar Ben Jelloun. *By Fire: Writings on the Arab Spring*. 2016. Back cover.
69. Sara Izzo. 2016. 77, quoting Martine Gozlan. *Tunisie, Algérie, Maroc: La colère des peuples*. Paris: L'Archipel, 2011. 15.
70. Martine Gozlan. 2011. 15. 'Mohamed Bouazizi's story will from now on be calligraphed as an immortal tale in Arab history. It took place at the end of the first decade of the twenty-first century, but it would not mar a story in the Arabian Nights. A fruit vendor from an unknown province defeated the tyrant who lived in velvet, gold and in the prostration of his viziers deep in his palace. And this, which will weave the legend, is not a legend but a reality which shot up from some days in the depth of Tunisia and which the entirety of Arab imaginaries immediately recognised as its own.'
71. All bibliographical information quoted from 'Jonas Lüscher'. *C. H. Beck*. No date (website – last accessed 25 April 2020).
72. Jonas Lüscher. *Barbarian Spring*. Trans. Peter Lewis. London: Haus Publishing, 2014.
73. See Lorella Ventura. 2017. 282–97; Stefan Borg. 2016. 211–27.
74. '"No," said Preising, "you're asking the wrong questions" …' *Barbarian Spring*. 2014. 1.
75. '"Once again, you're asking the wrong question," he said.' *Barbarian Spring*. 2014. 132.
76. The fact that the two can unambiguously be identified as patients at a mental hospital is due to Lüscher's editor. As the author states in an interview, this was much less unequivocal in his first draft. Jonas Lüscher. 'Den Widerstand der Welt erfahren – Interview mit Jonas Lüscher'. Interview by Gregor Szyndler. *Zeitnah*. 3 June 2013 (website – last accessed 21 April 2019).

77. Michel Foucault. *Folie et déraison: Histoire de la folie à l'âge classique*. Paris: Gallimard, 1972. 16. In *Folie et déraison* (1964/72), Michel Foucault argues that in societies which control, discipline and repress non-conformist behaviour, the domains of mental illness and the Orient – besides sexuality and dreams – serve as allegedly irrational foils for a positive, rational self-definition.
78. 'You could never be sure whether Preising's stories were true or not, but that wasn't the point. What mattered to him was the moral of the story.' *Barbarian Spring*. 2014. 10.
79. Peter Surber. 'Krisen-Showdown in der Oase'. *Saiten*. 8 January 2015 (website – last accessed 8 March 2018).
80. Michel Foucault [1967]. 'Of Other Spaces: Utopias and Heterotopias'. Trans. Jay Miskowiec. *Rethinking Architecture: A Reader in Cultural Theory*. Ed. Neil Leach. New York: Routledge, 1997. 330–6. 332. Interestingly, the two narrators are not only at a mental institution, but in its garden. Apart from its numerous other associations, for Foucault, '[t]he garden is the smallest fragment of the world and, at the same time, represents its totality, forming right from the remotest times a sort of felicitous and universal heterotopia …' 334.
81. J. A. Cuddon. 'Novella'. *Dictionary of Literary Terms & Literary Theory*. 3rd edn. London et al.: Penguin, 1999. 600–1. Italics in the original.
82. Susanne Kleinpass. 'Storytelling in Zeiten der Finanzkrise'. *Praxis Deutsch* 255 (2016): 33–6. 33.
83. Michel Foucault. *Wahnsinn und Gesellschaft: Eine Geschichte des Wahns im Zeitalter der Vernunft*. Trans. Ulrich Köppen. Frankfurt: Suhrkamp, 1973. 176–7.
84. Alain Ehrenberg [1998]. *Das erschöpfte Selbst: Depression und Gesellschaft in der Gegenwart*. Trans. Manuela Lenzen and Martin Klaus. Frankfurt and New York: Campus Bibliothek, 2015. 25–7. In contrast to depression, which is defined as usually resulting in self-contempt or even self-hatred, burn-out – a condition massively on the rise in all professional groups but still often stylised as a condition affecting the formerly successful – mostly expresses itself in an externalisation of anger and contempt. Anna Katharina Schaffner. *Exhaustion: A History*. New York: Columbia University Press, 2016. 169–82 and 202–32.
85. 'For the most part, his stories bore witness to his own prudence, of which he was inordinately proud. Yet Dr Betschart regarded Preising's prudence as a suitable case for treatment, a psychopathology for which she was still, three weeks after his referral to the institute, trying to find the correct clinical description.

The diagnosis appeared difficult, the symptoms unclear, and the obduracy of the patient, who veered between being charming and amiable on the one hand and tiresomely stubborn on the other, wasn't exactly helping either.' *Barbarian Spring*. 2014. 10.
86. Susanne Kleinpass. 2016. 34. The fact that Preising, both Swiss and rich, prefers not to actively interfere can be read as an ironic exaggeration of stereotypes about the protagonist's country of origin.
87. 'his team of thrusting high achievers and go-getters'. *Barbarian Spring*. 2014. 3.
88. Stefan Hofer-Krucker Valderrama points out that the name Prodanovic derives from the Croatian verb 'pròdati' ('sell') and the noun 'prodàvač' ('salesman'). Stefan Hofer-Krucker Valderrama. 2015. 48.
89. '"Maybe," he finally began, "none of this would ever have happened if Prodanovic hadn't sent me on holiday."' *Barbarian Spring*. 2014. 2.
90. 'A story … with a moral to it. A tale full of incredible twists and turns, nail-biting adventures and exotic temptations.' *Barbarian Spring*. 2014. 2.
91. 'When the same servant came back to impart the tragic news, I fully expected a traditional display of grief. Loud wailing, hair-tearing, extravagant clawing at faces contorted in pain, fainting fits and all that kind of thing. But instead the six daughters just looked at one another in silence, cleared away the tea glasses and the silver pot and deposited me out on the street with a half-eaten piece of baklava in my hand.' *Barbarian Spring*. 2014. 10.
92. '"I'll pass over the dinner at Malouch's house," Preising said. "Exquisite, elegant, exotic. And his wife, *très charmante*, but surprisingly modern. The house, a palace, was quite traditional, only with lots of televisions. All in all, a very nice occasion, but still a business dinner. Not that we discussed much business. But I'll skip telling you about that, it doesn't really have any bearing on the main story. Nor does my visit to the souk the next morning with Saida. Truly overwhelming. The smells. But that's another story. Oh, and the colours as well, quite breathtaking."' *Barbarian Spring*. 2014. 15.
93. 'And so, whistling the opening bars of Purcell's *Dido and Aeneas* to himself, he was escorted into the *Hôtel d'Elisha* by the manageress Saida Malouch. He insisted on calling it the "Hôtel Dido" – after all, he reasoned, that was the name by which the beloved queen was known to her subjects.' *Barbarian Spring*. 2014. 13.
94. Mark Cartwright. 'Dido'. *Ancient History Encyclopedia*. 29 June 2016 (website – last accessed 1 March 2018).

95. Stefan Hofer-Krucker Valderrama. 2015. 47; Susanne Kleinpass. 2016. 34. 'and anyhow camels were something of a leitmotif in his tale.' *Barbarian Spring*. 2014. 79.
96. 'Standing in front of the mirror with the oriental frame, he buttoned and unbuttoned the second-to-top button of his shirt five times, casting a critical eye over his appearance each time until finally, with his eyes shut, he managed to perform a complicated manoeuvre with his left hand which left it entirely to chance whether the shirt ultimately remained unbuttoned or not.' *Barbarian Spring*. 2014. 40.
97. *Barbarian Spring*. 2014. 7.
98. 'Preising would have been only too happy to turn the offer down flat, but the child labour thing wasn't as clear-cut as it seemed. He called to mind an evening at the neo-liberal business club Prodanovic belonged to, where the person next to him at dinner had explained what a delicate subject child labour was. Much more problematic than your average do-gooder might like to think, it really wasn't such a straightforward matter at all, and under certain circumstances it could even be the lesser of two evils.' *Barbarian Spring*. 2014. 7.
99. '[d]ab-handed little chaps'. *Barbarian Spring*. 2014. 12.
100. 'avowed cultural relativist of a completely unchauvinistic kind. His liberalism was a lukewarm variety of relativism. All the same, on our walks he was always ready to flaunt his ethics of virtue like some religious monstrance.' *Barbarian Spring*. 2014. 8.
101. 'his irritation led him to observe, chauvinistically, that Westerners might need to revise their view of the traditional role played by women in Muslim societies.' *Barbarian Spring*. 2014. 45.
102. J. A. Cuddon. 'Novella'. 1999. 600.
103. Stefan Hofer-Krucker Valderrama. 2015. 52.
104. Ibid. 47.
105. 'Camel'. *The Penguin Dictionary of Symbols*. Alain Gheerbrant and Jean Chevalier. Trans. John Buchanan-Brown. London: Penguin, 1996. 149.
106. Ironically, the novella's leitmotif and Preising also have a lot in common: not only does Preising claim that the desert is 'vielleicht die Landschaft, die mir am meisten entspricht' (*Frühling*: 21; 'the sort of landscape I relate to the most' *Barbarian Spring*: 16), but his insistence on his 'Besonnenheit' (*Frühling*: 15; 'prudence' *Barbarian Spring*: 10) is also reminiscent of camel symbolism: 'The camel is generally taken as the symbol of sobriety … and of awkward nature.' 'Camel'. 1996. 149.

107. Susanne Kleinpass. 2016. 34.
108. '"It was loud, it was hectic and pretty aggressive, too," Preising recounted with obvious disapproval. "And it went on and on, without the slightest hint of a resolution. In these parts of the world arguments carry quite a different weight and follow a totally different set of rules. Never, ever, try to get involved …"' *Barbarian Spring*. 2014. 19.
109. 'Preising held his breath, and a great sadness overcame him', 'the caravan leader's despair and grief had touched such a raw nerve in me …' *Barbarian Spring*. 2014. 20, 21. Translated literally, sadness and grief 'took possession' of Preising.
110. 'However, when I put my book aside for a moment to wipe my sunglasses, I saw her steal a sideways glance at what I was reading. "We seem to have the same interests," she said, holding up her own book to show me the dust-jacket. We were both reading Mahmoud Messadi's *The Birth of Oblivion*, she in an English translation and I in the German. My bookseller recommended it to me when I told her about my trip to Tunisia. She said it was the most important work of modern Tunisian fiction, in fact of modern Arab literature as a whole. Books are a wonderful ice-breaker.' *Barbarian Spring*. 2014. 28.
111. The contrast between Laura, Pippa's daughter, and her brother Marc perfectly illustrates the destructive force of cultural capitalism. While Laura, who works as a librarian on a Hurtigruten cruise ship, the paragon of cultural capitalism, is killed in a fire which also devours her books, her brother Marc, a banker, celebrates a luxury wedding at a desert resort which culminates in a fire but from which he is able to escape.
112. Jonas Nesselhauf. 'SpielGeldSpiel – Der Spekulant als Reflektionsfigur in der deutschen Gegenwartsprosa'. *Germanica* 55 (2014): 81–96. 88.
113. Edward W. Said. 2003. 52.
114. Ibid. 52.
115. 'Don't get me wrong; you know how keen I am on foreign civilisations, but after all the problems we'd had and the bother we'd caused, these cave dwellings were frankly a bit of a let-down.' *Barbarian Spring*. 2014. 58.
116. 'In an attempt to get Preising's attention again, Sanford served up the tale of the traditional Tunisian wedding feast. This basically consisted of a roasted camel with couscous. But the camel, which was cooked whole, was supposedly prepared in the refined manner of a Russian *Matroschka* doll, being stuffed with a whole sheep, which in turn was stuffed with a goat stuffed with a bustard stuffed with a dozen quails, each of which had been stuffed with barberries

and dates. Preising was sceptical. He had the feeling he'd heard this story, or something very like it, somewhere before, and in the context of a joke, what's more.' *Barbarian Spring*. 2014. 53–4.

117. 'Preising tried to impress some of the young people by telling them Sanford's story about the Berber camel roast; after he'd finished, two of the girls took to addressing him as "Mister Mungo Park". The reference was lost on him.' *Barbarian Spring*. 2014. 89.

118. Yvonne Hütter. 'Ethics and Aesthetics in Jonas Lüscher's *Barbarian Spring*'. *Primerjalna književnost* 40.2 (2017): 149–63. 155.

119. Mungo Park. *Travels in the Interior Districts of Africa* [1799]. Ware: Wordsworth, 2002.

120. 'The revellers had used their combined muscle power to haul the dead camel up by his hind legs and hang it over the gallows-like support for a large sunshade. There, they'd sliced open its belly, causing its innards to spill out over the glazed patio tiles. A slim brunette in skimpy shorts and a bikini was delving up to her elbows into the beast's entrails, while others were attempting to tear the felted hide off the cadaver. With a single well-aimed thrust, Quicky silenced the greyhound bitch, which was standing on the edge of the pool barking frantically at her master's lifeless body floating there. Then he picked up the whimpering puppies, one by one, and calmly slit their throats ... one group of maniacs lit a huge bonfire on the sand under the palm trees ... while others set about disembowelling the dogs. When they'd finished, in a gesture unparalleled in its sheer insanity, they stuffed the puppies back inside the slim body of their mother and then took the dead dog, her belly swollen with her butchered offspring, and shoved it into the bloody cavity they'd made in the camel.' *Barbarian Spring*. 2014. 123.

121. Laura Wade. *Posh*. London: Oberon Books, 2010.

122. Ingeborg Bachmann [1978]. *Das Buch Franza / Requiem für Fanny Goldmann. Texte des 'Todesarten'-Projekts*. Eds Monika Albrecht and Dirk Göttsche. Munich: Piper, 2004. 197ff. Quoted in Julian Reidy. '"Wie der Geist zum Kamele ward": Zu einem Leitmotiv in Jonas Lüschers *Frühling der Barbaren*'. *Colloquium Helveticum* 45 (2016): 157–73. 167.

123. Susanne Kleinpass. 2016. 34.

124. 'But instead of Saida, the only person he encountered there was the lifeguard, sitting glued to the television, on which a man was reading out an announcement. Preising waited patiently until the man had finished, at which point Rachid treated him to a long explanation of how an unlikely alliance of

renegade Muslim Brothers and the Marxist–Leninist Fourteenth of January Front had taken the opportunity provided by the crisis of capitalism to launch a second wave of the Arab Spring. This time, though, they were determined to see it through to the end, to have a proper clear-out that would rid the country once and for all of the fat cats and the toadies and lickspittles of the old regime, who'd survived the last revolution unscathed – in fact, who'd found themselves even better off in a democratic Tunisia after dividing up the spoils of those who'd been toppled – and redistribute their wealth among its rightful owners, namely the Tunisian people. The days of the powerful and rich family clans were numbered. Preising, who correctly assumed that these fat cats included the Malouchs, signalled his alarm at this, fearing not only for Saida's safety but also his own; after all, he was here as a guest of the Malouch family. Rachid reassured him that all the talk was of seizing property, not killing people – after all, they weren't living in Ben Ali's Tunisia any more – but failed to allay Preising's concerns.' *Barbarian Spring*. 2014. 114–15.

125. 'Four uniformed officers came to fetch Saida. Grabbing her by the hair, they dragged her past the long work benches, as the children kept their heads down and went on with their work … [Preising] saw Saida stumble and fall, and then the policemen were kicking her as she lay on the ground and dragging her across the tarmac by the collar of her René Lezard trouser suit, with her blouse torn and riding up to reveal her pale stomach and the blue bra she was wearing. He felt like he'd witnessed this scene before somewhere, in a different context, under quite different auspices, but he couldn't put his finger on it.' *Barbarian Spring*. 2014. 131.

126. Sarah Keller. 'Feminismus im Licht des Umsturzes in Ägypten'. *Arabischer Frühling? Alte und neue Geschlechterpolitiken in einer Region im Umbruch*. Eds Dagmar Filter et al. Herbolzheim: Centaurus, 2013. 112–32. 121.

127. Thomas Olesen. '"We are all Khaled Said": Visual Injustice Symbols in the Egyptian Revolution, 2010–2011'. *Advances in the Visual Analysis of Social Movements*. Eds Nicole Doerr et al. Bingley: Emerald Group Publishing Limited, 2013. 3–25.

128. 'ordinary Tunisian people sauntering through a luxuriously furnished villa. A villa just like the one where, not four days ago … Preising had been a guest.' *Barbarian Spring*. 2014. 129.

129. For the functioning of myths in essentialising, depoliticising and untiming social reality, see Roland Barthes. *Mythologies*. Paris: Seuil, 1957. 216–19.

130. Judith Butler. 2012. 138.

131. Anna Ball and Karim Mattar. 'Dialectics of Post/Colonial Modernity in the Middle East: A Critical, Theoretical and Disciplinary Overview'. *The Edinburgh Companion to the Postcolonial Middle East*. Eds Anna Ball and Karim Mattar. Edinburgh: Edinburgh University Press, 2019. 3–22. 10.
132. Susanne Kleinpass. 2016. 34.
133. Judith Butler. 2012. 137.

4

AFFECTIVE MASCULINITY AND THE ARAB UPRISINGS: ADAM THIRLWELL'S *KAPOW!* AND JOCHEN BEYSE'S *REBELLION: ZWISCHENBERICHT*

Don't get him wrong, argued Rustam. He was as sympathetic to political equality for women as the next man … but he was also keen to placate other people's notions of the polite. He'd for example found it difficult that when Nigora had recently met Mohamed, a friend of his, she'd been dressed in her normal jeans and shirt, accessorised with a headscarf. Mohamed had later commented on it. It was sexy, no doubt about it, but it was causing Rustam some concern …

'It frees you from the gaze of men,' hazarded Rustam. 'It protects you from the gaze of men.'

Can we gather up the reasons in one small place? Nigora's independence was the reason why Rustam felt so strongly the need to make her dependent – to educate her into being a possession.[1]

Even if the topic of gender equality is touched upon time and again in Western fictionalisations of the Arab uprisings, it is mostly present as a visible absence. As in this quotation from Adam Thirlwell's short novel *Kapow!*, the issue is mainly broached through an allegedly affect-driven and anxious male gaze: suffering from his non-conformance with predominant ideals of masculinity, Rustam, one of the characters in *Kapow!*, tries to disguise his own sexual insecurity by reasoning with his wife Nigora to wear the burka. On the stylistic level, the gender problematic finds its expression in the free indirect discourse which is used to render Rustam's speech. Although the greater part of his utterance remains unchanged in its free indirect form, the personal pronouns are adjusted. As a consequence, gendered personal pronouns ('him', 'he') dominate Rustam's monologue and underline how he approaches Nigora not in the roles of a 'you and I', but in their social gender roles as 'he and she'. One of the many footnotes in *Kapow!*, set at different angles from the main text and used to diversify the reading experience, further highlights that Rustam's repressed sexuality is the actual undercurrent of his new-found fundamentalist beliefs: just before he starts lecturing Nigora, the text's focalisation shifts towards Rustam to show how he stops listening to his wife and thinks about having sex with her: 'All too clearly, Rustam could picture Nigora lifting the hem of her dress, in the way he liked, with gentleness' (*Kapow!*: 68). While the footnote marks the direction of his fantasy, the main text shows how he glosses over these thoughts by speculating about the advantages of the burka ('Don't get him wrong …'). In this way, *Kapow!* does not only depict the duplicity of Rustam's Islamisation, but it frames both the uprisings in Cairo and the potential Islamist counterrevolution in terms of repressed sexual desire. Albeit in an ironising fashion, the text thus relies heavily on the figuration of the allegedly affective-driven Islamicate man.

Affective Masculinity and the Islamicate Man

In Western depictions of men from an actual or presumed Islamicate background,[2] sexual politics increasingly serve as a means of racist reductionisms and securitisation.[3] The epitome of erotic hedonism in colonial times, the construct of the Islamicate man has undergone an interesting reframing in recent Western media coverage.[4] Not (yet) a terrorist,[5] the supposedly unself-regulated lecherous and violent Islamicate man is a recurring figuration which builds on older Orientalist sediment and more recent developments in Western representations of allegedly affect-driven Islamicate masculinity.[6] Against the backdrop of the centuries-old stereotypes of the affective, irrational, sensual Oriental man who oscillates between the effeminate and the dangerous,[7] Western representations of Islamicate masculinity have now shifted towards a more sexually inhibited but aggressive register.[8]

In this aggressive register, representations of affective masculinity are instrumentalised as an argument against immigration.[9] Especially after the 2015/16 New Year's Eve sexual assaults in Cologne, the trope of an alleged 'predator sexuality'[10] of so-called 'rapefugees'[11] as a threat to women, Enlightenment values and to Western society in general has gained further momentum.[12] In fact,

> [m]oralized, criminalized, racialized, colonized masculinities in the Middle East are some of the most popular subjects of modern geopolitical hypervisibility, twinned with their fetishized Others or victims – the supposedly suppressed traditionalized veiled woman and the supposedly Occidentally-identified modernized gay man.[13]

As the continual Other to civilised Western sublimation,[14] the trope of the affect-driven Islamicate man builds on the allegedly problematic or backward sexuality of the Other.[15] Concomitant with the belief that the Islamicate world lives in a state of self-inflicted backwardness, the idea that people from an Islamicate background act according to the unbridled behavioural mechanisms of affectivity persists.[16] While Western history often reads as one of progress and growing rationality, Western media and elite foreign policy discourse frequently continues to present Islamicate countries as not having undergone any comparable development.[17] In a present-day discursive formation which Liz Fekete calls 'Enlightened Fundamentalism',[18] the Islamicate world thus continues to function as the unrestrained foil to portrayals of the West as the realm of enlightened rationality. While secularisation and Enlightenment are presented as foundational in shaping the construct of Western European culture, non-Western migrants are denigrated as too backward to grasp the meaning of these values.[19]

This juxtaposition of Western rationality and Enlightenment versus Islamicate affectivity and backwardness draws on a long tradition of Western narratives. These narratives portray Western history as a process of civilisation against the foil of an allegedly backward and inferior East.[20] For instance, in *Über den Prozeß der Zivilisation* (1939; *The Civilizing Process*), one of the most influential Western sociological works of the twentieth century, Norbert Elias famously claimed that between AD 800 and AD 1900, increasing thresholds of shame and rationality engendered the growing restraint of human affect in Western Europe. According to Elias, attitudes with regard to violence, sex, table manners and bodily functions consequently underwent considerable change.[21] Literature on the so-called Orient, on the contrary, served – particularly in overtly repressive ages such as the Victorian era – as a repository for the irrational, the sensual, the violent and lusty or, to put it briefly, for anything taboo.[22]

Not coincidentally, the starting point of this narration of civilisational change roughly corresponds with the emergence of Islam – a new, competing religion. Deeply entrenched in the Western imaginary, the Orientalist tropes of unrestrained affectivity date back to the seventh century, when the Catholic Church taunted Prophet Muhammad 'in the most virulent manner possible. Muhammed was described as an arch-seducer, who wore purple, coloured his lips, and delighted in scented things and coition.'[23] At the time of the emergence of Islam, this strategy of drastic Othering helped to create sufficient alienation from the new religion in the Christian subjects to prevent them from becoming apostates. The Church's allegation that Muhammad, in order to subjugate Christianity by means of sheer numbers, recommended sexual profligacy, functioned in a similar way. Moreover, Orientalists used the picture which the Quran paints of paradise as one early source to argue that Muslims strove for carnal gratification not only in this world, but in the afterlife as well.[24]

From the very beginning, discussions about the Orient thus contained a pronounced and highly instrumentalised element of sensuousness. Far from resulting in pejoration only, this element of sensuousness exerted an ambiguous sense of fascination. While in the nineteenth century, works such as Richard Burton's edition of *The Arabian Nights* (1885) helped to justify colonial rule by transmitting to a great readership the idea of a lascivious and lethargic Orient in need of reform, at the same time they turned gendered and sexualised Oriental affectivity into popular stock.[25] For one, this finds expression in the exoticist tradition of presenting the Orient as lascivious, full of dancing, heavily scented and voluptuous women or lewd men.[26] According to Said,

> the Orient was a place where one could look for sexual experience unobtainable in Europe … In time 'Oriental sex' was as standard a commodity

as any other available in the mass culture, with the result that readers and writers could have it if they wished without necessarily going to the Orient.[27]

Synecdochically represented by the harem,[28] the stereotypes of lasciviousness and male violence against the helpless but highly sexualised female often coexist in Western imagination. If violence is thus a second relevant and related trope in ethnosexist configurations of the affect-driven Oriental man, the Oriental woman is traditionally an object of desire allegedly in need of saving by the Western man – a pattern which Gayatri Chakravorty Spivak famously described as '[w]hite men … saving brown women from brown men'.[29] Recent migratory movements have, however, facilitated the rise of a modified pattern. Due to the allegedly aggressive sexuality of male migrants from Islamicate countries, there is now also a call for '[*w*]*hite men saving white women from brown men*'.[30]

Next to the long history of the trope of sexualised Oriental violence, it is assumptions of Muslim aggression which inform the figuration of the affect-driven Islamicate man. Highly visible in the rhetoric of, for instance, George W. Bush and Donald Trump, these assumptions frequently follow in the wake of arguments deployed by Orientalist Bernard Lewis. In 'The Roots of Muslim Rage',[31] an article published in *The Atlantic* in 1990, Lewis claims that there is a resentment against the West in many Islamicate countries. He attributes it to an alleged inferiority complex developed because modern Western political concepts do not work in Muslim countries. According to Lewis, this leads to a rejection and loathing of these concepts and ultimately results in a 'clash of civilizations'.[32] Adopting and popularising this term in a 1996 book of the same name,[33] Samuel P. Huntington shares Lewis' opinion that cultural conflicts 'will supplant ideological and other forms of conflict as the dominant global form of conflict'.[34] He especially warns against Muslims, arguing that 'Islam has from the start been a religion of the sword' and that '[t]he Koran and other statements of Muslim beliefs contain few prohibitions on violence, and a concept of nonviolence is absent from Muslim doctrine and practice.'[35]

In sum, affect-driven behaviour, especially with regard to sexuality and violence, continues to feature prominently in depictions of Oriental men. Because of the growing importance of the signifier Islam, however, the image of the Oriental man has shifted from the fantasy of erotic licentiousness and the capacity for sensual enjoyment to a repressed and violent register.[36] This chapter sets out to illustrate how, with this shift, the ambivalence of Orientalist projection has come full circle. If, for a long time, what was repressed in Western society was projected onto the Oriental and then exerted fascination, in Western discourse, the figuration of the Islamicate man now also incorporates a projection of the process of suppression itself: he has become the merging point of, firstly, Western projections of lasciviousness and, secondly, of a widespread Western discourse picturing Islam as opposed 'to the supposed sexual liberalism of secular societies'.[37] According to this reductionist logic, the Western individual sublimates sexual urges into higher scientific, artistic or ideological activities.[38] In contrast, the allegedly inhibited Islamicate man, presented as not having undergone this cultural development, can allegedly only resort to violence as an outlet for his pent-up sexual energy.[39] The result is an Orientalisation – and often an Islamisation – of both lust and repressed lust as securitised discourse.[40]

Kapow! and *Rebellion*: The Orientalisation of Repressed Lust and Violence

While the comparison between *Par le feu* and *Frühling der Barbaren* has revealed diametrically opposed ways of negotiating the construct of the Orient, Adam Thirlwell's *Kapow!* (2012) and Jochen Beyse's *Rebellion: Zwischenbericht* (2013; 'Rebellion: Status Report')[41] bear striking similarities. Both short novels investigate the Orientalisation of affective masculinity during the Arab uprisings. Although *Kapow!* and *Rebellion* are anchored in European capitals, London and Berlin, respectively, both texts also include the Egyptian uprisings in their plots. By means of embedded stories or imaginative projection, they weave the city of Cairo into their storylines. At the same time, they render this process of incorporation and Orientalisation visible. While *Kapow!* shows how its narrator transplants affectivity into his characters because he decides to write a love story, *Rebellion* imagines its autodiegetic narrator as vicariously acting out his affects when playing the first-person shooter *Tod in Kairo* ('Death in Cairo').

Adam Thirlwell: *Kapow!* (2012) and the Orientalisation of (Repressed) Lust

Adam Thirlwell, born in London in 1978, is a British novelist twice named as *Granta*'s Best of Young British Novelists.[42] He read English at Oxford and his work has been translated into thirty languages. Thirlwell also works as the London editor of *The Paris Review*. Besides *Kapow!* he has published three novels and a book on translation.[43]

Kapow! is set in London in 2011. The unreliable narrator, a writer who mainly survives on marijuana and coffee, listens to what Faryaq, a taxi driver, tells him about his brother Mouloud and the latter's friends in Egypt: Mouloud, after demonstrating on Tahrir Square, is severely beaten up, probably by the secret police. Rustam, a Cairo taxi driver, finds him unconscious in the street and brings him home to his wife. Using these characters, the London narrator begins imagining and starts to write a pulp love story. Against the backdrop of the protests in Tahrir Square, he invents the story of how Rustam's wife Nigora falls in love with a younger man named Ahmad.

Through the prism of this plot, *Kapow!* approaches the uprisings from an angle which explores affectivity in terms of lust and desire. At the same time, however, the book emphasises that it uses the frame of affectivity not because the characters themselves are affect-driven, but because of a predilection of the Western narrator. In fact, the question of a Western reframing and appropriation of the Arab uprisings is present from the beginning. Directly addressing this issue, the London narrator turns the process of how he decides to construct his 'own Arabic novel' into the topic of his frame narrative:

> He was a nickelodeon of stories, Faryaq – you peered in, and they flickered. And I wanted to steal them … although I wrote in English, obviously, although I was from the green London suburbs and I was Jewish or at least half-Jewish, as I listened to Faryaq I was still beginning to wonder if I could in some way construct my own Arabic novel. (*Kapow!*: 16–17)

Adopting the setting and characters Faryaq tells him about, the London narrator decides to turn them into a love story:

> So I began there, with Faryaq, in the freezing city of London, telling me about what was happening elsewhere, in the place of revolution. He wanted

to tell me the story of his brother Mouloud, who was one of the revolution's heroes. With his sidekick called Ahmad, and his new friend Rustam, they were going to remake the world. But while Faryaq was telling one story – the story of Rustam and Mouloud and their trajectory or path or whatever through the forest of revolution, I kept on seeing another story which Faryaq wasn't telling me. I was thinking of Ahmad, the sidekick, as the true hero of this other story – which was a love story, because all my stories end up as variants on love stories, and its other hero was Nigora, Rustam's wife. Inside Faryaq's story there was another story which he couldn't quite see. He thought it was about these revolutionary men, but me I had it slightly differently. I couldn't help it. (*Kapow!*: 19)

Even though Faryaq tries to talk to him about the revolution – a reality so alien to the narrator that he heterolingually marks it as 'this other world of *hoch* and *weltpolitik*' (*Kapow!*: 11) – he 'couldn't help' but process it in terms of romantic love. The ambiguity of the modal verb 'couldn't' implies that it would transcend both the narrator's ability and the norms of the Western book market not to adapt the story according to Western tastes.[44] The contrasting conjunction 'but', which occurs twice, moreover, establishes a clear dichotomy between the narrator's interpretation of what Faryaq thinks of the story and what the narrator makes of it ('But while Faryaq was telling one story … I kept on seeing another story …' and 'He thought it was about these revolutionary men, but me I had it slightly differently.') In the second instance, the 'but' is further stressed by a colloquial and modified duplication of the personal pronoun. Shifting from the object to the subject pronoun ('but me I'), this duplication both underlines the Western egocentricity of the narrator and his decision to turn himself from listener into narrator.[45] From the beginning, the text consequently highlights that it is a Western narrator who frames the revolution differently, that is, as a love story. So although *Kapow!* uses the Orientalisation of affective masculinity as a plot device, it simultaneously illustrates how it enacts this very process of Orientalisation and trivialisation.

By insisting on this process of trivialisation while at the same time contrasting it with important Arabic intertexts, *Kapow!* acts as a self-reflective critique of Western commodification and appropriation. The trivial appropriation into the Western view is accentuated both by the choice of the name Faryaq and by the story's taxi setting. A portmanteau of the names Faris and Shidyaq, the name goes back to *al-Saq ala al-Saq fim a huwa al-faryaq* (1855), a work by Lebanese writer Ahmad Faris Shidyaq (1804–87) often considered as the first Arabic novel.[46] While *Kapow!* thus names one of its characters after the protagonist of an influential Arabic *Bildungsroman* and while this character would like to talk about politics with the London narrator, the latter decides to condense the information he receives so as to adapt it as a love story. In addition to the choice of the name Faryaq, the taxi setting which the narrator creates for the frame narrative of his 'own Arabic novel' (*Kapow!*: 17) can be read as both a homage to and a self-reflective adaptation of Egyptian author Khaled Al Khamissi's 2006 bestseller *Taxi*.[47] As mentioned in Chapter Two, *Taxi* is a collection of short stories which gives a voice to the often dissident opinions of Egyptians from diverse social backgrounds.[48] In contrast to the sociological polyphony of this intertext, however, *Kapow!* opts for the form of what the narrator self-referentially calls a 'pulp novelette, a zoom of pure joyfulness' (*Kapow!*: 17).[49]

The Private and the Political
Although the narrator metafictionally highlights his intention of writing a love story, the resulting narrative also approaches the political implications of suppressed male lust. Thus interweaving the political and the private, *Kapow!* arranges its frame story and the embedded stories according to a logic which it renders more explicit through the use of the following footnote: 'He had once discovered, as Philip Roth once said elsewhere, that political events obeyed the same laws as private happenings. And so he invented his new forms' (*Kapow!*: 51). And in fact, in *Kapow!*, the issues of gender inequality and sexual harassment do not only repeatedly reappear as the background foil to Ahmad and Nigora's love story, but the arc of suspense of their allegedly private story also coincides with that of the political events: after Ahmad and Nigora fall for each other in Tahrir Square, their love is put to a halt when Rustam is imprisoned. Marking both the climax of their love story as well as that of the uprisings, they kiss only once – the moment that the president resigns. As the narrator indicates in a metafictional comment, they do so because he, the narrator,

can only imagine this love story at a slight angle to Faryaq's story, I cannot imagine it straight, what I am seeing at this high point of revolution is not the ex-President's face, his laughing face, la vache qui rit, no I am thinking instead of this. Ahmad, in the maelstrom or mess, suddenly kissed Nigora. (*Kapow!*: 41)

As this quotation illustrates, the narrator, even if he pretends to only think of the private story, cannot suppress the political. At the level of stylistics, this is shown by the negation ('what I am seeing at this high point of revolution is not the ex-President's face') and its modification 'his laughing face, la vache qui rit'): both enable the narrator to evoke a vivid visualisation of the political undercurrent which he purports not to describe.

What this political undercurrent shows is that, even if *Kapow!* advances a postmodern parody of the apolitical, it still merges the issues of love and desire as well as the politics of sexualisation and harassment in a common – and highly political – frame of affectivity. Oscillating between these two poles, the book's two-pronged approach mirrors the media coverage of the protests. According to Paul Amar's analysis of media representations of the protests,

> [t]he uprisings and mass protests that occupied Tahrir Square in central Cairo between 25 January and 15 February 2011 were haunted by the figure of 'sexual harassment' or, to put it more accurately, the sexualized assault and terrorization of women activists. Gender-sensitive coverage of the revolution by Egyptian, as well as Western, media outlets focused on two forms of representation. One was that Tahrir Square represented a utopian space that forged a new gendered social contract … In a second set of representations wholly incompatible with those above, Tahrir served as the mosh pit for a hypermasculine mob where Orientalist tropes of the 'Arab street' were bottled-up and concentrated, a space constantly bursting with predatory sexuality and not disciplined enough to articulate either coherent leadership or policy.[50]

In a combination of these two representational takes on gender issues in Tahrir Square, Nigora and Ahmad first spend time together and fall in love because of an incidence of verbal sexism uttered during the protests:

'We could do with some food,' interrupted Mouloud. It may have seemed incidental, because when Mouloud spoke he didn't speak as a modern man – no, folks, he was, I'm afraid, kind of sexist. When he mentioned this need for food in the form of a statement he meant Nigora and Aziza. But Nigora was not to be ordered, she was not to be determined by the world of male strangers. She chose cheekiness instead.

'You,' said Nigora to Ahmad, the pretty boy of the group. 'Come with me.' (*Kapow!*: 28)

Through an indirect speech act which barely conceals its sexist undertones, Mouloud tries to give orders to the two women of the group, Aziza and Nigora. By mentioning that Mouloud interrupts Nigora while she compliments Aziza on the beauty of her headscarf (*Kapow!*: 27), the text further visualises the gender categories at work in this scene. Moreover, directly addressing the reader ('no, folks'), the narrator establishes an implicit distinction between the supposedly non-sexist role of a modern man and the backward, sexist social male role which Mouloud plays in this situation: with the aid of a negative comparison ('he didn't speak as a modern man') instead of the simile ('he didn't speak like a modern man'), he contrasts Mouloud's entire social role – not just this individual utterance – to that of 'a modern man'.

Confronted with Mouloud's interruption and indirect order, Nigora reacts with counter-sexism. One of the many sentences in the short novel which is introduced by 'but' marks her opposition and grammatically mirrors how she processes her reaction ('But Nigora was not to be ordered, she was not to be determined by the world of male strangers'). Whereas the first part of the phrase remains a subordinate clause only, the mantra-like repetition of the information in the following main clause in free indirect discourse completes both the sentence and Nigora's self-assertion. Still trapped in the logic of gender hierarchies, however, Nigora does not direct her order at Mouloud himself, but at Ahmad. His pleasing but not hypermasculine outward appearance ('pretty' instead of 'handsome' or 'attractive') and his young age make him a possible target of Nigora's belittlement. Even though, at twenty-three, Ahmad is of age, thirty-four-year-old Nigora repeatedly thinks of him as a 'boy' (*Kapow!*: 30, 45, 63), and, as the agency and choice of verbs in her free indirect discourse illustrate, she enjoys being the leading one of the two:

> She liked this boy, thought Nigora. He was kind of definitely cute. She liked the idea of educating him. So before they went back to the others *she sat Ahmad down* on a beatup metal folding chair and *made him listen* to a tape. (*Kapow!*: 30; my italics)

If scenes such as the above highlight how, with regard to gender, the private is always political as well, *Kapow!* also approaches the political through the prism of the private. Most prominently, Ahmad and Aziza ask Nigora and Rustam to come to a meeting with them to discuss the place of women in the revolution. To Rustam's surprise, Nigora – who due to their prior revolutionary experiences in Uzbekistan (*Kapow!*: 9, 25) is sceptical with regard to joining the revolution in Egypt – wants to go. She agrees, however, not because of the meeting itself but because she wants to see Ahmad. In the meeting, the participants discuss strategies to protect women from sexual harassment, for instance by 'plot[ting] movements of harassment on an electronic map' (*Kapow!*: 45). When Nigora reacts hesitantly and is confronted by the other women, Aziza saves her by saying:

> 'Could we talk about more important things?' said Aziza. 'Could we like maybe talk about the virginity tests?'
>
> 'Exactly,' said Nigora.
>
> 'Because this is a wider problem,' said Aziza. 'I think this is a wider problem. They were keen for us to be there when we were demanding that the President should go. But now that he's gone, they want us to go home.' Aziza was being kind, thought Nigora, and it made her ashamed. 'There's a propaganda campaign against us,' said Aziza. 'They're saying that now isn't the time for women's rights.' (*Kapow!*: 46)

Approaching the issue of sexualised violence through this scene, *Kapow!* briefly foregrounds the issue of the 'virginity tests' as a 'more important' aspect. Embedded in the dynamics between Aziza and Nigora, its systemic implications are, however, quickly dropped when Aziza, in a move of female solidarity with Nigora, refocuses the discussion and identifies the 'wider problem' as the male protestors' attempt to uphold their superior position of power.

In its foregrounding of the gender issues among the protestors themselves, Aziza's rhetorical move follows the dominant pattern of representing sexualised violence during the uprisings. As Paul Amar explains, however, the latter cannot be understood without taking account of the critical role which the Egyptian security state played in the attacks on women during the revolts.[51] From 2000 onwards, the state systematically instrumentalised *baltagiya*, plain-clothes thugs, to infiltrate and delegitimise protests. In 2011, the 'virginity tests' (*Kapow!*: 46) in Tahrir Square were allegedly conducted so that women who were imprisoned during the protests could not claim to have been raped while in custody. In reality, these tests were a practice to discriminate against women in the revolution and to thus 'assault the respectability of its most effective dissidents through systematic sexual violence …'[52] While this aspect still found its way into explanations of the sexual violence in Tahrir Square at the beginning of the 2011 uprisings, such differentiated coverage soon yielded to racist and anti-Muslim patterns. In fact, the role of the security state eventually faded into the background of Western representations of the uprisings, and '[t]he predatory culture of Muslim men became the talking point.'[53] As a result, the image of protestors worsened considerably:

> Protestors were resignified as crazed mobs of brutal men, vaguely 'Islamist' and fiercely irrational, depicted according to the conventions of nineteenth-century colonial-Orientalist figurations of the savage 'Arab street'. And protestors became targeted as assemblages of hypersexualized terrorist masculinities.[54]

In *Kapow!*, the mention of sexualised violence thus at best shows how the systematic state practice successfully undermined the protests. Without any further contextualisation, however, it falls short of differentiating the highly gendered representations also found in most Western coverage of the uprisings.

Masculinity and Orientalism
Set against this delicate and highly political gender background, the love triangle between Nigora, Rustam and Ahmad represents different positions regarding the potential Islamist counterrevolution. While Ahmad fears the counterrevolution (*Kapow!*: 44–5), it serves Rustam both as an outlet for his male insecurity and as a chance to bind his wife closer to him. Before

the nexus between Rustam's suppressed lust and his increasing Islamisation is explored, however, *Kapow!* first presents the political and sexual violence of his arrest. Rustam is arrested 'on suspicion of subversion of the state. They couldn't give a precise idea of his location, nor of the date of his trial' (*Kapow!*: 59). After '[p]olice goons who were really army goons' (*Kapow!*: 59) confiscate Rustam's books, they blindfold him and lead him away. Then, they rape Nigora. While Rustam thus falls prey to political violence and has no real trial for months, Nigora is muted by means of sexual violence. By portraying sexual violence as an unfathomable 'it' which just 'happens', *Kapow!* alludes to the rape without depicting it. Thereby, the text reflects how '[t]he particular perversion practiced by the repressive security state'[55] deprives Nigora of words to describe the rape:

> And what happened in the apartment happened very slowly and very fast. When it was happening, it was very slow. When it was over it felt too fast. Nigora sat on the sofa. She stared at the illuminated squiggle in the bulb of Rustam's desk-lamp, until her eyes went out. (*Kapow!*: 59)

As in Aziza's representation, however, this framing of sexualised violence as a practice of the security state soon refocuses on the nexus between Rustam's increasing Islamisation, his male insecurity and his suppressed lust. After he is 'charged with insulting the military institution, and disturbing public security' and 'sentenced … to three months in prison' (*Kapow!*: 66) by a single military judge in a secret hearing, Rustam becomes more religious, dogmatic and intolerant – and he starts growing a beard. While he declares his beard as the outward signifier of his new-found beliefs, in secret, his transformation is mainly explained in terms of his insecurity with regard to his masculinity:

> It [the beard] gave definition to a face which, he thought, in secret, lacked definition. It lacked cheekbone. The podgy cuteness of his cheeks shamed Rustam. He longed instead for a masculine appearance, a skull dense with geography and history – not the blur which graced his photographs. So yes, he'd grown a beard. But there were more lavish reasons too … This dense, thatched, scribbled, stinking beard symbolised his separation from the usual things of the world. (*Kapow!*: 67)

Not only does Rustam consequently grow his beard out of a wish to look manlier, but 'his separation from the usual things of the world' turns out to be less religious seclusion, but more a painful experience full of jealousy and fear of loss (*Kapow!*: 69). In fact, both his beard and his attempt to reason with Nigora to wear the burka serve to conceal or alleviate his own insecurity (*Kapow!*: 68–70). This becomes particularly clear through the use of a footnote which directly juxtaposes his fear of loss while being imprisoned with the sexual performance anxiety which he felt the first time he slept with Nigora (*Kapow!*: 70, 53–4). Yoked together by means of this juxtaposition, Rustam's insecurities are presented both as an explanation for his transformation in prison and as an obstacle to his and Nigora's having a sexually fulfilling relationship. Although Rustam privately enjoys it when Nigora takes the lead (see, for instance, *Kapow!*: 33), he suffers from his inability but wish to behave according to dominant ideals of masculinity. Thus, when he feels the pressure of sexual performance, he foregoes the possibility of open dialogue with Nigora, glosses over his anxiety (*Kapow!*: 53–4) and tries to find solace in dogmatic ideas about gender roles instead.

Representing the pressure of complying with the ideals of dominant masculinity and for suppressed lust which chooses religion as its catalyst, Rustam's growing beard consequently does not just symbolise his increasing Islamisation, but it also illustrates the shift towards a more inhibited representation of the male Oriental and the conflicting roles which it entails. Choosing this mixed imagery, *Kapow!* both adopts and adapts a common Orientalist strategy of representation: while it uses Rustam's body as a signifying cluster,[56] at the same time it explores Rustam's motives for growing a beard. Thereby adding explanations which transcend his Islamisation, the text thus modifies the signification of Rustam's facial hair. As a result, *Kapow!* does not only avoid synecdochically representing Rustam by his beard, but it also tries to diversify the securitised stereotype of the bearded man as a potential danger to the West. Ultimately, though, this attempt at differentiation and ironic subversion does not act as a game changer with regard to the storyline: being the product of the Western narrator's mind, the plot still culminates in a Muslim male's Islamisation and his uttering of gender discrimination.

Besides showing that its frame of affectivity stems from a choice made by the Western narrator, *Kapow!* strongly relies on irony to differentiate the figuration of the allegedly affect-driven Islamicate man. For instance, the day after Rustam is released from prison, Mouloud tells Rustam and Ahmad a tale by the Persian poet Rumi:

> 'There was once a maidservant,' Mouloud said, 'who was possessed of a great erotic appetite.'
> 'Oh my precious love!' said Rustam, who was drinking a pomegranate juice, because it was good for the heart.
> 'And so she enticed a donkey to have sex with her,' continued Mouloud.
> 'Don't judge it too soon,' said Ahmad.
> But as well as being possessed of a great erotic appetite, Mouloud continued, she possessed an ingenious mind.
> 'Why's he talking like this?' said Ahmad to Rustam.
> 'It's an old story,' said Mouloud. 'It's literature.' (*Kapow!*: 76–7)

Mouloud continues explaining that the maid can safely have sexual intercourse with the donkey because she has devised a contraption which hinders the animal from fully penetrating her. Her mistress, however, dies after she sends the maid away on a pretence and entices the donkey to satisfy her lust – without using the contraption.

In his role as a representative of male sexism in the text (*Kapow!*: 28), Mouloud reinterprets the moral of the story. Surrounded by his male friends, he reduces the story to one in which the strong male and pornographic gaze is meant to entertain. To disguise this voyeurism and to uphold moral superiority, Mouloud presents the story as a warning against wanton women:

> You may think it strange, but nothing is strange to a woman. Lustful desire makes the heart deaf and blind, so that a donkey seems like Joseph, fire like light. Because the moral ... is that lust causes foul things to appear fair. The only remedy for this is marriage. The safest strategy is to withdraw. (*Kapow!*: 77)

While Mouloud thus turns the story into a criticism of female lust, the thirteenth-century Persian original by Rumi, 'The Woman Who Discovered Her Maidservant Having Improper Relations with an Ass', can be read as a tale about moderation, circumspection and perspectivity:[57]

In typical Rumi fashion, this is not a cautionary tale about bestiality or women's lust but one of understanding the whole situation on multiple levels before rushing in blindly, as the mistress could only 'see' part of the situation with her naked eye. Her carnal desires, in a sense, blocked her vision, including her intuition, thus resulting in her death.[58]

As a story-within-a-story, the use of this particular intertext mirrors the short novel itself. Similar to Rumi's story, *Kapow!* – although on the surface pretending to be about love and lust – is in fact about perspectivity.

Further illustrating the importance of perspectivity, Rustam and Ahmad's reactions to Mouloud's account serve as an attempt to differentiate the stereotypes of the sensual or affect-driven Oriental. Far from the stereotype of predatory Islamicate men,[59] both Rustam and Ahmad reveal that they are intimidated by the female hypersexuality described in the story. In fact, neither of the two men is presented as hypermasculine in appearance or behaviour. While Rustam is sexually inhibited, Ahmad – with his soft spot for technology, drugs and his hipster lifestyle – can be read as a stand-in for the London narrator or for youth culture in general.[60] When the two men try to understand the moral of the story, the word 'lust', repeated several times, astonishes both religious Rustam and hipster Ahmad. Rather than as something common to their everyday love lives in Egypt, they regard its lascivious undertones as an exotic curiosity. Recreating their alienation through the repetition of the word 'lust', the text suggests that it is as far removed from and as exotic to Mouloud's audience as it may be for the book's readership. In *Kapow!*, affective masculinity in the form of lust consequently emerges not as an Orientalist essence, but as an ironic and self-reflexive ingredient of choice of the narrator: instead of evoking the realm of scented erotic expertise perpetuated by classical Orientalism, *Kapow!* presents sex in ironic frames only and thus self-referentially ridicules its own genre expectations regarding pulp (Orientalist) fiction.

Form Countering Content: Stylistics as a Desecuritising Device?
Against this negotiation of the Islamicate man as a Western projection of the politics and dangers of lust and repressed lust, *Kapow!* presents an ambivalent stylistics which can be read as an attempt at desecuritisation. By means

of the ambiguity which stylistic strategies such as the use of heterochrony, heterolingual elements, incomplete sentences and epistemic modality create, *Kapow!* does not only try to challenge stereotypes of the sensual Oriental man and of predator sexuality, but it also seeks to undermine the stability of images of insecurity. Rather than presenting them as given facts, the short novel thus seeks to diversify issues of gender and sexual insecurity and relates them to the question of perspective.

To undercut the Orientalisation of affective masculinity, *Kapow!* relies on a strong temporal, spatial and linguistic layering which dilutes the notion of the Orient and foregrounds the interdependencies in a globalised world instead. As Alison Gibbons states about *Kapow!*,

> Thirlwell's recognition of 'this new mania for connections' might be read as an awareness of the 'complex connectivity' of the globalized world – that is, the way in which contemporary experience is characterized by the global interconnectedness of social, political, environmental, and economic interaction.[61]

Accordingly, the book features a diverse set of characters who, in their migratory experiences, their use of foreign languages and in their actions, already blur linguistic and geographical boundaries. Not only does the text feature numerous heterolingual elements, but both the characters' and the narrator's stories are translations already:[62] a cab driver in London, Faryaq, who is originally from Beirut, tells the narrator the story of his brother Mouloud, who lives in Cairo, which in turn includes the characters of Rustam and Nigora. The latter two, originally from Uzbekistan, had to flee their home country due to Rustam's revolutionary activities, and they become involved in the revolution in Cairo.

This effect of interconnected layering is further highlighted by the use of stories within stories. In an interview with *Granta* magazine, Adam Thirlwell summarises the recursive narrative structure of *Kapow!* in the following way:

> The narrator in London,
> listening to Faryaq the cab driver,
> describing and imagining the story of Nigora and her husband,
> within which story the characters are telling their own stories …[63]

Even apart from the numerous metafictional remarks, the spatio-temporal constructedness of the text thus quickly emerges as a topos in itself. Not only does the narrator actively comment on his handling of the multiple diegetic levels of his narration, but he does so with the startling speed which he creates by packing forty-nine chapters into eighty-one pages. As a result, the temporal dimension is, on the one hand, defined by diversity and acceleration – a fact which might also be attributed to the London narrator's considerable consumption of caffeine. At the same time, however, it is reduced by the narrator's habit of smoking marijuana – a combination which, by both extending and compressing his sense of time, results in a 'blissful state of suspension' (*Kapow!*: 5).[64] The catchy and fast-paced rhythm in the first paragraph of the book, which alternates between even binary and odd ternary stress patterns, illustrates this: 'it seemed like everywhere they were starting revolutions, or trying. Everyone who was everywhere was using a videophone' (*Kapow!*: 5). A quick and seemingly unfocused stream of free associations reinforces this impression and sets the tone for the entire book. The narrator's associations are triggered by the revolution (world events), then catapulted to the sky (the transcendental) before returning back to the narrator himself (a subject in crisis) and diverse coffee places in London (a globalised capital).

By emphasising anachronistic and allochronic elements in the swirl of the action – thereby blending different temporal planes in the same setting – *Kapow!* further amplifies the heterochronic nature of its temporality. In his rendering of the 'Battle of the Camel', for instance, the narrator flippantly utters his bewilderment with the fighting in Tahrir Square. In a Eurocentric frame ('biblical animals', 'Hollywood'), he amalgamates all the elements which he finds 'old-fashioned', and compares them to a 'Hollywood recreation of the east from the 1960s':

> The Square was a concrete field of tents. So Ahmad was very much to the forefront and foreground when an army of meatheads and lunks came riding in on their camels, those biblical animals, like a Hollywood recreation of the east from the 1960s. Some of them carried rocks, others had iron bars. A few arrived with pistols. Some believers in the Square began praying and sermonising. The men on camels came in and batoned everyone. They

cudgelled them. They did the old-fashioned things. They arrested some and took them off for torture. (*Kapow!*: 38)

At the same time, the narrator mentions the snipers on the roofs, and complements his anachronistic rendering by realigning it with the present: 'Up above, there were the snipers. On the ground, there were the crazy camels' (*Kapow!*: 38). So as to further highlight the influence of the entertainment industry on his own anachronistic framing, he inserts a footnote which juxtaposes his rendering with the even more ironically exaggerated account of a fictitious eyewitness:

> One soldier's holding a razor and hacking away at my hair and an officer's doing his Kung Fu moves on me and another soldier's hitting me with a wooden staff across my back and another soldier's electrocuting me!!!!! (*Kapow!*: 38)

At the semantic and syntactic level, *Kapow!* encodes heterochrony by 'manipulat[ing] temporal and spatial deixis'.[65] Alison Gibbons contends that

> [r]epetitions of 'everyone' and 'everywhere' emphasize the widespread scale of unrest, as does the way in which Thirlwell frequently starts sentences in *Kapow!* with the conjunction 'while' followed by a main clause (as in 'while X, Y'), only to omit that main clause. This gives the impression of events constantly happening somewhere else and simultaneously.[66]

This is, for instance, the case at the end of the short novel, when Ahmad decides to return to his girlfriend Aziza. By means of repetition and its incomplete structure, the last sentence leaves him on his way there and creates the loop of an open end:

> While Ahmad tripped over a protruding metal stub whose purpose no one, now, could have defined, collided at the door to an apartment block with a man who was kissing a speakerphone in his effort to be heard, ran headlong into a chair which had just been vacated by a vendor of imported DVDs from Morocco, knocked it over, picked it up, reknocked it over, repicked it up, and kept on going. (*Kapow!*: 81)

Like many others in *Kapow!*, the last sentence turns the subordinate clause, which begins with 'while', into a main clause, and omits the grammatical main clause.[67] With all the action in the subordinate clause, the level of grammar reflects the book's emphasis on how important perspective is: if a greater claim, the message of the main clause, remains untold, only a limited perspective reveals itself. The grammatical level thus corroborates the content level in that it does not provide one single message with a claim to truth. Instead, it indicates that if one version can be known, many others have to remain untold. Grammatically touching upon issues of knowledge and truth, the text's ironising frame can thus be read as an attempt at further de-essentialising the very tropes which it self-referentially Orientalises.

As Alison Gibbons points out, the use of epistemic modality, expressed by lexical items such as 'maybe' or 'might not know', in combination with the frequently used conjunctions 'or' and 'but', further convey the narrator's uncertainty as to the evaluation of the events which he portrays. With the aid of stylistics and design, she argues, Thirlwell 'comment[s] on the entanglement of revolution and counter-revolution, and how literary form can participate in present and future debates on the nature of the ethical, social, and political injustices of the contemporary world'.[68] Compared with the self-assured tone of the omniscient narrator in *Par le feu*, the foregrounding of epistemic modality in *Kapow!* appears as a tentative step in the direction of an epistemic exhaustion of old dichotomies. Instead of concentrating on time-distancing devices which relegate Egypt to the realm of allochronic time, the use of heterochrony and epistemic modality in *Kapow!* include it into the all-pervading zone of influence of existential doubt.

Besides the semantic and syntactic level, the numerous intertextual and historical references in *Kapow!* contribute to creating heterochrony and epistemic doubt – as well as to its inherent difficulty. Although turned on its head, the picture of Marie Antoinette on the book's title page already indicates that the French Revolution serves as one important heterochronic foil in the book. Indeed, the narrator, in reflecting on his own text, takes into consideration what he calls 'the old manuals of revolution' (*Kapow!*: 64). Ranging from, among others, Marie Antoinette and her role in the French Revolution (*Kapow!*: 21, 34, 64), Emiliano Zapata (*Kapow!*: 35), Joseph de Maistre (*Kapow!*: 58) and Edmund Burke, to Chateaubriand, Benjamin

Constant (*Kapow!*: 65) and Hannah Arendt (*Kapow!*: 71), the mainly Western and partly Latin American perspective to which the narrator aligns the Arab uprisings quickly becomes clear. He problematises this very standpoint and concedes that it is 'nuts ... to think that you can understand things not in terms of the actor or the agent, but from the standpoint of the spectator who watches a spectacle' (*Kapow!*: 71). By putting his remark in an upside-down footnote, he additionally underlines this reversal of perspective.

Its self-reflexivity notwithstanding, the text sets little else against its Eurocentric framing of the uprisings in terms of 'one dictatorship succeeding another'.[69] Instead, it reiterates this idea at great length by quoting from Benjamin Constant's *De l'Esprit de conquête et de l'usurpation* (1814): 'Usurpation brutalizes a people while oppressing it ... And if usurpation manages to endure for any length of time, it actually makes impossible any freedom or improvement after its fall' (*Kapow!*: 66). Although the following sentence, 'It was one way of describing the military takeover, after a dictatorship' (*Kapow!*: 66), qualifies this citation, it is ultimately just this 'one way of describing', which is time-worn and Eurocentric, with which *Kapow!* self-reflexively confronts its readers.

More than the individual historical and intertextual references themselves, it is their sheer accumulation into this 'one way of describing' which functions as a stylistic device in *Kapow!*. The numerous intertextual references in particular serve as a reminder that 'the Orient studied was a textual universe by and large ...'[70] Ultimately, the text itself addresses this difficulty by means of a quote on the possible intertextual use of the *Arabian Nights* and its problems – while the narrator at the same time dismisses them:

> No, I preferred the idea that Arab literature was me. I preferred the sad paradox as described by the thinker Jalal Toufic, and quoted by the artist Walid Raad, that a writer in English who freely used the *Thousand and One Nights* was foreign to him as an Arab intellectual precisely because of this proximity to and ability to use a classic of Arab literature – a book which was, for Toufic, on *the other side of the surpassing disaster*. Because, added Toufic, the day when, after the devastation of Lebanon, Iraq, Sudan, and Arab Palestine, etc, he felt he had the same close relation with *A Thousand and One Nights* as, say, Pier Paolo Pasolini, whose movie of the *Arabian*

Nights came out in 1974, he would either be a hypocritical Arab writer or already a Western one. Even though this stubbornness seemed to me still, well, still melodramatic. (*Kapow!*: 57; italics in the original)

The endeavour to create a mixed impression of speedy heterochrony, which the book's textual temporality and numerous references evoke, also extends to the level of the text's layout. Published by Visual Editions – which is also the home of Jonathan Safran Foer's highly praised experimental book *Tree of Codes* (2010) – and nominated for the London Design Museum's Design of the Year award in 2013,[71] the text comes in an unusual format. Particularly its bifurcated footnotes and fold-out pages are meant to intensify, diversify and accelerate the reading experience. The digressive additions and fold-out pages incite the reader to turn the book upside down or to hold it at a different angle, depending on the layout of the footnote. At the same time, however, they reduce the pace of reception. Although the plot itself often breaks with chronology, the layout – decided upon prior to the production of the text and designed to create a multimodal reading experience[72] – is essentially a conventional system of footnotes with the occasional fold-out page. While the layout is reminiscent of prior postmodern books such as Mark Z. Danielewski's novels *House of Leaves* (2000) and *Only Revolutions* (2006),[73] *Kapow!*'s page full of polka dots (*Kapow!*: 15) is so highly reminiscent of Laurence Sterne's experimentation with blank, black and marbled pages in his *The Life and Opinion of Tristram Shandy, Gentleman* (1759–67) that it further highlights this tension between intertextuality and innovation.[74]

In sum, *Kapow!* can be read as an attempt at stylistic and formal subversion. If at the level of content, it foregrounds affectivity, it counteracts and renders its Orientalisation visible at the level of form. The direct correlation which Alison Gibbons draws between the text's concern with global ethics and stylistic features such as 'perceptual deixis, free indirect discourse, and modes of address'[75] is, however, overly optimistic:

> [T]he recent fervor for ethical, political, social, and environmental commitments is telling in that it appears to indicate, at the very least, an epistemological shift away from the superficiality of postmodern irony, and, at its greatest, the onset of a more substantial post-postmodern turn.[76]

As the very stereotypes which *Kapow!* ironises serve as the springboard for its story, the book still reads like a cautionary inventory of Orientalist tropes of sensuousness as well as Neo-Orientalist tropes of affective masculinity. In its attempts to de-essentialise and desecuritise, the book's focus – although mostly ironically negated – consequently remains on the very issues which it tries to deconstruct.

Jochen Beyse: *Rebellion: Zwischenbericht* (2013)

Born in 1949, Jochen Beyse is a German writer. He studied history and art history as well as theatre studies, German philology and philosophy at the University of Cologne and completed a PhD on Siegfried Kracauer in 1977. In 1981, he published his first novel, *Der Ozeanriese*, followed by books such as *Der Aufklärungsmacher* (1985), *Ferne Erde* (1997) and *Fremd wie das Licht in den Träumen der Menschen* (2017).[77] In 2013, he published *Rebellion: Zwischenbericht*. Jochen Beyse lives in Berlin.

Rebellion can be read as an attempt to tackle the problem of representing the so-called Orient by straddling and reversing the stereotype of affective masculinity through its protagonist-narrator, a man who becomes active only when aggressive or violent. In Beyse's book,[78] the narrator spends a Saturday night in his small apartment. While getting increasingly drunk, he tries to write a *Zwischenbericht* of the Arab uprisings. However, he constantly interrupts his attempts to write by playing a video game which imagines the uprisings as a scenario from a first-person shooter. Since *Rebellion* hinges on this act of imagination, the analogy between the representative violence of Western literature and that of the first-person shooter quickly becomes obvious. Just as the narrator can virtually go berserk in a video game set in Egypt, he can do so literally by subjugating a world event to his own frustrated whims. While the book thus transfers passivity and violence to the autodiegetic narrator himself, at the same time it shows that the very recycling of this discourse is as passive and violent as Islamicate men are often presented to be.

By means of the invented shooter called *Tod in Kairo* ('Death in Cairo'), *Rebellion* takes the reader to a contemporary but virtual Cairo. By continually referring to Camus' *L'Étranger* (1942; *The Stranger*), the book's most prominent hypotext, *Rebellion* also evokes twentieth-century Algiers. Thus interweaving its different strands and settings, the text blurs all boundaries between reality and virtuality as well as between hypertext and hypotext, and arranges them in a literary puzzle of virtual and intertextual alter egos. As the narrative's sole unifying element, the mind of the first-person narrator only tentatively holds together the fragments of this puzzle:

> Ich dachte an den Fremden, ich dachte, der Fremde in mir würde besonders aus den melancholischen Fragmenten des Gesichts zu mir sprechen, ein paar Worte, leise, mit einem irre versöhnungsbereiten Flüstern, ich hatte mich getäuscht. Der Spiegel zerbrochen, aber er hielt. Ein Riss ging durch die Spiegelfläche. Ein Gesicht, darauf abgebildet, zerfiel in zwei Hälften, die Teile leicht gegeneinander versetzt wie beim Gesicht von *Jacqueline* aus der Hand von Picasso. (*Rebellion*: 10)[79]

While this reference to Picasso's second wife Jacqueline, who famously posed for Picasso's variations on Eugène Delacroix's 1934 painting *Femmes d'Alger dans leur appartement* (*Women of Algiers in Their Apartment*), reinforces the narrator's evocation of Algiers,[80] the narrator's fragmented image in the mirror already indicates that he has trouble coordinating his different projections. In fact, he does not only encounter difficulties in mastering his different narrative strands, but he also presents himself as unreliable:

> Ich erlebe das alles nicht in Wirklichkeit, und ich erlebe das alles unter dem Einfluss von reichlich viel Grand Verdier … Du bist in deinem Apparat im Kopf mit Alkohol so dermaßen in Fahrt gekommen, dass die Vernunft keine Zeit mehr finden konnte, sich zwischenzeitlich einzuschalten. (*Rebellion*: 109–10)[81]

Thus highlighting his irrationality and his increasing inebriation, the narrator distances himself from the realm of reason and begins to immerse himself into the realm of the affective – the border of which he projects into his construct of the Orient (*Rebellion*: 97).

Although the narrator actually sits – mostly passively – in his apartment in Berlin, he becomes activated by his affects when thinking about Algiers and when playing the first-person shooter set in Cairo: 'Alles wirkt wie entzündet, die Farben *brennen*. Meine Blicke können von den Sachen nicht lassen … Grelle Affekte durchzucken meinen Kopf, ich bäume mich sogar ein bisschen auf' (*Rebellion*: 79; italics in the original).⁸² Both Algiers and Cairo are hostile environments for him – however, it is precisely in their alleged hostility that they lure and activate him:

> kaum hier angekommen, hatte man bereits den ersten Feind! Es geht nicht ohne Feinde. Andere würden dazukommen, ein ganzer Haufen ... aber im Schatten der Feigenbäume, wo sich die unbekannten Feinde gerade aufhielten, im schwarzgrünen Halbdunkel der Blätter mit ihren fünf unförmig dicken Fingern war die Gefahr der Feindschaft ... war eine besondere Verlockung. Darum war man schließlich hier, wegen der besonderen Verlockung. Und außerdem –
>
> Schwarzgrünes Halbdunkel der Blätter, unbekannte Feinde, besondere Verlockung – es gibt ein paar Szenen im FREMDEN, die mir immer wieder hochkommen, über all die Jahre. (*Rebellion*: 13)⁸³

Combining the aspects of hostility and activation in this manner, the narrator does not only frame the two cities as the stimulus for his affect-driven behaviour, but he also pre-emptively relativises his responsibility for the violence which he is about to commit.

Representation and Responsibility
Even though the narrator continually tries to write a status report of the uprisings, he constantly interrupts his attempts by diving into his projections of Camus' *L'Étranger* and by causing a virtual carnage in the first-person shooter *Tod in Kairo*. Thus aligning the textual, the virtual and the affective, *Rebellion* raises important questions regarding the nature of contemporary Orientalist representations – and interventions. If the use of the first-person shooter in *Rebellion* extends the imaginary geography of the Orient from the textual into the virtual realm, at the same time it presents the Orient as a space of a mostly male Western imagination. What is more, the shooter also evokes the fact that, due to remote-controlled warfare technologies, the combat experience of Western soldiers, for instance in drone strikes, actually approaches such a virtual combat experience. In particular, through the use of the point of view of the first-person shooter, *Rebellion* explores the numerous problems of agency and responsibility which such a – mostly one-sided – cyber combat

> Ich würde gerne wissen, warum es hier so viele Menschen gibt, die sich wie Unschuldslämmer haben von mir abschlachten lassen, und komme auf den Gedanken, dass es an der Sonne liegen muss, an dem lähmend heißen Lichtsturz, der alle Kraft zur Gegenwehr zusammenschmelzen lässt. (*Rebellion*: 42)[93]

So as to divert the blame for the massacre he has committed to the victims themselves, the narrator turns his victims into the syntactic subject and, semantically, into the second agent of the subordinate clause. Through the use of causative verbs, he downplays his agency in committing the carnage even further. Presenting the whole act in the structure of a permissive causative ('die sich von mir haben abschlachten lassen'),[94] the narrator makes himself the syntactic object ('von mir')[95] of his victims' passivity. Looking for an explanation for their alleged passivity, he alludes to the intense sunlight which allegedly prevents retaliation. Not only does the narrator thereby merge his grammatical manipulation of agency with his intertextual line of referring to Camus' Meursault, but he also evokes tropes dating back to Montesquieu's climate theory and beyond – a line of argument which casts the so-called Orient as a realm in which the sun burns so relentlessly that all activity is allegedly muted to passivity and never-ending stasis.[96]

In addition to blaming his victims and the sun, the narrator names further agents to diffuse his responsibility by means of grammatical constructions. Starting from the neutral passive construction '*Und natürlich kann geschossen werden*' (*Rebellion*: 114; italics in the original),[97] he attributes the violence which he commits to agents such as '[d]er Lauf der FAMAS', 'der erste Schuss', 'der schmale hohe Balken Helligkeit' and 'die gewaltige Kraft der Einschläge':

> Der Lauf der FAMAS, der langsam immer höher steigt; das wutverzerrte Arabergesicht; der erste Schuss, der da eindringt, das Jochbein aufreißt und das Fleisch der halben Gesichtshälfte vom Schädel reißt; der schmale hohe Balken Helligkeit, wie der jetzt wirklich auf den Boden stürzt, dass der Körper des Arabers inmitten der Garben explodierenden Lichts hampelmannartig durchgeschüttelt wird; die gewaltige Kraft der Einschläge, die den Körper zurückbewegen, zurück zu den anderen Flüchtlingen … (*Rebellion*: 114)[98]

Syntactically aligning the Arab's face with the other agents of violence, the narrator assumes less responsibility for the shooting than he attributes to the man whom he kills. While the autodiegetic 'ich' ('I') does not function semantically as the agent here, it just watches the unfolding of the momentum created by the normally inanimate assault rifle. In a cruel persiflage of a purportedly technology-savvy Western rationality, technology is thus assigned agency and liability.

In contrast, the 'ich' only returns after his victims have died, and, in another nod to Meursault, it again mentions that 'die Sonne brennt' (*Rebellion*: 115).[99] While the return of the 'ich' might indicate that the narrator comes to his senses again after he has been seized with anger, the detailed but at times alienated description of the shooting (for instance, 'hampelmannartig durchgeschüttelt')[100] suggests that, even during the massacre, the narrator can attentively watch the violence inflicted by his shooter alter ego without identifying with him. Just as his intertextual model Meursault – the literary epitome of the allegedly emotionless murderer – the narrator thus watches the violence in a most detached way.

Rage, Race and Regress
In contrast to these representational strategies of evading responsibility, in a few passages, the narrator tentatively presents himself as responsible for the violence which he perpetrates. Suggesting that the question of responsibility is the preserve of the realm of reason, he marks it with the cognitive verb 'wissen' ('to know') and directly contrasts it with the affective realm:

> Auf der untersten Kommandoebene führt das schnell zu Frustrationen. Hier und da im Stadtgebiet hat es bereits Massaker gegeben, schwerste Gewaltexzesse, natürlich an der Zivilbevölkerung. Ich weiß, wovon ich rede. Es gibt eine Grenze, und wer die überschreitet, wird das rohe Tier, das seit Ewigkeiten darauf wartet auszubrechen. (*Rebellion*: 97)[101]

In the greater part of the short novel, however, the narrator shirks his responsibility by invoking his affects. Re-enacting the crossing of the boundary between the rational and the affective, the narrator describes how his affects take over after he has climbed the stairs of an old British imperial building, an ascent which feels like a triumphal march through the colonial past to him: 'Da befällt mich eine einzige Wut, und ich feuere eine lange Garbe ab –' (*Rebellion*: 108).[102] He enters into a rage – or rather, he states that the rage seizes him. By means of a causative verb, he turns himself into the patient of his affect, so that syntactically, it is his anger which acts. He follows this affect and starts to shoot uncontrollably, again muting the burst of fire by means of a dash.

Stylistically, the taking over of affect is signalised when the numerous incomplete sentences in *Rebellion* devolve into staccato style. In the following scene, they are combined with exclamation points and mimic a military tone of orders in which, again, the subject is often dropped:

> Die Konsole funktioniert über Bewegungssensoren ... tagelang auf dem Sessel habe ich den Arm in die Luft gereckt, den Körper nach recht gedreht, nach links, und alles im Dienst des Kampfes gegen eine aufkommende Empörung, eine schwelende Revolte, Rebellion: sämtliche Anführer an die Wand gestellt! keine Gnade! diese Revolte darf nicht überspringen! Wenn sie erst die angrenzenden Länder des Maghreb erfasst ... schon jetzt überall Tote ... liegen auf dem weißglühenden Land wie abgemähte Stängel einer Unkrautpflanze: In einer brutal in Herren und Knechte gespaltenen Welt kann man sein Heil vernünftigerweise nur im Lager der Herren suchen wollen, alles andere verdirbt den Spaß. Keiner soll mit irgendeinem humanitären Gefasel von dieser Wahrheit ablenken! Die Entlarvung alter Illusionen, darauf kommt es an – die falschen Wahrnehmungsweisen bekämpfen! Nach rechts werfen auf dem Sessel und den steifen Arm hochreißen. Falls die Sprachsteuerung aktiviert ist: ein Vorwärts! brüllen. (*Rebellion*: 35–6)[103]

Becoming completely disinhibited in his agitation, the narrator discloses the racist and violent gaze of the first-person shooter. Not only does he compare the corpses of revolutionary Egyptians to 'abgemähte Stängel einer Unkrautpflanze', but in the 'brutal in Herren und Knechte gespaltenen Welt' of *Tod in Kairo*,[104] the bodily movements which the game engenders physically illustrate how the narrator takes on an extreme right-wing position while playing it: he throws himself to the right and – reminiscent of a Hitler salute – yanks up his stiff arm before bawling 'Vorwärts!'[105]

If the Western narrator is thus presented as driven by his affects during the bloodbaths, the fact that he commits this violence in the virtual realm of the first-person shooter means that he can withdraw from the realm of affect at any time – even if this exit goes hand in hand with regression. By leaving the virtual Cairo of the game and by zooming back to Berlin, where the German soccer team has just lost a match, the narrator continuously interrupts the shooter. Thus detaching himself from the realm of affect, he recollects himself and surmounts his trepidation (*Rebellion*: 110–11). Before he returns to the bloodbath again, he renders his reflections in longer sentences and in calmer grammatical structures.

Despite this calmness on the surface, the reflections in his pauses, however, are in no way less epistemically violent than the rest of his behaviour. In fact, the task-oriented tone in which the narrator reiterates colonial myths, for instance that the people in Cairo need his help on their way out of chaos and into civilisation, indicate that his pauses give him the opportunity not to question, but to rationalise his affective behaviour: 'Da musste doch mit der FAMAS eine Ordnung reinzubringen sein! *Tod in Kairo* bietet ja einige Möglichkeiten, in dieses menschengemachte Chaos einzugreifen' (*Rebellion*: 102).[106] A similar feeling of Western superiority characterises his reasoning when he glorifies imperialist actions and voices the stereotype of the inability of the people to establish democracy:

> Die Straße breiter und breiter – ein Prachtboulevard eigentlich, bestimmt vor hundert Jahren angelegt, um dem Volk das großzügige Anlaufnehmen für den Sprung in die demokratisch verfasste Freiheit zu ermöglichen. Leider war er hoffnungslos zu kurz geraten, der Sprung, dieser und alle vorausgegangenen, denn jeder hat immer tiefer ins Chaos geführt! (*Rebellion*: 119)[107]

In combination with his affectivity and lack of empathy, the narrator's feeling of superiority helps him to rationalise his urge to kill. Unable to change his perspective, he projects his own rage into his male victims and interprets everything they do as motivated by hatred. In a gendered distinction, he continually mentions variations on 'hatred' when describing the men, whereas he presents the behaviour of the woman he has shot as 'gentle':

> Was bei der Frau eine Bewegung war, die alles abwehren wollte, was nicht bereits vom Tod berührt und darum eine letzte sanfte Vorbereitung auf das Sterben war, schien bei ihnen [den beiden verletzten Männern] eine vom

Just as in the example above, in which the narrator presents his voice as the acting instance which gives orders, in the following quotation, he describes the avatar of his arm as a prosthesis which is not part of his body and seems to act on its own:

> MUSIK, Fetzen von Tonfolgen, abgerissene Hirtengesänge – vorbei das stille Gleichgewicht des Tages. Mein Unterarm kommt ins Bild, jetzt das Sturmgewehr, die FAMAS F1, Verschluss und Magazin liegen hinterm Griffstück in der Schulterstütze, offene Visierung, leichter Rechtsdrall. Der Arm eine schwarze Waffe, eine schwarz-stählerne Stahlprothese ... steigt langsam hoch, Schweiß rinnt mir in die Augen. Immer noch diese belämmerte Musik: Töne, die man durchlöchern müsste, damit endlich eine Ruhe ist. Ich reiße das Gewehr nach oben. Die Töne sind überall und wollen mit ihrer irrsinnig schnellen Abfolge erreichen, dass man das volle Magazin verfeuert. Sogar Granaten verschießen kann das Gewehr, aber soll man Granaten gegen wildgewordene Töne einsetzen? Der Sicherheitshebel vorm Abzug: ich stelle ihn auf Dauerfeuer –
>
> Da brennt jetzt die Sonne ...   (*Rebellion*: 54)[89]

By means of the harsh alliteration and the polyptoton in 'schwarz-stählerne Stahlprothese',[90] which allows the repetition of the words 'stählern' and 'Stahl',[91] the narrator emphasises the inorganic material of his avatar's arm. At the same time, the combination of the two rhetorical figures reflects how his thoughts are focused on the weapon. Underlining the snatches of sound sequences and his irritation by means of fragmented syntax and an irregular rhythm, moreover, he presents the sounds not just as a reason for his irritation, but as an invitation for his aggression. Trying to silence the sounds, he starts shooting uncontrollably. When he finally mutes his constant firing by means of a dash (see also *Rebellion*: 108),[92] he renders the violence and deaths which he has caused invisible.

Besides advancing – as his intertextual model Meursault – the burning sun as an excuse for his behaviour, the narrator further shirks his responsibility by frequently reversing the semantic and syntactic roles of the agent and the victims of the violence. He does so by filling the subject position, which grammatically carries the main load of agency, with his victims:

experience entails. Because of this narrative choice, the text does not only include the reader in sharing the perspective of the one behind the remote control, but it also puts the main focus on how the autodiegetic narrator evaluates his responsibility for the violence which he commits in the virtual realm.

So as to negotiate this connection between representation and responsibility, the text shows how the autodiegetic narrator grammatically and stylistically distances himself from the violence which he commits through pronounced shifts in agency. Not only does he frequently speak in incomplete sentences and thus drops the subject pronoun 'ich' ('I'), but he also often takes cover behind the impersonal pronoun 'man' ('you/one'):

> Die Kluft zwischen mir und der Welt in diesem Teil von Kairo öffnet sich mit jedem Schritt ... Man hat ein Blutbad angerichtet. Danach stand man im Freien, deckungslos, das weiße Gestirn am Himmel war explodiert. (*Rebellion*: 43)[84]

> Man könnte mit der FAMAS von hier oben alles Leben auf der anderen Straßenseite auslöschen. Was ist nur passiert, dass einem schon wieder dieser Gedanke durch den Kopf geschossen kommt. (*Rebellion*: 103)[85]

Complementing this strategy, the narrator further diminishes his grammatical agency by turning the impersonal pronoun into the object of the sentence. In this way, 'Gedanke'[86] becomes the subject of the subordinate clause and thus of the verb 'geschossen'[87] – a lexical choice which further underlines the logic of war in the first-person shooter.

In order to further undermine his responsibility for the bloodshed which he causes, the narrator dissociates himself from the virtual representations of those parts of his body which are instrumental in inflicting violence:

> Bevor es gestern Nacht in Kairo losging, hatte ich mir kurz die Szenen in Memphis angeschaut, die herrlich sinnlosen Schießereien auf den ramessidischen Ruinenfeldern, zur Einstimmung ... trotzdem sehr öde, die Stunden, kein Sterbenswörtchen Dialog mit irgendwem, keine Zeit, alle mussten kämpfen. Man selber auch. Immer nur eine Stimme, *meine* Stimme, und die hat Befehle erteilt. (*Rebellion*: 19; italics in the original)[88]

blinden Hass diktierte Abwehrgeste, denn sie fuchteln mir mit knorrigen
Händen vorm Gesicht herum. Es kommt mir plötzlich vor, als habe ich
genug gelitten. Da zeigt der Linke von ihnen, der sich schmerzverzerrt das
Bein hält, auf die FAMAS und macht Zeichen, ihm das Sturmgewehr zu
geben. Ich weiß sofort, er will mich erschießen, und dass es ihm nicht nur
darauf ankommt, dass ich sterbe, sondern vor allem, *wie* ich zugrunde gehe:
langsam, qualvoll, nach dem Gesetz des Auge um Auge, Zahn um Zahn.
(*Rebellion*: 112; italics in the original)[108]

Reducing the two men to being led by blind hatred, the narrator – in
another reversal of roles – casts himself as the victim who has 'suffered
enough'. This continues on the next few pages: '[I]ch wartete bloß darauf,
dass er mir seine hasserfüllten Laute ins Gesicht schrie ...' (*Rebellion*: 113).[109]
Here, the man, whom the narrator starts calling 'der Araber/the Arab' is
deprived of all humanity. What he says is not language to the narrator,
just 'hate-filled sounds'. It is only through the subtitles of the first-person
shooter that the narrator understands the man's utterance: what seem to be
'hate-filled sounds' in fact turn out to be a critique of imperialism (*Rebellion*:
113).[110] In spite of this, the narrator continues to interpret everything as
hateful, even after the narrator has finished the massacre and has killed
the man. He hears that '[i]rgendwann drangen hasserfüllte Schreie zu mir
hoch, mit einzelnen fing es an, dann herrschte draußen regelrechter Terror'
(*Rebellion*: 116)[111] before he finally looks into 'hassverzerrte Gesichter'
(*Rebellion*: 117).[112]

So as to contextualise his massacre, the narrator conjures up a palimpsest
of the long history of Western interference while killing in the imperial
building:

Da steht die Zeit plötzlich still, rast still auf der Stelle und schneidet
schmerzhaft scharfe Bilder aus dem Augenblick heraus – die tote Mutter,
das tote Mädchen; die zerschossenen Palmen im ersten Morgengrauen,
der Qasr-al-Nil-Garten bei Sonnenaufgang; Lawrence unterbreitet dem
Hochkommissar von Ägypten erste weitsichtige Pläne zur Unterstützung
des arabischen Befreiungskampfs; der schlammgrüne Nil, sein blasiger
Teppich aus Schaum; das blasige Blut. (*Rebellion*: 114)[113]

Superimposing images from the colonial past with contemporary atrocities, this scene merges the past and the present in the raging energy of the moment. Culminating in the paradox of time which 'rast still auf der Stelle', it alludes to Paul Virilio's *L'Inertie polaire* (1990; *Polar Inertia*), translated into German as *Rasender Stillstand* (1992).[114] According to Virilio, the state of polar inertia – or racing stagnation – marks the paradoxical final stage of the history of human acceleration. After centuries of acceleration through new means of transport, transmissions in real time do not only result in even greater acceleration, but they also cause a regression: when human beings sit motionlessly in front of the racing events on the screen, this state of polar inertia unfolds.[115]

Perfectly embodying the state of polar inertia, the narrator, paralysed by all the information which reaches him on various channels and in real time, falls into a regression within the confines of his own living room. As he barely leaves his apartment, he is the receptive consumer *par excellence* of media representations of world events and more trivial news, for instance the weather: '[M]ir war ein bisschen kalt, obwohl das Wetter schön war, angenehm warm, ich habe gefroren. Ich konnte es nicht glauben. Ich stand auf und ging wieder zu einem der Apparate, ich überzeugte mich, dass angenehm warmes Wetter herrschte draußen.' (*Rebellion*: 17)[116] Once he turns off his electronic devices (*Rebellion*: 16), which he anachronistically or in a pun on the word 'app' calls 'Apparat/apparatus', his only activity consists of assembling the numerous intertextual pieces which he has collected from other sources. Not only does he thus take on the detachedness of his intertextual counterpart, Meursault, but with no other stimulus, he relies exclusively on the information which he receives via his electronic devices. In this sense, and as underlined by the allusions to Paul Virilio, *Rebellion* can also be read as a critique of the media and information society.

Sublimation and Projection
By transplanting the stereotype of affect-ridden male violence into the otherwise passive Western autodiegetic narrator, *Rebellion* tries to weaken the stereotype's close association with the Islamicate man. While the narrator's attempt at writing a *Zwischenbericht* can be read as an effort to overcome his passivity by means other than violence, that is, to channel his energy into a cultural product and to thus sublimate, he can barely concentrate on this

endeavour. So although the narrator's sexual urges inform his projections of Camus' *L'Étranger*, he does not manage to transform them into writing. Instead, he continually interrupts his attempts by causing a virtual carnage in the first-person shooter *Tod in Kairo*.

The whole set-up of the text thus serves to show how a Western attempt at sublimation ends up as a mere projection. Teeming with stereotypes, the narrator's representations of Arab men vividly illustrate how, instead of imaginatively sublimating, he continues to use them as proxies for his own projections. In contrast to the narrator – who has the representative power of putting on the character mask of affectivity at will – he imagines Arab men as uncontrollably affective, with regard to both sexuality and violence:

> [Maria] würde sich unmöglich dazu hergeben, zwischen einem *Haufen Männern* herumzusitzen und nur darauf zu warten, dass sie jemand zu einem Getränk einlädt, dabei kurz seine *Pranke* auf ihre Schulter legt, ähnlich wie da vorne jetzt der Araber den Unterarm einer mädchenhaften Frau drückt, mit einem Grinsen, sich wie ein *ordinärer Affe* vorbeugt und ihr etwas ins Ohr flüstert, dann folgt ihr Lachen. (*Rebellion*: 74; my italics)[117]

In this scene, set in Algiers and invented to bolster the narrator's projection of *L'Étranger*, the narrator does not only describe the men in animalistic lexis, but when he watches an 'Arab' whom he thinks of as a competitor, he depicts this man by resorting to stereotypes of a supposed predator masculinity:

> Der Araber blickt zu uns herüber … er kann wohl nur Maria taxieren. Es ist ein unverschämter Blick, das sehe ich an seiner Haltung: die Hüften rollen, beide Hände rucken durch die Luft, das Becken vorgeschoben – alles andere als die Haltung eines Träumers. Ich fahre im Sessel hoch. Was könnte man mit einer schönen FAMAS F1 auf dieser Terrasse alles anrichten! Mit einem metalltrockenen Metallgeräusch den Hebel auf Dauerfeuer legen, dann den Abzug durchziehen: Bei einer Magazinkapazität von dreihundert Schuss ließe sich alles Leben auf der Terrasse und im Innern des Cafés auslöschen … Aber ich weiß, ich bin nicht in Kairo, leider, sondern in Algier, und dass ich mit dem vielen Grand Verdier im Blut bestimmt auch zu betrunken wäre, um halbwegs sicher auf diesen Kopf zu zielen, seine höhnische Grimasse, die blendweißen Zahnreihen … (*Rebellion*: 76)[118]

Presenting the man with his pelvis thrust forward and flaunting his white teeth, the narrator paints him as uncivilised, at the mercy of his affects and in mostly physical terms. He denigrates his actions as 'Schmierentheater des Arabers' (*Rebellion*: 77)[119] and, following the pattern of white men saving women from non-white men, presents himself as the one who should have saved Maria: 'Ich wäre sonst längst auf Maria zugegangen und hätte sie angesprochen, hätte diesem Araber mit seinem ständig zwischen Raserei und Stumpfsinn oszillierenden Blick eindeutig die Stirn geboten –' (*Rebellion*: 78).[120] While it clearly is the narrator himself who is torn by his rage, his desire for Maria and his apathy, he projects his own state of being – 'zwischen Raserei und Stumpfsinn'[121] – into the other man, and both despises and envies his competitor for his allegedly affect-driven behaviour.

Heterochrony and the Chaos of Simultaneity
Besides showing how the narrator's attempts at writing fall short of sublimation and thus end up as stereotypical projections, *Rebellion* opens up a pronounced heterochronic dimension to dilute the stereotype of affective Islamicate masculinity:

> Die verschiedensten Informationen aus sämtlichen Tiefen von Raum und Zeit treffen in mir zusammen, aus dem Fernsehzimmer, dem Flur, hinten aus der Küche ... immer wieder aus Algier, immer wieder aus Kairo ... (*Rebellion*: 63)[122]

As illustrated in this quotation, Beyse's text produces temporal layering by means of intertextual reference. Indicating that the narrator's Orient is mainly an (inter)textual world,[123] his sources are both extradiegetically known and diegetic inventions: 'Algier kenne ich aus einem Buch, Kairo aus einem Spiel' (*Rebellion*: 93).[124] In *Rebellion*, the frequent references to *L'Étranger* and *Tod in Kairo* consequently do not only engender rapid changes of setting but – concomitant with these spatial shifts – they also create temporal changes, intertextual depth and excursions into virtual reality. Sometimes, they last for less than a sentence and end as abruptly as the narrator's thoughts, as for instance in 'KAIRO, als ich in Kairo – nein!' (*Rebellion*: 23).[125] Although the title of the second of the book's three section headings, 'Von Algier nach Kairo' (*Rebellion*: 65),[126] might suggest that these temporal and spatial shifts possess some chronological coherence, it quickly becomes clear that at any given moment, time and space can be turned upside down. While the narrator desperately tries to 'begin a new time' so as to no longer live in books (*Rebellion*: 26), living in an intertextual potpourri as well as in the real-time of diverse media representations is, in fact, exactly what he does. Even when he turns off the television and his other electronic devices, he remains caught in the news and stories which he has absorbed. In this, the text's heterochrony can also be read as a critique of the chaos of real-time simultaneity which has superseded the order of succession.[127]

Stuck in the chaos of real-time simultaneity, the narrator does not manage to write a *Zwischenbericht* of the revolution; all he is able to commit to paper are his thoughts and perceptions during his attempts to write. While as a character, the narrator remains elusive, he appears more clearly through his numerous metafictional comments on his writing process,[128] for instance the recurring 'Ich mache mir eine Notiz' and its variations (*Rebellion*: for instance, 9, 19, 23, 34, 59, 63).[129] Thus focusing on the protagonist-narrator's writing process, *Rebellion* shares important characteristics with the *Künstlernovelle* or *-roman* (artist novella or novel). And in fact, the title of the invented shooter *Tod in Kairo* does not only evoke Hans Christoph Buch's *Tod in Habana* (2007; 'Death in Habana'), but it also juxtaposes *Rebellion* with Thomas Mann's artist novella *Der Tod in Venedig* (1912; *Death in Venice*).[130]

Besides intertextual layering and the numerous metafictional comments, *Rebellion* creates heterochrony by means of stylistics. In a scene which starts in Camus' Algiers and ends in contemporary (albeit virtual) Cairo (*Rebellion*: 39–43), the narrator, for instance, uses a reference to the plot in *L'Étranger* to predict what will happen to himself: 'Ich *würde* ihn [Salamano's dog] kennenlernen …' (*Rebellion*: 39; my italics).[131] He first starts this external prolepsis in the past subjunctive, which indicates that his foreshadowing is at the same time grounded in a text already published and thus tied to the literary past. Then, however, via a longer passage in the present tense, the narrator modulates into predictions in the future tense. He then turns back the future tense into an immediate present tense, which becomes the here and now of the narration for a moment:

> Morgen *werde* ich auch Salamano im Treppenflur *begegnen* und bestimmt Maria auf der Straße. Wir *werden* mit dem Vorstadtbus ans Meer *fahren* ... Ich *sehe* mich schwimmen, eine Boje umklammern, Maria neben mir. Unsere Schultern *berühren* sich. Natürlich *begehre* ich sie. (*Rebellion*: 40; my italics)[132]

After the interlude of a longer flashback in the past tense and past perfect (*Rebellion*: 41–2), the narrator returns to his current state of being and the present tense. This presence is, however, placed in a different country: the virtual Egypt of *Tod in Kairo*. As this example representatively shows, different historical, literary and virtual layers are woven into a form and content which merge reality, imaginative projection, analeptic prolepses into the literary past, intertexts and excursions into contemporary Cairo. As a consequence, *Rebellion* does not only emphasise the interconnectivity of global events, but also directs attention to the historicity of the Arab uprisings: 'Jeder Tritt hat mächtig nachgehallt. Das Echo musste ja auch jede Menge Epochen durchlaufen, und jedes Mal traten einem neue Bilder entgegen' (*Rebellion*: 106).[133]

Affective Projections

Often presented as a potential danger to the so-called Western way of life,[134] the figuration of the affect-driven Islamicate man functions as a foil onto which Western affects and insecurities with regard to changing sexual and gender identities are projected by means of Orientalist tropes. Both *Kapow!* and *Rebellion* illustrate this Western projective fixation with the allegedly problematic and gendered Other by rendering the process of how affective masculinity is Orientalised (and Islamised) visible. Not only do the texts focus on how their narrators approach the uprisings from the angle of affectivity, but both books also show how the city of Cairo serves their narrators as a realm for their affective projections – of lust in the case of Thirlwell, of aggression in the case of Beyse.

By relocating affectivity from the level of the characters in the embedded story to that of the narrator, *Kapow!* demonstrates how the Western gaze Orientalises and ethnicises sexism. In particular, through Rustam, one of its characters, *Kapow!* visualises the double projection of Neo-Orientalism, that is, the Orientalisation (and Islamisation) of both lust and repressed lust: Rustam embodies how with the shift into a more sexually inhibited register attributed to the Islamicate man, the ambivalence of projection of Neo-Orientalism – its tension between the Western fantasy of a lascivious Orient versus a picture of Islam that is opposed to the alleged sexual freedom in secular societies[135] – is now completely outsourced into the construct of Islamicate masculinity.

Trying to weaken the close association of affect-ridden male violence with the Islamicate man, *Rebellion* shows how the Western autodiegetic narrator projects his own affects into his Arab counterparts. Otherwise remaining mostly passive, the narrator limits his affect-driven behaviour to situations in which he imagines himself in two cities in the Arab world – Algiers and Cairo. Moreover, by means of the first-person shooter, *Rebellion* illustrates how a peaceful uprising is turned into a virtual massacre. Thus presenting violence as a source of Western entertainment, the short novel criticises the representational violence which the narrator inflicts both in the first-person shooter and in his depiction of it.

Although both *Kapow!* and *Rebellion* broach the issue of affectivity on the level of content, they simultaneously demonstrate that it is their Western narrators – and, to a certain degree, their readers – who fabricate these affect-ridden images. In order to highlight this involvement in the construction of the narrators' respective personal Orients as affective realms, both texts include ergodic elements – that is, elements which place responsibilities on the recipients which transcend the mere thought process, eye movement and turning of pages, and thus require the recipient to actively participate in the construction of the text.[136] While by imaging the uprisings as a scenario from a first-person shooter, *Rebellion* illustrates on the diegetic level how its narrator becomes involved through the ergodic computer game, *Kapow!* also extradiegetically involves its reader by means of the ergodic elements in its layout. Thus further highlighting the interplay between narration and reception, *Kapow!* and *Rebellion* do not only involve their readers, but they also have their narrators reflect on their theoretical and representational decisions – and on their representational responsibility. By actualising their own construction of meaning, both books consequently try to raise awareness for the responsibility which a Western portrayal of the uprisings entails. At the same time, by having their narrators present themselves as intoxicated and thus unreliable, both texts illustrate how readily this responsibility is often shirked.

Further underlining their presentation of Islamicate affectivity as originating in the Western mind, *Kapow!* and *Rebellion* try to deconstruct the Orientalist traditions which precede them. To create irritation with these Orientalist traditions, both books parody them by means of irony, intertextuality and a pronounced metafictional level. Thereby, while involving their readers in the process of narration, the texts avoid addressing them on an identificatory affective level and negotiate affectivity at the content and metafictional level instead.

To challenge the stereotype of affective Islamicate masculinity further, *Kapow!* and *Rebellion* blur the boundaries between different temporal and spatial levels. Instead of focusing exclusively on the temporality of the Islamicate world as a distinct entity, both texts open up different spatio-temporal dimensions which transcend geographical boundaries. In order to do so, they make use of digressions and non-linear narration and create 'multiplicities of place and time that sit alongside and within each other'.[137] Even if filtered by a Western focaliser, they thus produce an effect of heterochronic time, that is, a 'layering of worlds and space-time parameters …'[138]

Despite these attempts to dilute spatial and temporal limitations, however, both *Kapow!* and *Rebellion* fall short of also incorporating what Slavoj Žižek calls 'signs from the future':[139]

> [I]nstead of analysing them [radical emancipatory outbursts] as part of the continuum of past and present, we should bring in the perspective of the future, taking them as limited, distorted (sometimes even perverted) fragments of a utopian future that lies dormant in the present as its hidden potential. According to Deleuze, in Proust 'people and things occupy a place in time which is incommensurable with the one they have in space': the famous madeleine is here in place, but this is not its true time.[140]

Remaining limited to a heterochronic representation of the past and the present, what both texts achieve could perhaps best be summarised by *Rebellion*'s subtitle, *Zwischenbericht*. Although both books try to transcend geographical and epistemological boundaries in their renderings of the

Arab uprisings, their distribution of representational space and straddling of stereotypes still follow the beaten track of Orientalist motifs – albeit with an inverted, that is, ironising, function. While signs from the future – that is, literary recontextualisations – are absent from both works, what the texts do is draw level with the status quo. As this status quo is filtered by a Western focaliser – and a subject in crisis[141] – *Kapow!* and *Rebellion* take stock of its stereotypical inventory in an ego- and consequently Western-centric way.

Both *Kapow!* and *Rebellion* consequently constitute intellectualised but counterproductive attempts to subvert – on the level of form – the stereotypes of affective masculinity which they evoke on the level of content. Through their self-reflexive use of postmodern narrative strategies, the texts do not only try to challenge the representation of affective Islamicate masculinity, but they also turn form into content. In this, they can be read as attempts at formal desecuritisation. As, however, both texts limit their attempt to highlight how the stereotype of affective Islamicate masculinity is constructed to simply reversing or transplanting the stereotype without shifting or widening its horizon of meaning, the stereotype keeps its position as the implicit norm. Just as in unconscious associations, in which negations are processed by still evoking what is *not*,[142] so this formal endeavour to subvert content by means of a straight irony of reversal does not override the stereotype itself. As it presupposes and reiterates what it tries to deconstruct, an ironic reversal by 180 degrees provides a mirror image of the stereotype but does not de-essentialise or change its sense.[143]

With regard to a poetics of desecuritisation, this implies that, so as to engender epistemological and representational shifts, ironic reversal does not suffice to overcome the categories which it parodies. In fact, in *Kapow!* and *Rebellion*, this kind of irony – together with the narrators' stress on their own intoxication and its attendant unreliability – can be seen not just as a distancing effect, but also as a strategy of avoiding responsibility. If, through their use of postmodern narrative strategies, both texts show how 'through a double process of installing and ironizing, parody signals how present representations come from past ones and what ideological consequences derive from both continuity and difference',[144] such an avoidance of responsibility, of endlessly recurring to the past, does not de-naturalise or de-doxify. While, as in much other postmodern fiction, a parodical rewriting of earlier texts is thus central in *Kapow!* and *Rebellion*, it is, however, not sufficient to overcome Orientalism.

In sum, the playful and ironic handling of responsibility in representations of sexualised securitisation by those who are not securitised is once again indicative of pronounced power imbalances which underlie the concept of security. Although the use of postmodern narrative strategies in the two texts could also be read as an endeavour to subvert the alleged stability of images associated with insecurity, because these strategies are so well-established, they do not extend the insecurity of those who are securitised to the level of form, but instead render the texts themselves invulnerable in their ambiguity: not threatened by being securitised themselves, they are positioned in a secure speaking position from which they can ironically raise the issue of responsibility without assuming any themselves.

Notes

1. Adam Thirlwell. *Kapow!* London: Visual Editions, 2012. 68. Henceforth quoted in brackets as *Kapow!* + page number.
2. For the wider usage of 'Islamicate' in this book, see n. 2 in Chapter One.
3. See, for instance, Sabine Hark and Paula-Irene Villa. *Unterscheiden und herrschen: Ein Essay zu den ambivalenten Verflechtungen von Rassismus, Sexismus und Feminismus in der Gegenwart*. Bielefeld: Transcript, 2017.
4. See, for instance, Gargi Bhattacharyya. *Dangerous Brown Men: Exploiting Sex, Violence and Feminism in the Age of Terror*. London and New York: Zed Books, 2008. 7, 14; Paul Amar. 'Turning the Gendered Politics of the Security State Inside Out? Charging the Police with Sexual Harassment in Egypt'. *International Feminist Journal of Politics* 13.3 (2011): 299–328.
5. For a criticism of sexualised explanations of terrorism, see, for instance, Pankaj Mishra. 'The Politics of Paranoia'. *The Guardian*. 17 September 2006 (website – last accessed 27 June 2017).
6. For works on affect which have received wide attention, see, for instance, Brian Massumi. *Politics of Affect*. Cambridge: Polity Press, 2015; Sara Ahmed. *The Cultural Politics of Emotion*. 2nd edn. Edinburgh: Edinburgh University Press, 2014. For more on the 'affective turn', see Patricia Ticineto Clough and Jean Halley, eds. *The Affective Turn: Theorizing the Social*. Durham, NC: Duke University Press, 2007.

7. The stereotype of the effeminate Oriental male is closely linked to climate theories dating back to Montesquieu and beyond. According to these assumptions, the hot weather allegedly resulted not only in a marked passivity of people living in the so-called Orient, but it also cost men their virile energy. Inge E. Boer. *Disorienting Vision: Rereading Stereotypes in French Orientalist Texts and Images*. Ed. Mieke Bal. Amsterdam and New York: Rodopi, 2004. 37–46. What both the stereotype of the effeminate Oriental and that of Islamicate predator masculinity share is the hypervisibility of sexuality as well as a general focus on supposedly affect-driven behaviour. Paul Amar. 'Middle East Masculinity Studies: Discourses of "Men in Crisis", Industries of Gender in Revolution'. *Journal of Middle East Women's Studies* 7.3 (2011): 36–70. 37, 40.
8. Gabriele Dietze. 'Sexualitätsdispositiv Revisited: Die Figuration des "Arabischen Mannes" als Abwehrfigur neoliberaler Freiheit'. *Der inspizierte Muslim*. Ed. Schirin Amir-Moazami. Bielefeld: Transcript, 2018. 215–45. 226.
9. Gabriele Dietze. 'Ethnosexismus: Sex-Mob-Narrative um die Kölner Sylvesternacht [sic]'. *Movements* 1 (2016): 177–85. 177.
10. Paul Amar. 'Middle East Masculinity Studies'. 2011. 37.
11. Lutz Bachmann, the founder of the German right-wing extremist group PEGIDA, helped spread this portmanteau word by wearing a T-shirt featuring the PEGIDA slogan 'Rapefugees not welcome'. 'Pegida-Chef wegen Volksverhetzung angezeigt'. *Zeit online*. 10 January 2016 (website – last accessed 26 September 2018). The website rapefugees.net offers a platform for hate speech (with keywords such as 'Vergewaltigungskultur' ('rape culture') or 'Horde Muslime' ('Muslim mob')) and a so-called 'rape map'. 'Gruppenvergewaltigung Essen/Vertuscht: Lauenburger Gang ist ein großer Muslimclan'. *Rapefugees.net*. 15 February 2018 (website – last accessed 26 September 2018).
12. Sabine Hark and Paula-Irene Villa. 2017. 82–5.
13. Paul Amar. 'Middle East Masculinity Studies'. 2011. 40. For more on the cooptation of ethnosexist tropes by originally emancipatory discourses, see Jasbir K. Puar. *Terrorist Assemblages: Homonationalism in Queer Times*. Durham, NC and London: Duke University Press, 2007; Sara R. Farris. *In the Name of Women's Rights: The Rise of Femonationalism*. Durham, NC: Duke University Press, 2017; Sabine Hark and Paula-Irene Villa, 2017.
14. Gabriele Dietze. 2018. 231.
15. Gabriele Dietze. 2016. 188.

16. Sabine Hark and Paula-Irene Villa. 2017. 85.
17. See, for instance, Lorella Ventura. 'The 'Arab Spring' and Orientalist Stereotypes: The Role of Orientalism in the Narration of the Revolts in the Arab World'. *Interventions* 19.2 (2017): 282–97; Stefan Borg. 'The Arab Uprisings, the Liberal Civilizing Narrative and the Problem of Orientalism'. *Middle East Critique* 25.3 (2016): 211–27.
18. Liz Fekete. 'Enlightened Fundamentalism? Immigration, Feminism and the Right'. *Race & Class* 48.2 (2006): 1–22. Quoted in: Sabine Hark and Paula-Irene Villa. 2017. 85.
19. Liz Fekete. 2006. 6 / Sabine Hark and Paula-Irene Villa. 2017. 85.
20. Edward W. Said. *Orientalism* [1978]. Ed. with new Afterword and Preface. London: Penguin, 2003. 7.
21. Norbert Elias. *Über den Prozeß der Zivilisation*. Vol. 1. Frankfurt: Suhrkamp, 1976. 312–454.
22. Rana Kabbani. *Imperial Fictions: Europe's Myths of Orient*. London, San Francisco and Beirut: SAQI, 2008. 26; Edward W. Said. 2003. 190.
23. Rana Kabbani. 2008. 36.
24. Ibid. 39.
25. Edward W. Said. 2003. 190.
26. Inge E. Boer. 2004. 53, 47; Meyda Yeğenoğlu. *Colonial Fantasies: Towards a Feminist Reading of Orientalism*. Cambridge: Cambridge University Press, 1998. 17. Edward W. Said. 2003. 190.
27. Edward W. Said. 2003. 190.
28. Rana Kabbani. 2008. 42; Inge E. Boer. 2004. 47.
29. Gayatri Chakravorty Spivak. 'Can the Subaltern Speak?' *Colonial Discourse and Post-Colonial Theory: A Reader*. Eds Patrick Williams and Laura Chrisman. New York: Columbia University Press, 1994. 66–111. 92.
30. Sabine Hark and Paula-Irene Villa. 2017. 85. Italics in the original. Considering how strong the association of the Islamicate male and homophobia has become, one might perhaps further sharpen this dictum and state that in mainstream discourse, it might also read as white men saving homosexual white men from brown men. On the issue of homonationalism, see Jasbir K. Puar. 2007.
31. Bernard Lewis. 'The Roots of Muslim Rage: Why So Many Muslims Deeply Resent the West, and Why Their Bitterness Will Not Easily Be Mollified'. *The Atlantic*. 1 September 1990 (website – last accessed 18 February 2015).
32. Ibid.

33. Samuel P. Huntington. *The Clash of Civilizations and the Remaking of World Order*. New York: Simon & Schuster, 1996.
34. Samuel P. Huntington. 'The Clash of Civilizations?' *Foreign Affairs* 72.3 (1993): 22–49. 22.
35. Samuel P. Huntington. 1996. 263.
36. Gabriele Dietze. 2018. 226.
37. Gargi Bhattacharyya. 2008. 9; Éric Fassin. 'National Identities and Transnational Intimacies: Sexual Democracy and the Politics of Immigration in Europe'. *Public Culture* 22.3 (2010): 507–29. 522–3.
38. Sigmund Freud. *Civilization and Its Discontents* [1930]. *The Complete Psychological Works of Sigmund Freud – The Future of an Illusion, Civilization and its Discontents, and Other Works*. Trans. James Strachey. London: Hogarth Press, 1961. Vol. XXI, 79–80.
39. Pankaj Mishra. 2006.
40. Both to underline the negative connotations inherent in the stereotype of allegedly unself-regulated Islamicate masculinity and because *Kapow!* itself highlights that it is about 'lust', I use the word 'lust', not 'desire'. Elaine Hatfield and Richard L. Rapson. 'Lust'. *The Oxford Companion to Emotion and the Affective Sciences*. Eds David Sander and Klaus R. Scherer. Oxford: Oxford University Press, 2009. 245.
41. Jochen Beyse. *Rebellion: Zwischenbericht*. Zurich and Berlin: Diaphanes, 2013. Henceforth quoted in brackets as *Rebellion* + page number.
42. Adam Thirlwell. 'An Interview with Adam Thirlwell'. Interview by Alison Gibbons. *Contemporary Literature* 55.4 (2014): 610–34. 611, 614.
43. 'Stories'. *Adamthirlwell.com*. No date (website – last accessed 2 June 2017).
44. For an analysis of the interdependencies between the construct of romantic love and consumer capitalism, see Eva Illouz. *Consuming the Romantic Utopia: Love and the Cultural Contradictions of Capitalism*. Berkeley and Los Angeles: University of California Press, 1997.
45. Also foregrounding different pronouns for the first person singular, the first of the numerous footnotes in *Kapow!* reflects on how this urge for Western over-assertiveness is closely linked to insecurities as to what constitutes the self. Alluding to the crisis of the European subject, this footnote stands upside down to the main text and presents a hipster narrator lost in trivial pursuits and losing his sense of self: 'It wasn't the usual or previous me, or I. But lately, to be honest, I'd been thinking that this thing called *I* wasn't anything at all. I was beginning to think that *I* was basically a pseudonym' (*Kapow!*: 5). For the crisis

of the European subject, see Julia Kristeva. *Crisis of the European Subject*. New York: Other Press, 2000.
46. Fakhri Saleh. 'Rethinking World Literature: The Arabic Novel in Non-Western Eyes'. *Qantara*. 6 May 2011 (website – last accessed 28 June 2018).
47. Khaled Al Khamissi [2006]. *Taxi*. Trans. Jonathan Wright. London: Aflame Books, 2008.
48. Khaled Al Khamissi and Stefan Weidner. 'Arabischer Frühling'. Trans. Günther Orth. *Qantara.de*. 19 May 2011 (website – last accessed 10 January 2020); Werner Bloch. 'Egypt's Culture on Four Wheels'. *Qantara.de*. 13 March 2011 (website – last accessed 10 January 2020); Caroline Rooney. 'Popular Culture and the Arab Spring'. *The Edinburgh Companion to the Postcolonial Middle East*. Eds Anna Ball and Karim Mattar. Edinburgh: Edinburgh University Press, 2018. 407–26. 421.
49. While the term 'novelette' has negative connotations, in English the term 'novella' is often used in a more general way to 'distinguish a long short-story from a short story and a short novel from a full-dress novel'. J. A. Cuddon. 'Novella'. *Dictionary of Literary Terms & Literary Theory*. 3rd edn. London et al.: Penguin, 1999. 600–1. 601. Both to avoid derogative undertones and to avoid confusion with close definitions of 'novella', I have opted for the term 'short novel'.
50. Paul Amar. 'Turning the Gendered Politics of the Security State Inside Out?' 2011. 300–1.
51. Ibid. 310.
52. Ibid. 310.
53. Ibid. 301.
54. Ibid. 308.
55. Ibid. 313.
56. Inge Boer. 2004. 69.
57. Mahdi Tourage. *Rūmī and the Hermeneutics of Eroticism*. Leiden and Boston: Brill, 2007. 243–50.
58. Staci Gem Scheiwiller. *Liminalities of Gender and Sexuality in Nineteenth-Century Iranian Photography*. New York and Abingdon: Routledge, 2017. 185.
59. Paul Amar. 'Turning the Gendered Politics of the Security State Inside Out?' 2011. 301.
60. Naomi Lubrich. 'The Art of Tahrir Square: Adam Thirlwell's Kapow!' *Jewish Museum Berlin*. 1 February 2013 (website – last accessed 14 April 2015).

61. Alison Gibbons. '"Take that you intellectuals!" and "kaPOW!" Adam Thirlwell and the Metamodernist Future of Style'. *Studia Neophilologica* (2015): 29–43. 36.
62. For more on Adam Thirlwell's take on the role of translation in the production of literature, see *Multiples: 12 Stories in 18 Languages by 61 Authors*. Ed. Adam Thirlwell. London: Granta Books, 2013; Rebecca L. Walkowitz. 'Epilogue: Multiples'. *Born Translated: The Contemporary Novel in an Age of World Literature*. New York: Columbia University Press, 2015. 235–45.
63. Adam Thirlwell. 'Interview: Adam Thirlwell'. Interview by Ted Hodgkinson. *Granta*. 19 June 2012 (website – last accessed 28 March 2015).
64. Ibid.
65. Alison Gibbons. 2015. 33.
66. Ibid. 34.
67. Ibid. 34.
68. Ibid. 35.
69. Hamid Dabashi. *The Arab Spring: The End of Postcolonialism*. London and New York: Zed Books, 2012. 10.
70. Edward W. Said. 2003. 52.
71. 'Kapow! by Adam Thirlwell'. *Visual Editions*. No date (website – last accessed 24 September 2018).
72. Alberto Hernández. '"Kapow!" An Experimental Collaborative Book of Upside-Down Texts and Fold-Out Pages'. *The Publishing Lab*. 8 May 2013 (website – last accessed 27 March 2015).
73. Mark Z. Danielewski. *House of Leaves*. New York: Pantheon Books, 2000; Mark Z. Danielewski. *Only Revolutions*. New York: Pantheon Books, 2006.
74. In the much earlier *Tristram Shandy, the* novel of digression, heterochrony features in numerous ways, not least by the narrative twist of the autodiegetic narrator's reaching the point of his birth in volume III only. Laurence Sterne [1759–67]. *The Life and Opinions of Tristram Shandy, Gentleman*. Oxford: Oxford University Press, 1983; Jonathan McAloon. 'Middle Immaturity: Adam Thirlwell, Kapow!' *Jonniemcaloon.com*. 17 July 2012 (website – last accessed 8 March 2015).
75. Alison Gibbons. 2015. 31–2.
76. Ibid. 30.
77. 'The Ocean Giant', 'The Bringer of Enlightenment', 'Distant Earth', 'As Foreign as the Light in People's Dreams'; Sascha Kiefer. *Die deutsche Novelle im 20. Jahrhundert: Eine Gattungsgeschichte*. Cologne, Weimar and Vienna:

Böhlau, 2010. 472–3; 'Jochen Beyse'. *Diaphanes*. No date (website – last accessed 7 December 2020).

78. Although it has the subtitle *Zwischenbericht* ('status/interim report'), *Rebellion* can best be categorised as a short *Künstlerroman* ('artist novel') or an *Erzählung* (a literary form which is longer than a short story but shorter than a novel and is sometimes translated as 'novella'). Unlike a *Novelle*/novella in its stricter sense, however, the form of the *Erzählung* is not characterised by the use of a concrete symbol or an *unerhörte Begebenheit* ('event without precedent'). J. A. Cuddon. 'Novella'. 1999. 600.

79. 'I was thinking about the stranger, was thinking, the stranger in me was speaking to me above all from the melancholic fragments of that face – a few words, quietly in a crazily conciliatory whisper – I was mistaken. The surface of the mirror had a crack running down it. A face, appearing thereupon, rent asunder, the two parts slightly out of kilter, much like the face of *Jacqueline* by Picasso.' All translations of the quotations from Jochen Beyse's *Rebellion* are courtesy of Michael Banks (University of Trier). Some translations were adapted to make them more literal in order to facilitate the understanding of the close readings in the German original.

80. Alexandra Matzner. 'Museum Barberini: Picasso. Das späte Werk. Aus der Sammlung Jacqueline Picasso'. *ARTinWords*. 6 March 2019 (website – last accessed 9 May 2019).

81. 'I don't really experience all of that and I experience all of that under the influence of copious quantities of Grand Verdier … You have got yourself going so much in the apparatus in your head through alcohol that reason sense was no longer able to assert itself.'

82. 'Everything seems like it is on fire, the colours are *burning*. I cannot tear my eyes away from the things … Garish affects flash through my mind, I even rear up a little.'

83. 'scarcely arrived and already the first enemy! Gotta have an enemy. Others would join them, a whole load … But in the shade of the fig trees where these unknown enemies were currently at large, the green-black half-dark of the leaves, with their five unshapely, fat fingers, the threat of enmity was … was a particular temptation. That's why here had been come to, because of this particular temptation. And moreover – green-black half-dark of the leaves, unknown enemies, particular temptation – there are a few scenes in the STRANGER which arise in me over and over again, across all the years.'

84. 'The rift between me and the world in this part of Cairo yawns ever greater with every step … There has been a bloodbath. Afterwards, one was standing outside, no cover, the white star in the sky and exploded.'
85. 'One could extinguish all life on the other side of the street from up here with the FAMAS. What on earth has happened to make this thought come shooting through this head again.'
86. 'thought'.
87. 'shooting'.
88. 'Before it all started in Cairo last night, I watched the scenes in Memphis briefly, the gloriously senseless shootings on the Ramesside ruins, to get me in the mood … Still most tedious, the hours, not the slightest hint of dialogue with anyone, no time, everybody had to fight. As one does. Only ever one voice, *my* voice, and that was the one giving the orders.'
89. 'MUSIC, snatches of sound sequences, disjointed shepherd's song – over, the silent equilibrium of the day. My forearm appears in the picture, now the sub-machine gun, the FAMAS F1, breechblock and magazine behind the handle in the shoulder support, sight at the ready, leaning slightly to the right. The arm, a black weapon, a steel-black steel prosthesis … rising up slowly, sweat running into my eyes. This wretched music still: sounds that you would need to blast to pieces to finally have some peace and quiet. I yank the weapon up. The sounds are everywhere and want to use their crazily quick succession to cause the firing of the entire magazine. The weapon can even shoot grenades but should you use grenades on tones gone crazy? The safety before heading out – I set it to sustained fire. The sun is burning now …'
90. 'steely-black steel prosthesis'.
91. 'steely', 'steel'.
92. Albeit without the ambiguity, this strategy of using the dash to avoid a direct portrayal is reminiscent of Heinrich von Kleist's novella *Die Marquise von O…* (1808). See Thomas Nehrlich. '*Es hat mehr Sinn und Deutung, als du glaubst'. Zu Funktion und Bedeutung typographischer Textmerkmale in Kleists Prosa*. Hildesheim: Olms, 2012. 152–62.
93. 'I would like to know why there are so many people here who let themselves be slaughtered by me like innocent lambs, and have the idea that it must have something to do with the sun, with the paralysingly hot shaft of light that causes all strength to resist to melt away.'
94. 'who let themselves be slaughtered by me'.
95. 'by me'.

96. Published in his 1748 treatise *De l'Esprit des lois* (*The Spirit of the Laws*). Inge E. Boer. 2004. 37–8.
97. 'And of course it is okay to shoot.' The narrator appropriates a statement by Red Army Faction leader Ulrike Meinhof here.
98. 'The barrel of the FAMAS, which slowly climbs higher and higher – the rageful face of the Arab – the first shot, which gets right in there, tearing the cheekbone apart and the flesh of half of the side of the face off of the skull; the thin high shaft of light, how that really slams down to the floor, shaking the body of the Arab from side to side like a jumping jack in the midst of the burst of exploding light; the violent force of the incoming shots which beat the body back, back to the other refugees.'
99. 'the sun is burning'.
100. 'shaking the body of the Arab from side to side like a jumping jack'.
101. 'On the lowest commando rank this quickly leads to frustration. There had already been occasional massacres here and there within the city limits, the most extreme excesses of violence, of course on the civilian population. I know what I am talking about. There is a line and anyone who crosses it turns into that savage beast that has been waiting for an eternity to break out of its cage.'
102. 'I am overcome by all-consuming rage and I fire off a long burst.'
103. 'The console functions by means of motion sensors … I have been sitting in the armchair with my arm thrust up in the air for days, my body twisted to the right, to the left, and all in service of the fight against rising outrage, smouldering revolt, rebellion: all ring leaders up against the wall! No mercy! This revolt must not spread! If it reaches the bordering Maghreb countries … dead people everywhere as it is … lying on the white-hot ground like scythed stalks of weeds. In a world brutally divided into servants and masters, it only makes sense to seek salvation in the masters' camp – everything else ruins the fun. Nobody should attempt to distract from this truth with some kind of humanitarian claptrap! Unmasking outdated illusions, that's what it's about – fighting false modes of perception! Throw to the right in the armchair and jab the stiff arm upwards. If voice control is active, shout *Forward march!*'
104. 'scythed stalks of weeds', 'world brutally divided into servants and masters'.
105. 'Forward march!'
106. 'It had to be possible to create a kind of order with the FAMAS. *Death in Cairo* does present a few ways of intervening in this human-created chaos.'
107. 'The street wider and wider – a grand boulevard no less, certainly created a hundred years ago to give people a generous run-up ready to make the

jump into democratic freedom. Unfortunately, it was hopelessly too short, the jump, this one and all of the preceding ones, for each one led ever deeper into chaos.'

108. 'What for the woman was a movement intended to block everything that had not already been touched by death and was therefore one last gentle preparation for death, appeared in their case [the two injured men] to be a blocking move impelled by blind hatred, for they wave their gnarled hands in front of my face. I suddenly feel as though I have suffered enough. Then the one on the left, who holds his leg in agony, points to the FAMAS and gestures that I should pass him the semi-automatic. I know at once that he wants to shoot me to death, and that he does not just care about my dying but above all *how* I perish – slowly, agonisingly, in accordance with the law of an eye for an eye, a tooth for a tooth.'
109. 'I was just waiting for him to scream his hate-filled sounds in my face …'
110. 'hate-filled'.
111. 'At some point hate-filled cries forced their way up to me, it started with a few, then the air was filled with downright terror.'
112. 'faces twisted with hatred'.
113. 'Then time suddenly stands still, still races on the spot and cuts painfully sharp images out of the moment – the dead mother, the dead girl; the palm trees shot to pieces at the first hint of dawn, the gardens of Qasr El Nil at daybreak; Lawrence giving the High Commissioner to Egypt initial, wide-ranging plans to support the Arab struggle for liberation; the algal green Nile, its bubbling carpet of foam; bubbling blood.'
114. Paul Virilio. *L'Inertie polaire*. Paris: Christian Bourgois, 1990; *Rasender Stillstand* [1990]. Trans. Bernd Wilczek. Frankfurt: Fischer, 1997.
115. Ibid; Christof Forderer. 'Der rasende Stillstand'. *Taz*. 8 September 2012 (website – last accessed 15 July 2018).
116. 'I was a little cold, even though the weather was nice, pleasantly warm, I was freezing. I couldn't believe it. I got up and went back to one of the apparatuses, I convinced myself that the weather outside was pleasantly warm.'
117. 'There is no way [Maria] would entertain sitting around in a *pile of men*, just waiting for somebody to offer to buy her a drink while putting his *paw* on her shoulder, just like the Arab over there is squeezing a girlish-looking woman's arm, with a grin, leaning in like a *vulgar ape* and whispering something in her ear, followed by her laughter.'
118. 'The Arab looks over at us … he must be looking Maria up and down. It's a shameless gaze, I see this in his posture: his hips rolling, both hands jerking

through the air, pelvis thrust forward – anything but the posture of a dreamer. I start up in the armchair. All the things that could be done with a lovely FAMAS F1 on this patio! Setting the trigger to continuous fire with a leaden clunk, then pulling it: a magazine holding 300 shots would be enough to extinguish all life on the patio and inside the café … But I know I'm not in Cairo, unfortunately, just in Algiers, and would certainly be too drunk to take aim at his head, at his scornful visage, at those dazzlingly white rows of teeth, what with all this Grand Verdier in my system …'

119. 'Arab farce'.
120. 'I would otherwise have approached Maria long ago, would have spoken to her, would have clearly stood up to this Arab with his expression constantly oscillating between frenzy and apathy.'
121. 'between frenzy and apathy'.
122. 'The most diverse array of information from all the depths of space and time coalesce within me, from the TV room, the corridor, from the kitchen out the back … over and over from Algiers, over and over from Cairo …'
123. Edward W. Said. 2003. 52.
124. 'I know Algiers from a book, Cairo from a game.'
125. 'CAIRO, when in Cairo, I – no!'
126. 'From Algiers to Cairo'.
127. Paul Virilio. 1997. 112. Italics in the original.
128. Sascha Kiefer. 2010. 476.
129. 'I make a note.'
130. Hans Christoph Buch. *Tod in Habana*. Frankfurt: Frankfurter Verlagsanstalt, 2007; Thomas Mann [1912]. *Der Tod in Venedig*. Frankfurt: Fischer, 1992.
131. 'I *would* get to know it [Salamano's dog] …'
132. 'I *will bump into* Salamano on the staircase tomorrow and, no doubt, Maria in the street. We *will get* the city bus to the seaside … I can *see* myself swimming, my arms wrapped around a buoy, Maria next to me. Our shoulders *touch*. Clearly I *desire* her.'
133. 'Every footfall echoed powerfully. After all, the echo had to make its way through a vast number of epochs and new images emerged every time.'
134. Peter Morey and Amina Yaqin. *Framing Muslims: Stereotyping and Representation after 9/11*. Cambridge, MA: Harvard University Press, 2011. 1.
135. Gargi Bhattacharyya. 2008. 9.
136. Espen J. Aarseth. *Cybertext: Perspectives on Ergodic Literature*. Baltimore: Johns Hopkins University Press, 1997. 1–2.

137. Alison Gibbons. 2015. 33.
138. Ibid. 33.
139. Slavoj Žižek. *The Year of Dreaming Dangerously*. London and New York: Verso, 2012. 127.
140. Ibid. 127.
141. *Kapow!* addresses this issue in its very first footnote by stating: 'It wasn't the usual or previous, or I. But lately, to be honest, I'd been thinking that this thing called *I* wasn't anything at all. I was beginning to think that *I* was basically a pseudonym.' (*Kapow!*: 5; italics in the original).
142. Martina Feurer. *Psychoanalytische Theorien des Denkens: S. Freud – D. W. Winnicott – P. Aulagnier – W. R. Bion – A. Green*. Würzburg: Königshausen & Neumann, 2011. 23.
143. K. Brian Sonderquist. *The Isolated Self: Truth and Untruth in Søren Kierkegaard's On the Concept of Irony*. Copenhagen: C. A. Reitzel, 2007. 81.
144. Linda Hutcheon. *The Politics of Postmodernism*. London and New York: Routledge, 1989. 93.

5

FIGURATIONS OF TERROR: THE ISLAMIST RAGE BOY IN KARIM ALRAWI'S *BOOK OF SANDS* AND MATHIAS ÉNARD'S *RUE DES VOLEURS*

I imagined an attack, an explosion, with his Pakistani friends from the mosque, as he [Bassam] called them; a revenge for the death of Bin Laden, a coup to destabilize Europe further at a time when it seemed to be wavering, cracking like a beautiful, fragile vase, vengeance for the dead Syrian children, for the dead Palestinian children, for dead children in general, that whole absurd rhetoric, the spiral of stupidity, or simply for the pleasure of destruction and fire, what do I know, I watched Bassam in his solitude and his seclusion, ricocheting like a billiard ball in the Street of Thieves against the sad whores, the addicts, the verminous, and the bearded men of the mosque, I saw him again absorbed in resentment in front of that decadent photograph on Rambla Catalunya, لعلَّ السَّاعَةَ تَكونُ قَريباً, I saw him ogling Maria's sex on her doorstep, I pictured him carrying suitcases to Marrakesh, and as the killer with the sword in Tangier, and as a fighter in Mali or Afghanistan, or maybe none of the above, maybe just a man just like me lost in the whirl of the Carrer Robadors, a hollow man, a walking tomb, a man who sought in flames the end of an already dead world, a warrior from a theatre of shadows, ... moved by the last breath of hatred, in a cottony emptiness, a cloud, a silent man, a mute man who would blow up in a train, in a plane, in a subway line, for no one, لعلَّ السَّاعَةَ تَكونُ قَريباً, perhaps the Hour is approaching, I saw Bassam's perfectly round head in prayer, I no longer expected answers to my questions, no more answers, an unknown surgeon would soon open Judit's skull to remove the disease from it, around us the world was on fire and Bassam was standing there, motionless like a snake charmer's cobra, an empty man whose hour would soon toll, a soldier of despair who carried his corpses in his eyes …[1]

Interweaving attacks, explosions, weapons, revenge, hatred, destruction, bearded men, prayer, fire and flames, Lakhdar, the protagonist of *Rue des voleurs*, conjures up a mosaic of atrocities, fear and doubt. When he thinks of his best friend Bassam, he does not only picture him as an unpredictable threat, but he also sexualises and Orientalises him. Like a 'charmed snake' without any ratio of his own, Bassam is presented as driven by his repressed sexual urges, hatred and by Islamist indoctrination – in short, by what Lakhdar describes as 'that whole absurd rhetoric, the spiral of stupidity, or simply … the pleasure of destruction and fire …'[2] This depiction of terror as 'savage and irrational, an irruption of the primitive'[3] is not transcended by any alternative framings. Despite the markers of doubt which Lakhdar includes ('que sais-je', 'ou peut-être rien de tout cela') and although the introductory 'J'imaginais' denotes the whole long sentence as Lakhdar's projection, terror is mostly presented as Otherness. The repetition of an Arabic phrase from the Quran, which Lakhdar turns into an incantation of threat, further frames terror in terms of religious and linguistic difference. Thus stripped of its complexity, terror is condensed into the flat character of Bassam. Pathologised, sexualised, securitised and Orientalised, he is configured as what could be called an Islamist Rage Boy – a recurring narrative figuration which helps to break down the complexities of terrorism and Islamist radicalisation into the seeming simplicity of a sexually and ideologically lost young man.

Focusing on the figuration of the Islamist Rage Boy, this chapter illustrates through what narrative strategies Islamist radicalisation and terrorism are projected into the ahistorical distance and difference of complete Otherness. As exemplary readings, the following literary analyses show how in Karim Alrawi's *Book of Sands* (2015) and Mathias Énard's *Rue des voleurs* (2012),[4] terror figures implicitly but prominently. Instead of depicting terrorism directly, these novels foreground the danger of Islamist radicalisation by means of a pronounced antithesis in their constellation of characters.

Both texts feature a secondary character – a deuteragonist – who embodies radicalisation, irrationalism and fundamentalism. Unlike these flat characters, the novels' protagonists are round, rational and sympathetic characters who invite understanding and identification. While the protagonists are consequently cast as understandable, 'good' or non-Muslims who feel drawn to the West, the deuteragonists serve as their negative foil and carry all the weight of securitisation and Orientalisation.

Figuring Terror

Of the numerous levels at which the securitisation of people from an Islamicate background operates, narrative patterns of Islamist radicalisation and terror are the most naturalised. Despite its omnipresence in the 'Age of Terror',[5] however, there is no official definition of terror.[6] In fact, since the first widespread occurrence of the term during the French Revolution, the meaning of terror has fundamentally changed:

> [In the] Terror of the French Revolution, ... Terror was the effect of the state, the first instance in which the state itself became the instrument of terror on its subjects, who lived in fear of execution, imprisonment, and torture. Just as the meaning of terror moves from cause to effect, and from the effect on the public to the terrorist, so terror as a term migrated quickly from being a description of practices of the state, the violence of the state perpetrated against its own citizens, as originally in the French Revolution, to practices aimed against the state from below.[7]

In spite of or perhaps just because of its blurry boundaries, terror has become 'the West's current self-consolidating enemy par excellence',[8] whose often undifferentiated discursive instrumentalisation helps to uphold pronounced power asymmetries in the postcolonial world:

> To cite the observation of ... Simon Jenkins, the 'War on Terror' has become an ideal post-Cold War tool. It allows Western states to reinstate the condition, presumably taken from colonial times, of wielding sovereignty through war-without-end. In both situations, colonial and contemporary, terror becomes all pervasive and completely non-specific, as well as deeply contradictory.[9]

Stating that '[w]hat is bad about all terror is when it is attached to religious and political abstractions and reductive myths that keep veering away from history and sense',[10] Edward Said critically underlines how the complexities of terrorism are often reduced according to a Eurocentric and ahistorical logic. As Tarak Barkawi and Mark Laffey point out, it is not only Western political and media discourse, but also traditional security studies themselves which frequently fail to acknowledge the historical and systemic aspects of terrorism. Despite recent developments in the international system, research in security studies still mostly focuses on great powers. As a consequence, it often fails to grasp the phenomenon of non-state attacks and remains caught in 'contradictions between old security logics and new security problematics'.[11] As traditional security studies furthermore often neglect to contextualise the emergence of terrorism historically,

> [t]he taken-for-granted historical geographies that underpin security studies systematically misrepresent the role of the global South in security relations and lead to a distorted view of Europe and the West in world politics. Understanding security relations, past and present, requires acknowledging the mutual constitution of European and non-European worlds and their joint role in making history.[12]

Not only do security studies thus often remain limited to the issues of Western defence against terrorism and immigration, but because of this, they neglect the insecurity of the securitised.[13]

Even if Eugene Victor Walter's dictum that '[o]ne person's terrorist is another person's freedom fighter'[14] quickly comes to mind here, this chapter is not intended to justify terrorist attacks. The undeniable material dimension of terror in the form of attacks notwithstanding, it serves as a reminder of how importantly frame and perspective must feature in any analysis of terror and its representation. After all, the relationship between the material and discursive dimensions of terror is highly complex. Not only does terrorism strongly depend on the images it produces,[15] but besides the political violence of terrorist attacks, there is also the epistemic violence of reducing it to the logic of self and other: up until today, terrorism has continued to be 'more often than not described as the revolutionary expression of a counter-modernity rather than of modernity'.[16] However, in order to better understand acts of terrorism, an alternative perspective needs to 'turn back to the colonial archive of violence and repression, to records of the colonial formations of sovereignty, policing, and surveillance, which find such prominent afterlives in counter-terroristic formations today'.[17] It is only through such a more comprehensive angle that we can 'examine [the] occurrence [of terror] in the reciprocally violent historical contexts of colonialism and global neo-colonialism rather than of the ahistorical "war on terror" …'[18]

Text and Terror

In the representational domain of fiction, the mere fact that literature depicts terrorism does not necessarily amount to securitisation. In reverse, however, there can be epistemic violence in the narrative choices and frames by means of which fiction negotiates and explains the origins of terror. Even if violence is not shown directly, there is often, to borrow Judith Butler's words,

> violence in the frame of what is shown. That latter violence is the mechanism through which certain lives and certain deaths either remain unrepresentable or become represented in ways that effects [sic] their capture (once again) by the war effort. The first is an effacement through occlusion; the second is an effacement through representation itself.[19]

It is this kind of 'effacement through representation itself' which we find in flat and decontextualised representations of terror as epitomised by the Islamist Rage Boy. As a literary figuration,[20] he unites widespread stereotypes of the allegedly angry and irrational young Muslim man:[21] through him, radicalisation is presented as the result of a suppressed sexuality which, unsublimated,[22] mounts into rage and finds its outlet in Islamism.

Following this reductionist logic, the Islamist Rage Boy functions according to a process of commodification also visible in the case of Shakeel Ahmad Bhat. A Kashmiri activist and cult figure on the Internet, Bhat was nicknamed 'Islamic Rage Boy' by several right-wing bloggers.[23] Not only are he and his activism thereby reduced to representations of his angry face, but two US bloggers even turned Bhat into a cartoon character which they commodified 'on T-shirts, beer mugs, hoodies and Valentine cards in a variety of bloodthirsty and furious poses, and copyrighted it'.[24] The figuration of the deuteragonists in the two novels analysed in this chapter work from a similar – albeit less blatant – starting point.[25] In order to highlight these stereotypical overlaps and the reductive function of this figuration, it could be called Islamist Rage Boy – with the important difference, however, of not serving as a label for any real people but to describe and deconstruct the reductionist and ahistorical representation of terror which finds its aestheticised expression in this figuration.

Karim Alrawi: *Book of Sands: A Novel of the Arab Uprising*

Karim Alrawi was born in Alexandria. His family emigrated first to England, then to Canada.[26] Alrawi completed two degrees in Structural Engineering at University College London and at the University of Manchester, and he earned an MFA in Creative Writing at the University of British Columbia. He is mostly known as a playwright and worked at several theatres in the UK and the US. Alrawi also taught in the theatre department of the American University in Cairo, but his plays were banned in Egypt, and he was arrested because of his human rights activism. He rejoined his family in Canada and taught at the University of Victoria. During the uprisings in 2011, Alrawi returned to Egypt and participated in the uprisings in Cairo. *Book of Sands: A Novel of the Arab Uprising* is his first novel and won the inaugural HarperCollins/UBC Prize for Best New Fiction.

Set during the protests in Egypt in 2011, *Book of Sands* negotiates the Arab uprisings by juxtaposing freedom and Islamist radicalisation. The novel's protagonist, Tarek, a former political prisoner, flees from Cairo when he is about to be arrested by the police. He takes his nine-year-old daughter, Neda, with him but has to leave behind his wife, Mona, who is in the late stages of pregnancy. However, like other babies during the uprisings, her child refuses to be born. Once the contractions start, Omar, who is described as 'her deeply troubled and religious brother',[27] is supposed to bring her to the hospital. In the meantime, Tarek and Neda travel through the countryside and encounter people from Tarek's past. While in a long flashback, during which the reader learns that Neda is not Mona's biological daughter, the situation in Cairo comes to a head. Mona finally goes into labour, but instead of taking his sister to the hospital, Omar – intoxicated and in a frenzy – almost shoots her. At the last minute, however, he changes his mind.

Tarek: Between Maths and Mazes

By means of the protagonist Tarek and his brother-in-law Omar, *Book of Sands* creates a pronounced antithesis. From the beginning, in the way it introduces Tarek and Omar, Alrawi's debut novel establishes two strikingly different stylistic and metaphorical frames – one near, open and full of possibilities, the other one far, extreme, narrow and closed. Tarek, whom *Book of Sands* introduces first, is linked with love, freedom, rationalism and the ability to think in alternatives. Likely to win the reader's sympathies, the protagonist does not only run a puppet theatre for children, but he also makes a first appearance as a loving father: before the focalisation shifts to Tarek, the novel slowly and sympathetically approaches him through the gaze of his daughter.

Through Neda's focalisation, the opening scene prepares the backdrop for her father's experience of the uprisings:

> On the morning babies decide not to be born, and mothers cease to give birth, Neda, seven weeks and four days to being ten, late for school, skelters through a flurry of starlings that scatter from the sidewalk, take flight to gather on balconies and rooftops. At the corner of the alley she stops. A wall of concrete slabs, four meters tall, seals off the street. Its pitted surface spray-painted with slogans for an end to the rule of soldiers. (*Book of Sands*: 1)[28]

Thus, the opening of the novel introduces the unfathomable refusal of the unborn to enter this world, the inexplicably high number of birds as well as the walls erected by the government throughout the city and the people's protests against them through the eyes of a precocious child ('seven weeks and four days to being ten'):

> In the schoolyard she slips her hands into the pockets of her hoody, bites her lower lip, pretends not to listen as the janitor, a retired army corporal, tells her father of troubles – walls constructed overnight by the military to block streets against protestors gathered from college campuses beyond the bridge of crouching lions. At the city's central square, crowds tore sheets of corrugated steel and scaffolding from construction sites, raised barricades, hung flags from lampposts and banners across buildings that declare: *The People Rise and Tyrants Fall*. (*Book of Sands*: 2; italics in the original)

Without explicitly naming Cairo, the evocations of Qasr El Nil Bridge and Tahrir Square, both central sites in the 2011 uprisings, conjure up the city's revolutionary geography. Reinforcing the magic realist mode of the novel, Qasr El Nil Bridge is paraphrased as 'the bridge of crouching lions'. It is thus simultaneously recognisable and abstract enough for the story to work both on the concrete, realist, as well as on the fictional and even magic realist level. At the same time, the paraphrase complements the pronounced animal imagery which slowly unfolds throughout the novel and which, from early on, creates the impression that the city is teeming with activity beyond comprehension.

Against this backdrop, the novel sets different scenes in which Tarek is presented as a freedom-loving individual struggling with the injustice of corruption and repression in Egypt. Metaphorically, the oppressive omnipresence of the regime is symbolised by the walls which the government had erected in the streets as a countermeasure to the protests. Having to navigate in narrow lanes predetermined by the regime, Tarek feels 'like a rat in a labyrinth ...' (*Book of Sands*: 4) or like a calf about to be butchered: 'At the ministry's customer service department, Tarek joins a line bounded on either side by iron rails – a calf corralled at a slaughter-house waiting its turn for the knife' (ibid.). Feeling as powerless and exploited as laboratory or farm animals and completely at the mercy of those in power, Tarek 'follows wall after wall with a growing sense of impotence' (*Book of Sands*: 7). When he dreams about his arrest and the torture to which he had been subjected years earlier (*Book of Sands*: 34–5), this imagery reappears. Like the repetitive structure in Tarek's free indirect discourse, these recurring images suggest that Tarek fears there is no escape from the maze of repression: 'They will just build a new wall, as they have wall after wall after wall actual or virtual, to cut off streets, seal off a man from his neighbour, a husband from his wife, a father from his child' (*Book of Sands*: 6).

Both at the level of content and form, *Book of Sands* links repression to corruption and religious dogmatism and contrasts these elements with Tarek's thoughts and behaviour. For instance, when Tarek goes to the ministry to bribe the official to have his meter read so that his inflated electricity bill can be corrected, he encounters an unsympathetic clerk who personifies the self-righteous injustice of the regime:

'We're closed to the public.' An officious woman glares at Tarek, pulls forward her yellow scarf to make certain every last hair is covered. God forbid a man should see the slightest curl. To think there was once the possibility of his working in such a place with such people, each an autocrat ruling over a desk, phone and filing cabinet, dispensing favours with a rubber stamp and a signature. (*Book of Sands*: 4–5)

Tarek's cynicism in reaction to the clerk ('God forbid a man should see the slightest curl') positions him in opposition to religious dogmatism.

As Omar disapprovingly notices, Tarek is neither religious himself nor does he raise his daughter religiously (*Book of Sands*: 37). Nonetheless, the protagonist does have a system of belief: mathematics. Although Tarek could not finish his university degree because he participated in the student protests of that time, in the face of repression, he continues to resort to his mathematical knowledge. This is emphasised by the use of mathematical formulae in letters which he and Mona wrote while he was in prison. So that their letters would not be understood by his jailers, he and Mona communicated by means of this different type of heterolingual element:

> The first [letter] includes an equation adapted by Mona from a textbook. It reads, M ∩ T ⇒ n. He took it to mean Mona, M would share, ∩, responsibility with him, T, for Neda, n.
>
> … Below it he writes the equation from the second letter, in which he replied, N ∈ T ⇔ n ∈ M, then added T ⇔ M. As Neda is a part of, ∈, Tarek, so she is of Mona, if they are both to be true to each other.
>
> In the next letter she wrote M ∪ T = ∪ { M, T }, restating her love and that together they will face life's challenges. (*Book of Sands*: 62; see also 97–8)

Not only does *Book of Sands* thus link love and science – especially when Tarek starts copying all their letters so that a mathematical love poem emerges (*Book of Sands*: 63) – but by means of the mathematical formulae, the text also visualises Tarek's rationalism and sets it apart from oppression and religion.

In contrast, in the passage which introduces Tarek to the reader, there is only one heterolingual Arabic element, '*Maleesh*' (*Book of Sands*: 8; italics in the original). Like the other heterolingual elements in the novel, '*Maleesh*' is set in italics. Although not translated, the meaning of the word is contoured through an enumeration of expressions which denote emotions and which intimate early on that Tarek is a character with high emotional granularity: 'A knot of a word that can be spoken by way of reassurance, encouragement, apology, irritation, defiance, excuse, pardon, love. A word that fills many a gap in language. A word that, in effect, means nothing' (ibid.). Tarek's angry helplessness in the face of his problems notwithstanding – a helplessness which is also reflected in the phrase 'means nothing' – the novel thus paints him as a sympathetic character with emotional depth.

As the metaphoric counterpoint to the walls in the city, the large flocks of birds which have started gathering in the city, further position Tarek in the novel. While the government has walls erected in the streets as a countermeasure to the protests, both the protestors and the birds fight these walls. As expressed in the clauses introduced by 'as though', the birds stand for both alternative realities and the hope for freedom:

> Outside the school, birds flit then settle along a wall that severs the street. They scrape their claws and peck, as though to chip away at the concrete. He [Tarek] cannot recall when last they gathered in such numbers. (*Book of Sands*: 2)
>
> Starlings jab at the blocks as though their beaks could crack concrete. (*Book of Sands*: 6)

Spreading across the city despite the government's walls, the birds could also be seen as a symbol of some of the protestors' use of social media – especially because the social networking service Twitter, both in its name and its emblem, makes direct reference to a bird. Moreover, the characters' differing reactions to the birds align them with either the hope for freedom or repression. Although the birds interrupt everyday life (for instance, *Book of Sands*: 28, 55), Tarek encounters them not with rejection, but with open astonishment. Indicating that Tarek's puppet theatre is a space of open ideas, the birds gather around it in great numbers. An elderly woman from the neighbourhood even blames Tarek for their presence and threatens to report him to the authorities (*Book of Sands*: 56). Unlike her brother, Tarek's wife Mona 'thinks them [the birds] beautiful, free and unconquerable' (*Book of*

Sands: 289) and has Heba, their domestic help, feed them. So while Tarek and the people to whom he is close welcome them, Omar hates the birds and the authorities try to poison them (*Book of Sands*: 147).

Through the birds and through Tarek's perspective on the protests, *Book of Sands* presents the uprisings and the locations of the protests in a mostly peaceful and positive light. In contrast to the rest of the city – static because of the constricting walls – Tahrir Square is described as a wide expanse, with birds flying over it: 'an expanse that keeps on widening, spreads in all directions to a far horizon of trees and grey buildings' (*Book of Sands*: 14). A vast emptiness in the congested city, the square appears as a utopia in both its senses: as a good and as a non-place; it functions as a heterotopia where different rules apply.[29] All the people Tarek encounters on the square are portrayed as friendly and considerate. In contrast, the smell of tear gas serves as a reminder of the violence of the previous night's fight with the police. Synaesthetically rendered in the form of a lingering smell which taints the utopic square of peaceful protestors, violence is only alluded to indirectly. Instead of staging drastic battle scenes, *Book of Sands* thus foregrounds a peaceful first representation of the uprisings.

Against the backdrop of this portrayal of peace and quiet on the square, the sudden intrusion of a tank appears even more violent. Defending themselves against it, the protestors share a moment of intense solidarity. Tarek is shown as one of the protestors. Indicating the tension which he feels between free choice and predetermination, another 'as though' comparison presents Tarek as predetermined to look for freedom in the confined possibilities he has: 'Not for the first time he feels as though an unseen thread tugs him in a direction he does not want to go, like a character in a story of someone else's making, an element in a set of numbers bracketed by barriers about the square' (*Book of Sands*: 18).

Omar: Between Prosternation and Prostitution

While Tarek is presented as the sympathetic positive norm at the beginning of *Book of Sands*, the second chapter introduces Omar, his negative foil. Not only does the chapter create a direct opposition to Tarek, but it also sets the tone for Omar's radicalisation. Starting in the midst of events without any explicit prior introduction, the first sentence casts Omar *in medias res*, that is, while praying. Providing variations on and thus emphasising the word stem 'pray', a *figura etymologica* repeatedly links his name to prayer: 'Omar prays the morning prayers at the airport's masjid, a carpeted room to one side of the duty-free store advertising perfume and whisky' (*Book of Sands*: 19). While the setting in which Omar first makes an appearance immediately characterises him as religious, it also establishes a frame of closed narrowness. In contrast to Tarek, who is introduced outdoors, Omar is depicted indoors, in presumably narrow surroundings. Located next to the duty-free store with its perfume and whisky, the prayer room ambiguously situates him both in the realm of religion and at the margins of consumerism. Thereby, it foreshadows his being torn between the world of luxury goods, heavily made-up sex workers and inebriation on the one hand and his religious dogmatism on the other hand.

Because of this inner conflict and in order to resist temptation, Omar presents himself as ostentatiously religious. For instance, not only does he use a ring tone which 'sounds the call to prayer, broadcasting his piety before every telephone conversation' (*Book of Sands*: 45), but the novel also quickly draws attention to Omar's wearing a beard (*Book of Sands*: 20). As an outward signifier, this beard marks Omar as religious – but also as different. While it aligns him with the Islamist characters in the novel, it distinguishes him both from the protestors on the square and from Tarek, who wears a moustache or no facial hair at all. Against the backdrop of the airport, Omar's beard, moreover, evokes associations of the bearded bomber, who, although Islamist suicide bombers would ritually shave off their hair before an attack,[30] has paradoxically become one of the epitomes of Neo-Orientalist discourse. This is particularly the case because, from the beginning, Omar is portrayed at a high affective level, as a loner who channels his deep narcissistic insecurity into hatred and indulges in violent fantasies (*Book of Sands*: 21).

Omar's hatred – directed against the birds which cause delays in the airport schedule – positions him in a frame in contrast to Tarek's: 'How he hates those feathered emissaries of the devil – *the malevolent whisperer, whispering in the breasts of men*' (*Book of Sands*: 19; italics in the original). While Tarek is presented as approachable, Omar is thus mainly characterised by what he dislikes and condemns. Presented in such negative terms, he is a socially isolated character. His sister, Mona, is his only other contact, but even she only reluctantly keeps in touch with him. Omar attributes this to the fact that he objected to his sister's marrying Tarek, whom Omar despises because he is not religious and has a child with another woman out of wedlock. As the story gradually reveals, however, the main reason for their estrangement lies in the trauma of Mona's genital mutilation.[31]

Marking Omar as not fully integrable and alien in the running text, the passages written from his perspective contain numerous elements in italics. These elements help to constitute his frame of Otherness and underline the antithesis between Tarek and his brother-in-law: where, as indicated by the use of the mathematical sign system in the novel, the protagonist tries to overcome hardship by means of mathematics, that is, by means of rationality (see for instance *Book of Sands*: 62–3, 97–8), the deuteragonist resorts to religion to sort out his identity problems, particularly to reciting the Quran. Although Omar has great difficulty reading from scripture (*Book of Sands*: 24, 283) and often falls short of cognitively understanding its meaning, he nevertheless practices his daily recitations. To mark Omar's struggle to remember the precise wording of Quranic verses, *Book of Sands* highlights his incomplete quotations by means of italics (for instance, *Book of Sands*: 20, 284). Moreover, while *Book of Sands* presents Tarek's strategy of turning to mathematics in a positive light, the text – by also italicising the voices in Omar's head – typographically aligns the difficulties which Omar has with the verses with his paranoia. In combination with italicised heterolingual elements from the semantic fields of danger and gender inequality, these typographical emphases thus do not only pathologise and securitise Omar, but by creating a distance from his character, they prevent identification with him even in the passages in which he serves as the focaliser.

Throughout the novel, the use of heterolingual elements in connection with Omar is mostly negative – fundamentalist first, violent later. It frequently occurs in conjunction with the sex workers and Islamists who almost exclusively constitute Omar's acquaintances. Directly drawing attention to Omar's deeply troubled relationship with women, the first heterolingual element which appears in Omar's focalisation is *awra*:

> What does Omar care what foreigners do with each other in hotel rooms? His is a job collecting and delivering clients and women who earn more money in an hour with their bodies than he does in a day driving his cab.

He feels sullied doing so. But what choice does he have? Lord have mercy. Women are *awra* – the seduction of the eyes, the allurement of sight, the sin of temptation Eve caused Adam. He will not be blinded by woman. He keeps his body unsullied, conscience clear by prayer. (*Book of Sands*: 20–1)

Unlike in Tarek's case, the free indirect discourse in Omar's depiction does not allow him to present himself in a differentiated way. Whereas the double discourse of Tarek's own words as mediated by a sympathetic narrator presents the protagonist in a favourable light, the supporting voice of the narrator is absent from Omar's free indirect speech. Instead, as in the example above, Omar's free indirect discourse reifies his simplistic reasoning and the double standard regarding his job and his religion. What is more, by representing him not by means of the first personal pronoun 'I', but with the aid of the gendered personal pronouns 'he' and 'his', his free indirect discourse linguistically underlines the important role of gender in his thinking. By juxtaposing this 'he' not with a 'she' but by the more conceptual generic plurals 'woman/women', the text further stresses the gender oppositions in Omar's head.

As indicated by the use of heterolingual elements, from the beginning, *Book of Sands* foregrounds the role which Omar's sexual insecurity plays in his radicalisation. When Omar meets the Salafist Maulana, 'an elderly man in a traditional black *bisht* robe braided with gold thread, dark glasses, a black prayer callus on his forehead, prayer beads in one hand' (*Book of Sands*: 40), the latter's misogynist preaching falls on fertile ground. Speculating about the rumour that babies continue to refuse being born, Maulana assumes that the unborn cannot be the reason. According to him, it is more likely the mothers' fault, which 'would be a heinous case of *nushuz* – the sin of female wilfulness. 'Women refusing motherhood in defiance of the Almighty God'" (*Book of Sands*: 41), and Omar echoes that '[i]ndeed, woman is *nushuz* and *awra* – wilfulness and temptation' (ibid.).

Obsessed with the topic of female depravity, Maulana preaches about hardly anything else:

'*Men are a degree above women*,' Maulana quotes scripture. 'What, you may wonder, is a degree? ... Not less equal to, but above. Above means more.

More means better' ... 'Yes, she [woman] is less in strength. Less in spirit? Yes, that too. That much is meant, by way of metaphor said, Eve created from Adam's rib. A woman's strength and wisdom come from the man by her side. Her father and brothers in the first place, and but after them her husband. Her spirit from the spirit of men in her family – anything else is *nushuz*, wilfulness. Thus, her ignominy is their ignominy. Her dishonour, their dishonour.' (*Book of Sands*: 108–9; italics in the original)

Teeming with simplifying literary devices such as anadiplosis and graded parallelisms ('but above. Above means more. More means better.'), rhetorical questions and ellipses, Maulana's argumentation illustrates how by means of sheer affective repetition, he further indoctrinates Omar. In fact, Omar's admiration of Maulana relies on precisely this reductionist world view: he considers the verses which Maulana quotes 'as the *very essence* of *every* science' (*Book of Sands*: 41; my italics). Maulana ends his lecture with some words on the birds in the city, whose presence he interprets as a sign that the 'end of days' is near:

> Howbeit, we know from holy text and must wonder, the Lord sent swarms of birds to cast brimstone on Abraha the Abyssinian with his elephant in the desert. The Lord did so but as warning and sign that the Prophet, God's prayers and peace be upon him, was but soon to begin his mission. And so we do ask what lessons from then for now? For lo, the birds return to signal this new age of ignorance and disorder, of sacrifice and struggle, in which once more there be strife between believer and the infidel. (*Book of Sands*: 109–10)

To dismantle Maulana's authority and the values which he epitomises, *Book of Sands* uses alternating scenes. Even before Maulana begins to indoctrinate Omar, the novel undermines the credibility of his words about 'female wilfulness' (*Book of Sands*: 41) by showing the Salafist's behaviour first: it describes how he strokes the thigh of a young 'boy in a brightly coloured shirt and hennaed hair' (*Book of Sands*: 40). Although Maulana interprets the birds as a sign of the end of days, the way in which he is depicted reduces his literal interpretations to absurdity. To further question the ambiguous impact of his teachings, *Book of Sands* contrasts a scene in which the Islamist indoctrinates four young students against women with a scene directly afterwards, in which the students poke fun at him and buy a pornographic magazine which they look at in a both overcompensating and shame-ridden way (*Book of Sands*: 109–10).

At the metaphorical level, Maulana's negative influence finds its expression in the spread of cockroaches. With their hard shell and mostly hidden but inveterate infestation, they embody ingrained dogmatism. Occurring mostly underground and unable to fly, the cockroaches do not only epitomise the dogmatic inability to sublimate, but they also stand in stark opposition to the birds. Associated with filth and darkness,[32] the insects are first introduced in a description of Omar's sparse apartment, where he keeps a cockroach in a box under his bed. He thinks it is the devil's minion, calls it 'Pilgrim', talks to it and tries to convert it by reading to it from the Quran. When Omar spots a cockroach at Maulana's apartment after the latter's religious lecture, the novel begins to brim with the metaphor. Maulana's black prayer callus, negatively described by the doctor and/or narrator as 'swollen like a third eye, blinded and black' (*Book of Sands*: 112), does not only resemble a cockroach, but it also marks him as the origin of both the actual cockroaches and of their figurative meaning, that is, of blind and dark indoctrination. When the doctor asks for any signs of indigestion to rule out a gastric carcinoma as the cause of the callus, Maulana does not tell him he defecates cockroaches in such high numbers that they have infested the whole building. Instead, in his own narcissistic interpretation of his callus, Maulana casts it as a sign of righteousness:

> [T]he prayer callus on his forehead will shine a divine light to guide the faithful [on the Day of Judgement ...] He imagines it will be like the light of lanterns carried by children during the month of Ramadan when they go round to their neighbours' apartments asking for cake and candy in return for telling a riddle-me-rhyme. Then with the light shining forth from his forehead all the world will wonder and know him for one of the righteous for whom a place has been reserved for eternity by the side of the Lord. (*Book of Sands*: 113)

The spreading of the cockroaches thus visualises how the Islamist self-righteously indoctrinates others: the increasing number of cockroaches which

Omar encounters during his time with Maulana demonstrates how he is infested by the Salafist's arguments.

A scene in which Omar accompanies 'three bearded men with prayer calluses' (*Book of Sands*: 150) to the square to fight the protestors further reinforces and links the metaphor to the Islamists. Omar understands that, for the moment, the Islamists have joined forces with the army to prevail against the protestors, whom they attack with metal tubes. Before a gruesome scene in which a group of Islamists jointly and cruelly beat up individual protestors, Omar notices that 'tiny roaches from the gutters' (*Book of Sands*: 152) feed on the blood of the protestors spilled by the Islamists. Whereas Tarek, who goes to the square to help, is portrayed in the wide expanse of the square as well as surrounded by birds, Omar is consequently linked to the perfidious violence which the Islamists inflict at the dark and roach-ridden rims of the square:

> Every so often a wave of hard hats wielding metal tubes and wooden staves surges from the museum wall, through the State Security barriers. They drag a protestor back, beat him until he collapses. Officers arrive to arrest the prisoner. Omar's phone sounds the call to prayer ... Too exhilarated, he ignores the call, turns off the ringer. Another protestor is dragged through the barriers to the museum wall, beaten, clothes torn, bleeds from his face and mouth. He sobs as the tries to reason, screams as he pleads between the beatings. Omar feels a surge of excitement, watches the terror on the man's face as speech splinters into whimpers and cries. A metal tube cracks his skull with a sound like wood snapping. He drops to the ground. A crowd of hard hats and beards kick the body, stamp and spit. (*Book of Sands*: 152)

Here, the repeated rendering of the Islamists as a 'wave of hard hats' or a 'crowd of hard hats' depersonalises them and creates an analogy with the shells of the cockroaches. Both move in groups and emerge from sinister places, and – literally or figuratively – gorge on the protestors' blood: in the face of the people mistreated in front of him, Omar feels elated; even his religious ring tone does not stop his sadistic exhilaration, but instead marks the hypocrisy of his dogmatic religiosity. When he is about to join the Islamists in their violence, Omar only backs off because a medic, who Omar is afraid might be his cousin Yara, asks to be allowed to treat one of the victims.

Although used in a different way in *Book of Sands*, the metaphor of the cockroaches vividly evokes Lebanese-Canadian author Rawi Hage's 2008 novel *Cockroach*.[33] Because of his role in his sister's death, the protagonist in this earlier novel suffers from a trauma which results in a dissociative identity disorder: he thinks he is half cockroach. In *Cockroach*, both the themes of the insect and that of sibling betrayal can in turn be read as references to Kafka's *Die Verwandlung* (1915; *The Metamorphosis*). Despite these intertextual undertones, however, the use of cockroach imagery in *Book of Sands* is problematic. Especially due to the way in which 'the vermin metaphor was made literal in the Nazis' treatment of the Jews',[34] it is difficult to ignore the long history of abuse of vermin metaphors. As even today, certain neo-Nazi campaigns still use the imagery of the cockroach to launch attacks against immigrants,[35] this imagery in itself – and its inherent 'semiotics of extermination'[36] – has an uneasy parallel with far-right extremist imagery. As in *Book of Sands*, the cockroaches epitomise Islamist fundamentalism, they are not employed as a generally anti-Muslim trope. Nevertheless, the choice of such a drastic and historically highly charged metaphor – with its associative proximity to both historical and contemporary forms of group-focused enmity and its echoes of infiltration and extermination – remains extreme and sharply reinforces the structural antithesis of the novel.

As the cockroaches are linked to Maulana's defecation, they also underline a representation of Omar's radicalisation process which, to borrow Pankaj Mishra's words, could be criticised as a 'genitals-centric analysis (constipation and sexual frustration) of radical Islam'.[37] Not only is Omar's increasing radicalisation fuelled by the Islamists' sermons about the evils of women, but – further interweaving securitisation and sexualisation – the text presents the psychological problems from which Omar suffers as a result of his sister's genital mutilation. When Omar feels strangely attracted to the young boy with the hennaed hair, who will later on masturbate Omar (*Book of Sands*: 172), this moment of conflicting emotional and sexual arousal triggers a flashback to Omar's repressed childhood memories:

> Omar feels a moment's vulnerability he takes for weakness. It summons vague, disjointed images of childhood. A memory too dense to picture clearly of a day when, thirteen or so, he sat at a streetside café, in imitation

of men much older, smoked a shisha pipe, watched kids play soccer in the alley. Then, he does not recall how, he was in the bathroom of his parents' apartment, the local barber wiped with a rag blood from a straight razor. Mona, maybe seven years old, screamed and sobbed as she lay on the stone tiles. (*Book of Sands*: 44–5)

Although not named directly, the 'vague, disjointed images' and gaps in Omar's memory serve to visualise how the psychological stress created by his sister's suffering caused dissociative amnesia in Omar. Narratologically, the novel represents the reasons for Omar's dissociative disorder by means of a shift in focalisation. To fill in the information which is missing in Omar's intrusion, a scene in which Mona serves as the focaliser complements her brother's fragmented and repressed memory: Mona remembers that she was one of the children playing soccer and that it was Omar who took her by the hand and led her to the local barber in their apartment (*Book of Sands*: 65). In combination with Omar's other symptoms – his flashbacks, mood and sleep disorders and, in particular, his aggression – his dissociative amnesia suggests that the shock of his sister's suffering and his repressed guilt have caused a post-traumatic stress disorder.[38] What is more, by highlighting Omar's aggressive behaviour as one of the most severe symptoms of his post-traumatic stress disorder, the text does not only link Omar's pathology to his radicalisation, but presents his disorder as the root of his increasing fundamentalism.

Before Omar's frenzy reaches its climax, the novel inserts a long flashback similar to Omar's individual flashback, thereby creating a collective and cultural parallel to Omar and Mona's trauma. Unlike the rest of the novel, part III (*Book of Sands*: 189–263) is written in the past tense. It focuses almost entirely on culturalised violence against women and, because of the change in tense and setting, it creates an allochronic distance to the temporality of the reader. Providing a pronouncedly magic realist exploration of the role of female genital mutilation in the countryside, it serves as the cultural background against which Omar's individual trauma – and his radicalisation – are set. In terms of plot, it is again Tarek who functions as the link between the allochronic past of part III and the narrative present of the rest of the novel. With his daughter Neda, he flees from the secret police into the desert. During his flight, he meets people from his past, and they trigger the analepse to his time in prison. Through Tarek's confrontation with a former fellow prisoner, the novel fills in the gap of who Neda's biological mother is, and her representation is linked to the cultural trauma of violence against women.

In this whole episode in the past, Tarek fares mostly well, and is contrasted here with a reduplication of Omar, Yaqzan. Yaqzan is the old rainmaker of the valley close to where Tarek was imprisoned. Tarek falls in love with Yaqzan's young third wife, Reham, Neda's biological mother. As in most of the novel, the focalisation is mainly a male one. While the archaic traditions of cutting and suturing female genitals are briefly described from the point of view of Umaya, the woman who carries out the 'cleansings' (*Book of Sands*: 193–5), their impact is most drastically illustrated by means of the figure of old Yaqzan. Although he does not enjoy causing his young wife, Reham, pain, to uphold tradition and fulfil his duty, he brutally injures her on their wedding night. Unable to penetrate Reham because he cannot burst open her sutured vagina, Yaqzan resorts to a knife:

> He forced her legs apart, eased the blade into the seam. She writhed in the darkness, screamed, sobbed as he climbed on top of her to insert herself into her fresh wound. Her warm blood flowed along his scrotum and thighs, lubricated his penetration. She pleaded for him to stop, tossed from side to side, her face wet with tears. He thrust to come, to discharge himself in her and be done. (*Book of Sands*: 214–15)

When Reham's bleeding does not stop, Yaqzan protests when Umaya tells him to give his wife time to heal:

> He protested. He was not to blame for his wife's condition, caused by the cleansing and not by anything he had done. After all, he did not care, one way or another, if girls were cut and sutured. It was all a matter of custom. Why should he take the blame? Such matters were best left to women to decide upon and arrange. He did not interfere in women's matters. (*Book of Sands*: 215–16)

By means of Yaqzan's indifference to his young wife's suffering as well as the detailed and violent description of the way that Yaqzan rapes Reham, the novel drastically illustrates the sexual consequences of female genital mutilation. At the same time, however, *Book of Sands* does not explore its further implications, nor does it give a voice to Reham other than in her role as a victim. While after the rape, she becomes the focaliser for a short passage, the rape itself is told from a male perspective. Moreover, its critical stance towards female genital mutilation notwithstanding, the text adopts a voyeuristic, if not pornographic gaze: while Yaqzan feels how Reham's blood flows along his genitals and 'lubricate[s] his penetration', the scene shows how Reham screams and cries but does not delve into her thoughts and feelings. Whereas her bodily reactions during the penetration are thus described, it is her husband's mind which takes priority.

If one could argue that in this way, the text tries to illustrate Reham's pain without penetrating her mind in addition to her physical body, it is still striking how in the novel, she mostly serves as a female bodily foil against which Yaqzan's and Tarek's conceptions of gender roles can be illustrated. Thus, Reham's body, for instance, is instrumentalised in order to juxtapose Yaqzan's belief in tradition with a crude conception of romantic love as epitomised by Tarek. Soon after Reham's severe genital wounds have healed, she sleeps with Tarek. While the novel mentions that both have an orgasm – a fact which, so soon after the rape, is in itself reminiscent of the quasi-magical healing processes of rape victims such as de Sade's prototypical Justine[39] – it is again the man's perspective which the text adopts: 'Once they had come, he lay on his back on the cave floor, closed his eyes to retain for as long as he could the sensation of release and pleasure. When he opened them she was gone' (*Book of Sands*: 216). Even before Reham becomes pregnant and dies in childbirth, her own role consequently remains limited to that of a receptacle. Emptied of the child after giving birth, she has fulfilled her role in the novel and dies.

Just as Omar dissociates the traumatic experience of his role in Mona's female genital mutilation, so the novel – at the level of its macro-structure – dissociates the long flashback to Reham's story in part III. Because of its fragmentary, allochronic and often oneiric quality, at the figurative level, this part could even be read as one of Omar's dissociations. In this, the magic realist mode serves to explore how the repressed reality beneath the magical surface is the tradition of female genital mutilation. Relying on magical elements to incite the reader to question what is real and what is not,[40] the magic realist mode renders Omar's difficulty remembering his trauma visible. By providing a broader background to Omar's individual experience, the drastic depictions of the consequences of female genital mutilation furthermore reinforce the impression that his pathology and his subsequent radicalisation are rooted in a deeper general gender trauma. Focusing on the behaviour which genital mutilation causes in men rather than exploring what this practice means for women, the mainly male focalisation in part III corroborates this reading. Instead of subverting Orientalist patterns by exploring other possible origins of Islamism, part III thus provides a culturalised and atavistic explanation of Omar's radicalisation.

In line with a common tendency towards magic realism, the use of intertexts by Jorge Luis Borges in *Book of Sands* does not only inscribe the novel in the 'globalized hybridizing inflection' of postcolonial literature,[41] but especially in the South American origins of the magic realist tradition. Further blurring the lines between fact and fiction, the fictional intertexts by Borges, moreover, substantiate the reading of part III as a possible dissociation by Omar. The fact that Omar's sister, Mona, reads *April March* (allegedly 1936), a fictional novel which allegedly consists of a third part only,[42] indicates that it is no coincidence that in *Book of Sands*, it is part III which provides the cultural backdrop to her genital mutilation. Although a fictional book by fictional Irish author Herbert Quain, whose works Jorge Luis Borges pretends to survey in the short story 'An Examination of the Work of Herbert Quain' (1941), *April March* manifests as a real hardback novel which Mona reads in *Book of Sands* (*Book of Sands*: 57). As a 'fragmentary story made up of one conclusion with nine possible origins',[43] *April March* reinforces the themes of alternate worlds. Furthermore, this reference to Borges' hypotextual work draws attention to the multiple options of reading alternative realities – in general, but also with regard to Mona's and Omar's subjective realities and traumas. Apart from *April March*, the title *Book of Sands* and its layout with its rough-cut edges additionally refer to Borges' 1975 short story and short story collection *El libro de arena* (*The Book of Sand*). The latter is about another fictional book, a book without a beginning or an ending, an idea which clearly influences part III of *Book of Sands*: part III of Alrawi's novel comes to an end when Kasem, one of the minor characters, reads the fictional *Book of Knowledge*, only to find that it contains everything that is happening around him. He challenges his fate by choosing a different life, and as he makes this decision, the book's pages start to crumble (*Book of Sands*: 258–62): 'All the while the storm intensified, beyond anything described in the book. Like an hourglass upturned, a torrent of sand poured into the valley' (*Book of Sands*: 262). Both with the references to Borges and by the simile of the hourglass, *Book of Sands* underlines its negotiation of freedom and predetermination and their role in Omar's trauma and radicalisation.

Against the foil of the collective cultural trauma explored in mostly magic realist terms in part III, part IV returns to the present tense. A taut succession of different scenes and settings mirrors Omar's rising tension and accelerates the narration towards the climax. Omar is highly agitated by Maulana's sermons and by the sexual encounter which he has with the young androgynous boy. In his emotionally unstable state, the '[v]oices multiply in his head …' (*Book of Sands*: 284). Afraid that one of the protestors from the square might recognise him, Omar purchases a gun, which the text renders by means of the heterolingual element *fard*. After one of the sex workers rejects him (*Book of Sands*: 300), Omar's tension rises further. When he calls Mona, Yara tells him that Mona is already in labour but does not tell him which hospital she is in. Feeling helpless, Omar starts rocking back and forth (*Book of Sands*: 301) and increasingly works himself into a frenzy. Rhetorical questions mark his deep insecurity, as does an enumeration of people who he feels have rejected him. His hurt feelings finally find an outlet in a fantasy of violence against the sex worker who rejected him:

> As he waits in a line of slow-moving cars, his thoughts drift to the boy smoking *bango*. He wonders why he has not called. Did Omar, unintended, cause offence by something he said or did? His thoughts jump to recollections of his humiliation by that whore. He imagines the hurt he could cause her with razors and knives. The suddenness of his rage disturbs him. He should attend the *moulid* by the mosque to seek the calming influence of the saint. It will soon be nightfall and a little time spent there would distract him from the rejection he feels by everyone, from Mona and Yara to the boy and the blonde. (*Book of Sands*: 302)

In an attempt to overcome this intense feeling of rejection, Omar smokes marijuana during the celebrations and picks up a sex worker in a black *niqab*. The following sex scene further illustrates how torn Omar is between the fundamentalist degradation of women and his repressed sexual desire and need for intimacy. During their intercourse, Omar assumes the passive and submissive part, while the sex worker straddles him and gently but efficiently leads him to a quick orgasm. When she asks him whether he wants her to stay, even this minimal bit of human proximity, bought by money, makes '[h]is chest burn …' (*Book of Sands*: 303). In the middle of the night, and under the influence of the marijuana which he smoked, he inspects the woman's body and 'sees a sparrow nestled between her legs …' When he performs cunnilingus on her, '[t]he sparrow's neck grows and hardens in his mouth' (*Book of Sands*: 303).

The next morning, he is 'no longer certain what of the previous night was hallucination and what actual' (*Book of Sands*: 303), and a conversation with Tarek brings forth his rage again: 'Rage ignites as soon as he hears his voice' (*Book of Sands*: 304). Because of his excessive fatigue and his drug usage, his physical condition worsens and his sanity diminishes: 'With the boundaries of sleep and wakefulness transgressed since the previous night, thoughts arise in one state, continue in another' (*Book of Sands*: 305). Arguing with the cockroach, Omar again smokes a joint and

> [v]oices arise to debate, cut across, interrupt and argue with each other in his head – voices around and in him. So many voices he cannot hear himself think –
> *A man like me above such things as sin   anyone been tempted as much*
> *   resist all manner   dare no not at all and but though*
> *   like suffocate that's what   better ask   out of you fuck*
> *I would just like that with the bitch   a believer Pilgrim cos if   I can't think*
>   (*Book of Sands*: 305; italics and indentations in the original)

By means of the elements in italics, the text visualises how Omar is no longer able to think straight. He starts to cry and, overwhelmed by this 'onslaught of voices' (*Book of Sands*: 306), he kills the cockroach. The repellent description of his reaction, oscillating between triumph and terror, intimates that violence is his only coping mechanism to silence the voices in his head: 'He stares at the dead cockroach. The voices fall silent. He feels the stickiness between fingers and thumb, inhales the sickly-sweet scent, feels triumphant at killing the devil, terror at having done so' (ibid.).

While the danger emanating from Omar increases towards the climax of the novel, his frame is simultaneously Orientalised. Teeming with dancing dervishes and snake charmers, the frenzied atmosphere of a *moulid*, a Sufi celebration held at al-Rifai Mosque, mirrors Omar's growing inner tension. Abducting his sister, Mona, from the hospital, he tells himself that he is bringing her to the festivities in order to get the saint's blessing for the unborn baby. The personal narration in this passage, however, shows that it is in fact the power over his helpless sister which he enjoys. Normally superior to her brother, Mona is under an analgesic and completely at her brother's mercy:

> He watches Mona, her mind still in a haze, sees the sickening look on her face, feels satisfaction at her discomfort. She stumbles past whirling dancers. Dervish sway as others chant. Unsteady, she steps into a man draped with snakes about his shoulders. A serpent shoots forward, hisses, bares fangs, its forked tongue lashes at her face. (*Book of Sands*: 308–9)

When Mona's contractions start, Omar takes her to the Jewish cemetery. There, the tension further increases when the voices he hears again start to multiply. Completely out of control, Omar thinks he sees ghosts and 'hears voices coming from the graves. Their susurrations call his name, call him to them, while other voices urge him on … The voices pierce his skull, grow louder' (*Book of Sands*: 310). When he tries to shoot at the shadows, the ejected cartridge case hits him and exacerbates his fury: 'All rage, he crawls to take cover behind a gravestone. Now the voices loud and unrelenting demand he kill. Yes, yes, he must kill the hunted wraith. One bullet spent, five remain, more than enough for *afrit* or man' (*Book of Sands*: 311). Here, the adjunct 'all rage' indicates the complete takeover of affect in Omar; rage dominates, obliterating other facets of his personality. The short staccato and often elliptical sentences in the scene convey the excitement which the power of the handgun gives him. Furthermore, they time his thinking with his actions and thus present it as reduced to the question of life and death:

> Omar cocks the *fard*. Voices tell him to fire in case it be a demon, before it looks up and sees him. He resists the urge to kill until he can be certain …

> Omar aims the handgun at her [his sister, Mona], feels an onrush of pleasure, an unfamiliar sense of power – she a broken-winged sparrow, her life at his disposal. The ability to summon death his alone. (*Book of Sands*: 311–12)

At the climax of the staccato sentences, the novel does not only merge the issues of radicalisation and gender trauma, but it also revives the bird metaphor. In the scene with the sex worker, Omar sees the woman's clitoris as an unmutilated sparrow. As he is about to kill Mona, Omar presents his sister in terms of her mutilated clitoris by describing her as a 'broken-winged sparrow' (*Book of Sands*: 312). Representing the hope for freedom, the metaphor of the birds is thus not only connected to the uprisings, but also to questions of gender equality. If the cockroaches represent indoctrination and are linked to Maulana's defecation, the metaphor of the birds is thus also double-coded, with one level of meaning pertaining to the genital region. Both at the level of content and form, the tension between the demands of the Arab uprisings and Omar's radicalisation is thus negotiated through a genitals-centric lens.

Just before her brother is about to shoot her, Mona 'takes a deep breath, braces herself, opens her eyes, fixes him with her gaze' (*Book of Sands*: 312). She tells him that she never forgave him for letting them cut her. In the extreme stress of the moment, he falters; his trauma is re-enacted and he finally remembers:

> Lashed by the haunting voices, and his struggles with the devil in and among the infidel dead, memory surges and he watches as the blade draws blood from a child held on the bathroom floor, her screams pierce like breaking glass, as though from the gravestones … (*Book of Sands*: 312)

Then, after two blinks of the eye, he comes to his senses again: 'He blinks, blinks again, returns himself to the present of Mona pregnant in the graveyard' (*Book of Sands*: 312). He drops the gun and by means of a few rhetorical questions, the novel intimates a different, more nuanced side of his personality. None of this personality or Omar's deradicalisation, however, is shown. Instead, after a few moralising words, *Book of Sands* ends abruptly. Although at the last moment, Omar refrains from shooting his sister, his deradicalisation is thus only fleetingly and unconvincingly rendered on the penultimate page of the novel.

With the exception of the last few pages, Omar's radicalisation process consequently determines the entire novel.[44] Evocative of the logic of a 'sexual clash of civilizations',[45] which turns sexual freedom into the linchpin of freedom in general,[46] Omar's radicalisation is both set in contradistinction to the uprisings and ascribed to sexual trauma. Not only does the cause of his pathology – his subjective trauma and the cultural trauma of female genital mutilation – suggest that a whole generation of potentially dangerous irrational men like him must exist, but the text's metaphorical network also aestheticises this genitals-centric representation of Islamist radicalisation.

Mathias Énard: *Rue des voleurs*

Born in 1972, Mathias Énard is a French novelist and translator. He read Persian and Arabic and lived in different countries in the Middle East. He has won several literary prizes, most notably the Prix Décembre and Prix du Livre inter for his single-sentence novel *Zone* (2008; *Zone*) and the Prix Goncourt for his novel *Boussole* (2015; *Compass*). Moreover, he translated, among others, an anthology of erotic texts by Mohamed ibn Mansûr al-Hilli.[47] Énard lives in Barcelona.[48] *Rue des voleurs* (2012) won the 2013 Prix littéraire de la Porte Dorée, awarded for Francophone fiction dealing with issues of exile. Additionally, it won the Prix Liste Goncourt/Le Choix de l'Orient (2012) and the Prix du Roman-News (2013), an award for French-speaking fictionalisations of current events.[49]

Set against the Arab uprisings and the Indignados movement in Spain, *Rue des voleurs* imagines the so-called Arab Spring as a coming-of-age story. Lakhdar, the novel's autodiegetic narrator, is a young Moroccan who leaves Tangier and, via the Strait of Gibraltar and Algeciras, fights his way to Barcelona. Originally not one of the adolescents desperate to leave Tangier and to emigrate to Europe, Lakhdar grows up in a conservative and religious working-class family (*Rue*: 12–14). He spends most of his days reading mainly French detective fiction, smoking marijuana with his friend Bassam or observing Spain on the other side of the Strait of Gibraltar, a mere fourteen kilometres away. Lakhdar flees from Tangier when, at the age of seventeen, he is caught in bed with his cousin Meryem. While Meryem is sent to the countryside, where she dies after an amateur abortion, Lakhdar, beaten up and humiliated by his father (*Rue*: 16), is too ashamed to return home. He travels south instead, eking out a living by begging and prostituting himself. After a while, he returns to Tangier. Completely exhausted and dispirited, he is grateful to develop a new routine for himself as the librarian of the 'Diffusion de la Pensée coranique',[50] a fundamentalist group which his friend Bassam has joined in the meantime. Lakhdar falls in love and begins a relationship with Judit, a Spanish tourist and student of Arabic. When, after a bomb attack in Marrakesh, all the members of the group disappear and the building of the 'Diffusion' burns down, Lakhdar finds himself homeless once again. He starts working for a French language publisher in Tangier, and then, in an attempt to reach Europe, he signs up to work on a ferry. The shipping company, however, goes bankrupt. Lakhdar takes up work for a Spanish undertaker specialising in the repatriation of drowned refugees. When his boss commits suicide in front of him, the protagonist flees to Barcelona. There, he sees Judit and Bassam again. Afraid that his friend is about to commit a terrorist attack, Lakhdar kills Bassam and is convicted for murder. Lakhdar reconstructs these happenings from the retrospect of his prison sentence – in, as he remarks himself (*Rue*: 122), a more or less reliable way.

As this summary indicates, *Rue des voleurs* focuses on the hardships of Lakhdar, an illegal alien, and sets them against the background of the political protests in several Arab countries and in Spain. The novel depicts Lakhdar's struggles to make a living for himself, and it does so by creating – both at the level of content and stylistics – a frame of liminality for its protagonist. As it alludes to the large numbers of drowned refugees through Lakhdar's work for the undertaker and as it delves into the fate of Lakhdar, the novel can be read as an attempt to illustrate the insecurity of those who are often securitised and to thereby desecuritise the figure of the illegal alien. At the same time, however, the book drafts the figure of the illegal alien in extreme contradistinction to the figure of the Islamist terrorist. So, while *Rue des voleurs* shows the insecurity from which Lakhdar suffers and casts him in a frame of liminality, it reduces his friend Bassam to a stock character and portrays him in a frame of terror. An extremely flat character and Islamist Rage Boy, Bassam represents the danger of Islamist radicalisation and terrorism reaching Europe. Despite the fact that Bassam is the focaliser's friend and could thus be expected to evoke some sympathy, the representation of his character limits itself to infantilising and pathologising him. In this clear-cut constellation, Lakhdar's frame of liminality only functions in opposition to Bassam's frame of terror, and the former is always on the tipping point of terror.

Lakhdar: Betwixt and Between

Throughout the novel, Lakhdar's development is profoundly influenced by the experience of liminality:[51] the feeling of being torn between two worlds characterises not only most of the protagonist's subjectivity, but also structures the plot and setting. Betwixt and between,[52] Lakhdar meanders between adolescence and adulthood, between Morocco and Europe, between fact and fiction, between ideology and disillusionment, between ideals and desire, between different languages, between world and personal history as well as between life and death. As both the different settings and the titles of the three parts of the novel indicate, he does so in an environment marked by liminality, passage and hybridity. While the first part of *Rue des voleurs* is tellingly entitled 'Détroits' ('Straits'; *Rue*: 9) in the plural, the title of the middle part is 'Barzakh' (which means 'barrier' and is roughly similar to the Christian concept of limbo (*Rue*: 167)).[53] Referring to a ethnically mixed street in Barcelona, the last part is entitled 'La Rue des Voleurs' ('The Street of Thieves'; *Rue*: 237).

From the first part of the novel onwards, the protagonist faces radical change and a number of straits, both literal and figurative. Growing up in the in-between place that is Tangier, a nexus between Africa and Europe known for its long-time mixed international status,[54] Lakhdar experiences the geographical, linguistic, sexual and economic ambivalence of the city. In particular, Lakhdar is torn between his suburban family's strict moral codex and sexual taboos, and his wish for, especially sexual, freedom. Although Lakhdar sees his premarital sex with Meryem as the 'peché originel' (*Rue*: 119)[55] which provokes his subsequent misfortune, he hears about a different side of Tangier as well – and thus of a city which, for those with sufficient financial means, is an icon of international sex tourism and a homosexual or bisexual lifestyle:[56]

[J]'ai croisé des types qui rêvaient de s'y rendre, en touristes, louer une jolie villa avec vue sur la mer, boire du thé au *Café Hafa*, fumer du kif et baiser des indigènes, des indigènes masculins la plupart du temps mais pas exclusivement, il y en a qui espèrent se taper des princesses des *Mille et Une Nuits* … et s'ils avaient su que le seul cul que j'ai dévisagé avant d'avoir dix-huit ans c'est celui de ma cousine Meryem ils en seraient tombées par terre ou ne m'auraient pas cru, tant ils associent à Tanger une sensualité, un désir, une permissivité qu'elle n'a jamais eue pour nous, mais qu'on offre au touriste moyennant espèces sonnantes et trébuchantes dans l'escarcelle de la misère. (*Rue*: 12)[57]

As alluded to by this act of double projection, in which it is unclear to what degree Lakhdar extends or imagines the Orientalist fantasies of the men he met, the sexual ambivalence in the novel does not simply stem from the differences between tourists and inhabitants in Tangier, but also results from the sexual ambivalence of the inhabitants themselves. If the portrayal of his family positions him as involuntarily standing on the conservative shore of the sexual strait, the narrator at the same time renders visible the tension and hypocrisy inherent in the morality of his sociocultural background. Not only does he himself alternate between watching pornography and reading the Quran (*Rue*: 29), go to a sex worker (*Rue*: 112–13) or ogle scantily clad tourists with his friend Bassam, but he also describes the sexual hypocrisy in his home town at large. When, for instance, he organises a book sale in front of the mosque, he speculates why *La Sexualité en Islam* is a bestseller: 'sans doute parce que tout le monde pensait qu'il y aurait du cul, des conseils de positions, ou des arguments religieux de poids pour que les femmes admettent certaines pratiques …' (*Rue*: 27–8).[58]

To dismantle his family's hypocritical notion of honour, Lakhdar resorts to an irony which illustrates the friction between his family's attempts to save appearances and their actual situation, between what is said and what is done. Thus, for instance, he undermines the direct verbal characterisation of his father by juxtaposing it with an indirect characterisation, laconically inserted after the dash: '[M]on paternel était un homme pieux, ce qu'on appelle un homme bien, un homme d'honneur qui ne maltraitait ni sa femme, ni ses enfants – à part quelques coups de pied dans le fondement de temps en temps, ce qui n'a jamais fait de mal à personne' (*Rue*: 12).[59] Lakhdar's wording further plays on his family's notion of honour. Although in the rest of the novel, the autodiegetic narrator frequently uses the colloquial word 'cul' ('ass'), in the description of his family, he ironically echoes their euphemisms and instead chooses the more abstract and formal 'fondement' ('backside'). Nonetheless, this use of irony only unsuccessfully masks the numerous stereotypes in the description of Lakhdar's pious but strict father and subservient mother (*Rue*: 12–13): they appear as hardly more than a pair of stock characters who represent the expectations of their gender roles.

Both in order to mark Lakhdar's renunciation of his family's morals and to reproduce the orality of his speech, *Rue des voleurs* frequently takes recourse to sexualised and vulgar vocabulary. This results in a pronounced sexual explicitness which does not only distance the young man from his family background, but which also stands in opposition to the stereotypical sensuality of Tangier. Although the novel pretends to be told by a twenty-year-old who has prematurely aged due to the difficulties he has gone through, Lakhdar's tone is not that of someone telling the tale of his fate from a prison cell. The pomposity of Lakhdar's frivolousness paints him not as sensuous and sensitive, but as a stereotypically lascivious and flat Orientalist projection of suppressed wantonness. Even at the most unlikely moments of the plot, he is instrumentalisd as the focaliser of a male gaze engaging in extended pseudo-witty blazonings of female bodies. Thus, at a time of intense worry for both Bassam and Judit, Lakhdar takes a whole page to retrospectively enumerate and group women's bodies according to their skin colour:

> Je lui [Bassam] offrais généreusement la plus belle collection de culs de la terre. Allongées dans la même direction, … seins nus ou non, certaines en string, d'autres en chastes maillots une pièce, tout un arc-en-ciel de filles se déployait sous nos yeux – des blanches comme le lait en train de se passer de la crème ; des roses, qui avaient des chapeaux pour protéger leurs visages ; des légèrement hâlées, des bronzées, des noires, un dégradé de fesses, de pubis rebondis dans les costumes de bain, de seins de toutes formes et de toutes couleurs … à un mètre de moi j'avais, les cuisses légèrement écartées sur une serviette multicolore, une Nordique dont le cul bien rond commençait à rosir sur les côtés du maillot – on devinait son sexe qui plissait légèrement l'étoffe, la bosselait dans des vagues de douceur où pointaient,

> à la lisière du tissu, contre la chair, quelques minuscules poils blonds … j'avais l'impression d'avoir la tête entre ses jambes et je me suis demandé si mon regard aurait un effet sur ce con si proche ; si, en le fixant longtemps, je parviendrais à l'échauffer, comme le soleil enflamme la paille à force de rayons … La fille du Nord s'est gratté le bas du dos, comme si je l'avais dérangée, et j'ai brusquement détourné le regard, par un réflexe idiot – à moins qu'Odin n'ait pourvu des créatures de capacités inédites, l'œil unique qui m'observait derrière le polyester grenat était aveugle. (*Rue*: 317–18)[60]

For this long description, Lakhdar chooses the *phrase migrante*[61] ('migrant sentence'), a stylistic feature for which Mathias Énard is famous and which stylistically determines the novel from the beginning. As a 'sentence in permanent movement'[62] which meanders for a long time before reaching the full stop, it stylistically mirrors Lakhdar's perambulations. In this instance, however, the *phrase migrante* drowns Lakhdar's pressing problems in a flood of sexualised and racialised corporealities. Far from reflecting the protagonist's own meandering as a migrant, the sexualised excursion to the beach serves as a retarding moment at best. In its mix consisting of vulgar words, hyperboles, the complacent reference to Odin and the parallelisms of skin colours, it oscillates between the colloquial and the ironically erudite or ironically poetic. This tone indirectly characterises Lakhdar as someone who enjoys hearing himself talk. At the same time, it calls into question to what extent the author, as he claims in an interview with *Le Monde*, tried to put himself in the shoes of the protagonist in order to show the interdependencies of Europe and the Arab-speaking world:

> Ce qui m'a poussé à me mettre dans la peau de Lakhdar, c'est cette complexité du monde d'aujourd'hui, la diversité de ces cultures qui se mélangent. Montrer qu'il existe des points communs entre les aspirations des jeunesses catalane et marocaine, par exemple. Que le destin de l'Europe est aujourd'hui inséparable du destin du monde arabe ; qu'ils se mélangent.[63]

Despite these intentions, moments of intense encounter or passages in which the reader gains an insight into the emotional life of the protagonist are extremely rare (*Rue*: 323). As in the example above, Lakhdar's representation often remains limited to a high degree of sexualisation – a choice which, in the case of a young Moroccan man serving as the focaliser, seems stereotypical at best.

In contrast to the sexual permissiveness and sensuality presented to the tourists in Tangier, Lakhdar's own experiences with prostitution are marked by illicit desire, deprivation, poverty, humiliation, disgust and shame. When wandering through the country after being found in bed with his cousin, he has to prostitute himself and is deeply ashamed of it; when he decides to pay for sex himself, he feels too ashamed to consume the sex for which he has paid. Not only do Lakhdar's first sexual encounters – his intercourse with Meryem included – thus often end with him fleeing (for instance, *Rue*: 41–2 and 112–13), but the issues of shame and sexual hypocrisy are further underlined by an intertextual reference. Judit, a Spanish tourist with whom he begins a relationship, gives him an Arabic copy of *For Bread Alone* by Mohamed Choukhri (*Rue*: 83, 147). *For Bread Alone*, one of the most important intertexts in *Rue des voleurs*, is an autobiographical novel first published in its appropriation/translation by Paul Bowles in 1973.[64] Due to its explicit depiction of teenage sex and drug abuse, it was long censored in Morocco. By creating an analogy between Lakhdar's and Choukhri's experiences, the reference helps to fill in narrative gaps to which the protagonist's account only alludes (*Rue*: 41–2). Moreover, as the intertext vividly evokes the sexual libertinage of which the Beat Generation took advantage in the Tangier of the 1950s, it reinforces the issues of sexual hypocrisy and ambivalence in the protagonist's home town.[65]

In addition to the exterior liminality which Lakhdar experiences, the protagonist is an in-between character himself. Being in his adolescence, he is at a liminal age. While he describes himself as childish, the fact that, though barely twenty, he is already turning grey illustrates his premature suffering (*Rue*: 94). Moreover, with regard to the Arab uprisings, as a Moroccan from Tangier, Lakhdar oscillates between being impacted directly and being an outside observer. Although there were uprisings in Morocco as well, they ended much earlier than in other countries due to concessions made by the king. As a consequence, Lakhdar experiences the uprisings mostly as mediated by television: 'À la télévision, on voyait les manifestations en Égypte, en Tunisie, au Yémen, le soulèvement en Libye. C'est pas gagné, j'ai pensé. Le Printemps arabe mon cul, ça va se terminer à coups de trique, coincées entre

Dieu et l'enclume' (*Rue*: 41).⁶⁶ Both his age and his country of origin consequently result in his viewing himself in a liminal position. In fact, the stylistic to and fro of his wandering phrases reflects that Lakhdar feels lost between two worlds and seeks his private revolution in winning over Judit:

> [I]l était temps d'être un homme, d'avancer vers elle comme un homme et de l'embrasser sur la bouche puisque c'était cela dont j'avais envie, cela dont je rêvais, et si nous ne faisons pas d'effort vers nos rêves ils disparaissent, il n'y a que l'espoir ou le désespoir qui changent le monde, en proportion égale, ceux qui s'immolent par le feu à Sidi Bouzid, ceux qui vont prendre des gnons et des balles place Tahrir et ceux qui osent rouler une pelle dans la rue à une étudiante espagnole, évidemment ça n'a rien à voir mais pour moi, dans ce silence, ce moment perdu entre deux mondes, il me fallait autant de courage pour embrasser Judit que pour gueuler Kadhafi ! Enculé ! devant une jeep de militaires libyens ou hurler Vive la république du Maroc ! seul au beau milieu du Makzen à Rabat ... (*Rue*: 86–7)⁶⁷

This in-between position is also what characterises Lakhdar's jobs – all of which oscillate between the profit reaped by those in charge and the precarity of those whom they exploit. While Lakhdar works as the bookseller of the 'Diffusion de la Pensée Coranique' and even lives at its headquarters, he is only marginally involved in the group's activities. After the 'Diffusion' burns down and all the other members disappear, the protagonist starts working at the subsidiary of a French publisher in the Free Zone of Tangier. While he is situated between religion and fundamentalism with his job at the Islamist group, Lakhdar works between the different realities of the books which he digitalises for the French-language publisher. When he signs up to work on a ferry which crosses the Strait of Gibraltar, the protagonist continually moves between Africa and Europe. When Lakhdar is exploited by Cruz, a Spanish mortician who specialises in repatriating the remains of drowned illegal immigrants, the protagonist finally works between life and death.

Both Cruz's name and the book's epigraph are intertextual references to Joseph Conrad's novella *Heart of Darkness* (1899). After watching hour after hour of videos about violent deaths on the Internet (*Rue*: 214, 226), Cruz commits suicide by poisoning himself in front of the unsuspecting protagonist. In his mental illness, his exploitation of others and in his gruesome death, Cruz is reminiscent of Kurtz, an ivory trader and the central character in *Heart of Darkness*, and Kurtz's famous dying words – '[t]he horror! the horror!'[68] By means of this intertextual reference, *Rue des voleurs* suggests that Lakhdar's stay with Cruz leads the protagonist into his personal heart of darkness, and it draws an analogy between Marlow, the narrator in Conrad's novella, and Lakhdar. While Marlow witnesses the workings of imperialism on his way to the Inner Station, Lakhdar is confronted both with the atrocious deaths and corpses of the drowned refugees and with harrowing scenes of torture and war through Cruz's consumption of violent videos. Insofar as *Heart of Darkness* can be read as a critique of the evils of imperialism,[69] this intertext underlines the neo-imperial dimension of Cruz's business with the drowned refugees: making money every time one of them dies, Cruz benefits from the insecurity of those who try to cross the Mediterranean Sea (*Rue*: 212).[70] At the same time, however, the uncritical reference to the controversial intertext of *Heart of Darkness* aligns *Rue des voleurs* with an uncritical celebration of a Eurocentric literary canon.[71]

Both in order to diversify its own literary frame of reference and to further underline Lakhdar's frame of liminality, *Rue des voleurs* uses a plethora of diverse intertexts in addition to *Heart of Darkness*. Besides references to *For Bread Alone*, mentions of Ibn Battuta, a medieval explorer from Lakhdar's home town, and his travelogues (*Rue*: for instance, 85, 114, 142, 156, 218, 235, 347) permeate the entire novel, and Lakhdar crosses the Strait of Gibraltar on a ferry of the same name, the Battuta. Other intertexts range from Casanova (*Rue*: for instance, 132, 295, 301) and Melville (*Rue*: for instance, 284) through French detective fiction (*Rue*: for instance, 31, 94, 267, 276), Paul Bowles, William Burroughs and Àngel Vázquez (*Rue*: 110) to Naguib Mahfouz (*Rue*: 93, 258), Abû Nuwâs, Tayeb Salih (*Rue*: 258), Nizar Kabbani (*Rue*: 106, 134, 139) and the Quran. Explicitly evoked, these intertexts do not only close narrative gaps, but they also present Lakhdar's reality as one of books and words. Moreover, they demonstrate the diversity of influences on which Lakhdar draws. Due to his wide reading, the protagonist is able to transcend borders which would otherwise remain closed to him, so that he can move between different worlds and languages. At the same time, the books he reads serve him as a means of education, language learning, self-stylisation and as escapisms (*Rue*: 276–7; 325).

When it comes to the aesthetics of the novel, the intertexts diversify the reading experience not just at the diegetic level, but also at the level of reception. This holds particularly true when they appear in combination with heterolingual elements, another feature which constitutes Lakhdar's frame of liminality. Thus, the novel incorporates individual verses in Arabic by Nizar Kabbani (*Rue*: 106, 134, 139), and only gradually provides their translation into French: on page 106, the verses appear in the Arabic original, without translation. When they are repeated on page 139, they *are* translated. As a consequence, any reader who does not speak Arabic is only slowly granted access to the meaning of the citation – and is thus briefly put in a position similar to Lakhdar's, who, throughout the course of the novel, progressively improves his understanding of French and Spanish. If most references are explicitly mentioned in the novel, one important intertext which remains implicit is Tahar Ben Jelloun's *Partir* (2006; *Leaving Tangier*). Besides the fact that it was Ben Jelloun who translated Choukri's novel in 1980,[72] *Rue des voleurs* has numerous parallels with Ben Jelloun's novel *Partir*. In both novels, the characters want to leave Tangier, and as Azel in *Partir*, Lakhdar becomes involved with Islamists. However, whereas Azel is killed by a Muslim Brother, *Rue des voleurs* reverses the ending: in an attempt to prevent a terrorist act in Barcelona, Lakhdar kills Bassam.[73]

To further diversify Lakhdar's frame, *Rue des voleurs* inserts many heterolingual elements from Arabic, English or Spanish (for instance, *Rue*: 68, 94, 106, 120, 134, 137, 139, 157, 181, 212, 214, 262, 268, 273, 278, 284, 290). Sometimes, these elements are used to create an effect of reality, for instance when a brief fictional newspaper article is rendered in Spanish without a translation (*Rue*: 181). In a similar situation, however, the novel includes a Spanish newspaper article in French (*Rue*: 255). Similarly, Arabic words are sometimes transliterated in the Latin alphabet, and sometimes replicated in Arabic letters. The heterolingual elements in the novel accordingly do not follow any coherent strategy. Instead, their abundance, diversity and situational difference mirror how Lakhdar linguistically adapts to the multilingual reality of his life.

Despite the novel's attempt to cast its protagonist as a liminal character both at the level of content and style, it frequently explodes the limits of Lakhdar's autodiegetic narration. Especially in the third part of *Rue des*

Voleurs, where a narrative 'nous' ('we') often substitutes the narrative 'je' (*Rue*: 247ff., 'I'), many of Lakhdar's utterances undermine his credibility as a character. When, in a lecturing tone, Lakhdar stylises himself as 'l'intellectuel de la rue des Voleurs' (*Rue*: 277)[74] or he speaks in clichés such as 'je prenais une petite avance sur le Paradis, que Dieu me pardonne, il ne manquait que les houris' (*Rue*: 263),[75] he appears more like an ideological mouthpiece than like a round character in his own right. The same holds true for a series of digressions on topics ranging from the strike in Spain to the Catholic Church and the issue of contraception (*Rue*: 280–1). Furthermore, as Lakhdar's frame of liminality works only against the foil of Bassam's frame of radicalisation, it is portrayed as always being on the point of tipping into the disastrous in an increasingly dangerous world.

Bassam: Becoming a Bearded Bomber

Although *Rue des voleurs* is Lakhdar's coming-of-age story, the novel retraces his development against the foil of Bassam's radicalisation. Like Omar in *Book of Sands*, Bassam is sketched as an Islamist Rage Boy. Unlike Omar, however, Bassam is granted no focalising space at all. This makes him not only an even flatter character, but also reinforces the impression of mutism in which the novels casts him. Although Bassam is presented through the eyes of his best friend Lakhdar – a point of view which could be expected to elicit some sympathy for Bassam – his portrayal is mostly depreciative. In a tone which is not amicable but condescending, Lakhdar depicts his friend as dumb, infantile, irrational, sexualised and brutish. Bassam is thus drawn as a character who cannot express himself verbally, and who lets violence speak instead.

Whereas Lakhdar's frame abounds with words, books and languages, Bassam's frame is one of Islamism, radicalisation, speechlessness and terror. The Islamists first make contact with Bassam at the mosque, and – as the lapidary 'et voilà' and Bassam's oversimplified explanation illustrate – Bassam is an easy target: 'Il avait rencontré ce Groupe de la Pensée à la prière du vendredi, avec son père. À force de les voir, ils avaient sympathisé, et voilà. C'est des gens comme il faut, disait Bassam. Ils reviennent d'Arabie et sont pleins de fric' (*Rue*: 25).[76] From the beginning, Bassam is consequently presented as easily manipulable. Not only does Bassam blindly follow the group's leader,

Cheikh Nouredine, but by appealing to Bassam's double standards, Lakhdar also knows how to instrumentalise his friend. Despite Bassam's being a part of the Islamist group, it does not take much for Lakhdar to persuade his friend to ogle girls or drink alcohol with him (*Rue*: 30).

When after his flight to the south, Lakhdar returns to Tangier and Bassam introduces him to the group, the reader first encounters the bearded and sombrely dressed Islamists (*Rue*: 24). The charismatic and sophisticated Cheikh Nouredine, who studied in Saudi Arabia and Pakistan (*Rue*: 29), listens to Lakhdar's story. He blames Meryem and Lakhdar's father for what happened and accuses the latter of not having exerted effective control over the female members of his family. After Lakhdar becomes the bookseller of the group and is asked to sell Islamist pamphlets under-the-table, among them writings by Sayyid Qotb (*Rue*: 29), he becomes aware of the group's radical ideas.

Although Lakhdar is beguiled by Cheikh Nouredine and does not know where else to seek shelter, he soon begins to present the group as a threat. When he learns that the Islamists aim for free elections to seize power and Islamise the constitution and the law, he for instance presents them as a wild force of nature, as the untamable Other: '[L]e groupe voyait les révoltes arabes comme la marée verte tant attendue. Enfin des vrais pays musulmans du Golfe à l'Océan, ils en rêvaient la nuit' *Rue*: 33).[77] Although it could also be the group's own words which Lakhdar reiterates here, the simile of the 'marée verte' which the novel uses is nonetheless problematic. Not only does the simile evoke widespread images which compare the Islamists to a flood inundating entire countries,[78] but it also reverberates with fears of an alleged 'Great Replacement' fuelled by far-right authors such as Renaud Camus.[79]

Animal imagery further underpins this frame of infiltration and danger: 'Le Groupe était un vrai tas de bestioles en cage, ils tournaient en rond en attendant le soir et le moment de l'action' (*Rue*: 36).[80] As in *Book of Sands*, the Islamists are compared to animals which need to be contained; they are equated with vermin and shown as moving around in groups (also *Rue*: 271). Once let out of their 'cage', the group uses the chaos of the demonstrations to begin the 'nettoyage du quartier' (*Rue*: 36).[81] Heavily relying on intensifying repetitions, the novel shows how the sheikh indoctrinates his followers with his rhetoric of otherworldly glory:

> Bassam, pressé de se venger sur le premier venu son nez cassé de l'autre jour, était à la proue des bastonneurs. Ils sortaient par bandes d'une dizaine, armés de gourdins et de manches de pioches après un sermon belliqueux et éloquent du Cheikh Nouredine, où il était question des expéditions du Prophète, du combat de Badr, du Fossé, de la tribu juive des Banu Qaynuqa, de Hamza le héros, de la gloire des martyrs en Paradis et *de la beauté, de la grande beauté* de la mort dans la bataille. Puis, bien chauds après cette mise en jambes théorique, ils partaient presque en courant dans la nuit, les nerfs et la trique de Bassam en tête. (*Rue*: 36; my italics)[82]

Incited by Cheikh Nouredine's sermons and eager to avenge himself, Bassam is at the forefront of the attackers. In the group's activities, he is presented as an eager but headless henchman who, 'avec beaucoup d'élan' (*Rue*: 38), violently beats up a bookseller:

> Bassam l'a frappé bien fort, sur l'épaule, un bruit mat a résonné, il a hurlé de douleur, ... Bassam a abattu le gourdin sur ses côtes, avec beaucoup d'élan, le libraire a hurlé de nouveau, blasphémé horriblement, Bassam a remis ça sur sa cuisse, en visant l'os, l'homme s'est mis à gémir. Bassam souriait, son bâton brandi. Je me suis demandé un instant s'il n'allait pas me péter la gueule aussi. (*Rue*: 38–9)[83]

Because of Bassam's radicalisation, he and Lakhdar become increasingly alienated. While before and after attacking the bookseller, Bassam tries to make eye contact with the protagonist (*Rue*: 38, 39), his smile after violently hurting someone deeply frightens the protagonist. Although at first, when Lakhdar hesitates to hit the bookseller and Bassam steps in, the scene has the potential to convey emotional depth, Lakhdar's subsequent portrayal of Bassam's smile thwarts any form of ambiguity or emotional differentiation. Bassam, whose name roughly translates as 'the one who smiles',[84] is not presented as a complex character with conflicting emotions. Instead, brandishing his weapon while smiling, his smile – and, by implication, his name and his entire being – are inextricably linked to the violence he has committed.

From the beginning, Lakhdar continually refers to those aspects in his friend's physiognomy which paint him as simple-minded. In particular,

Lakhdar focuses on Bassam's round head and small eyes and connects them with both his friend's religiosity and simplicity: 'Bassam avait une bonne tête de pauvre, ronde à petits yeux, il allait à la mosquée tous les jours, avec son vieux' (*Rue*: 15; see also *Rue*: 57, 137, 308–9, 322, 323, 336, 345, 348–9).[85] In the course of the novel, Lakhdar turns them into the outward signifiers of his friend's increasing indoctrination and unpredictability; he describes Bassam's eyes as 'weaselly' and as shining 'with strange madness, in the center of his thick peasant's head':[86]

> Il était surexcité, comme d'habitude. Il tournait en rond comme un *chiot autour du panier de sa mère.*
> Qu'est-ce qui t'arrive encore? j'ai demandé. Un type de plus à tabasser?
> Non, cette fois-ci, c'est plus gros que ça.
> C'est la sabre du Prophète?
> Arrête tes blasphèmes, mécréant. C'est l'heure de la vengeance.
>
> J'ai cru un instant qu'il rigolait, mais après avoir allumé la lumière j'ai pu vérifier que *ses yeux de fouine brillaient d'une folie étrange*, au milieu de *sa bonne grosse tête de plouc* … Il m'a servi un embryon de théorie paranoïaque selon laquelle seul un attentat qui frapperait les esprits ferait bouger les choses en précipitant l'Occident, la population et le Palais dans la confrontation. C'était tout à fait Cheikh Nouredine, mais très peu Bassam. Il avait *un petit pois à la place du cerveau* … En plus je savais très bien qu'au fond l'Islam politique lui était égal. (*Rue*: 47–8; my italics)[87]

The frequent references to Bassam's head function as a materialist barrier at the surface of which Lakhdar stops short. He makes no effort to understand what goes on inside Bassam's head – and as a consequence of the first-person narration, the reader is not granted insight into Bassam's thoughts either: 'Son œil s'est allumé. Ça réfléchissait dur, dans sa tête' (*Rue*: 48).[88] The grammatical agency by means of which Lakhdar chooses to represent his friend – with 'œil' and 'Ça' in the subject position – highlights that Lakhdar does not believe that it is Bassam's mind which leads him, but the mechanics of his fragmented body and the influence of others. Further foregrounding Bassam's corporeality, Lakhdar depicts his friend mainly in terms of his relationship to women or food. Often combining these two focuses, the protagonist presents Bassam's crapulous eating habits as a vicarious satisfaction for his unfulfilled sex drive. Counting on his friend's 'faible pour les histoires de houris toujours vierges qu'on pouvait baiser pour l'éternité au bord du Kowthar, le lac d'abondance de l'au-delà' (*Rue*: 48),[89] Lakhdar pretends that he has a date with two Spanish tourists. When the two Tangerians coincidentally do encounter two Spanish women, Judit and Elena, at a café, the novel conflates the culinary and the sexual. Using the ambiguity of Bassam's tongue movements, the text presents him as staring at the two women while simultaneously gorging on food like an animal: 'Bassam se léchait littéralement les babines, sa grosse langue glissait sur sa lèvre supérieure pour profiter des derniers copeaux de chocolat …' (*Rue*: 53–4).[90] This depreciatory portrayal continues when Lakhdar approaches the tourists. After the four of them have started a conversation, Bassam constantly stares at Elena's breasts (*Rue*: 57–61). Thus, reducing Bassam to his corporeality, *Rue des voleurs* creates a pronounced mind–body dichotomy between the protagonist and the deuteragonist.

By presenting Bassam by means of animal metaphors, Lakhdar further irrationalises his friend. This use of animal metaphors results in a patronising tone which, reminiscent of an animal documentary, debases Bassam. Even if in themselves, comparisons such as the one with the puppy might appear to present Bassam in an, as yet, harmless light, they further underline his subservience to the authority of male figures such as his father and Cheikh Nouredine, and they foreshadow that – unless domesticated – Bassam can grow into a full-blown threat. Especially as the dog imagery continues to appear in conjunction with Bassam's complete devotedness to the dangerous sheikh, it helps to prepare his framing as an irrational threat. In fact, towards the end of the novel, Lakhdar does not compare his friend as a puppy anymore, but likens him to a dog. When Lakhdar sees Bassam again in Barcelona after their long separation, he asks Bassam where he has been. His friend does not answer but looks at him with 'ses yeux vides, ses yeux d'aveugle, ses yeux de chien. C'est Nouredine qui a répondu à sa place : il était avec moi, en train de parfaire sa formation' (*Rue*: 309).[91] While Bassam has resorted to mutism (*Rue*: 316, 319, 329, 331, 333), the sheikh answers in his stead. Like a trained dog, Bassam reacts to the sheikh's voice only, and Lakhdar denies his friend any thoughts of his own: 'Son œil de chien battu a replongé dans l'assiette, est-ce qu'il pensait à la guerre, non, il devait se contenter de mastiquer, le crâne vide' (*Rue*: 323).[92]

Having introduced Bassam as simple-minded, brainless, wanton yet inhibited, affect-driven like an animal and prone to violence, the novel intensifies his frame of terror. Although Lakhdar does not paint his friend as inherently evil, he presents him as increasingly dangerous. To hint at Bassam's future development, *Rue des voleurs* uses foreshadowing. When Bassam himself states that the time of vengeance has come (*Rue*: 47), a joke which Lakhdar makes about his friend's weakness counterbalances this hint by briefly questioning Bassam's fundamentalism: 'Si toutes les recrues du Cheikh Nouredine sont aussi facilement manipulables que Bassam, la victoire de l'Islam n'est pas pour demain …' (*Rue*: 49).[93] However, Lakhdar soon loses faith in his friend, and finds more and more signs which intimate that Bassam constitutes a threat. For instance, while Cheikh Nouredine pays Lakhdar in cash, Bassam, deprived of any financial means, will be paid in the currency of violence and danger: 'Bassam me regardait avec envie, le Cheikh Nouredine avait sorti ces billets sans se cacher, lui il avait droit à un autre genre de salaire, celui de la violence et du danger' (*Rue*: 79).[94]

After an attack at a café in Tangier, Lakhdar sees a police sketch of the culprit and thinks it might be Bassam: '[I]l avait la tête ronde et la figure enfantine de Bassam, ça aurait pu être lui' (Rue: 137).[95] Using the *phrase migrante*, the protagonist starts a reflection on Bassam's motivation, on his hatred of the West and the love of his religion. Lakhdar identifies Cheikh Nouredine as the reason for Bassam's radicalisation, and Bassam's compliance with the sheikh turns him into a threat:

> Mais en y réfléchissant bien j'étais aussi conscient que, *a contrario*, ce n'était pas parce qu'il aimait les filles ou rêvait d'Allemagne et d'États-Unis que cela empêchait quoi que ce soit. Je savais que le Cheikh Nouredine avait grandi en France, et lorsque j'en parlais avec lui il appréciait certains aspects du pays et il reconnaissait que, quitte à vivre au milieu des *kuffar*, des Infidèles, il valait mieux vivre en France qu'en Espagne ou en Italie, où, disait-il, l'Islam était méprisé, écrasé, réduit à la misère. (*Rue*: 138; italics in the original)[96]

Stating that the sheikh grew up in France, the novel evokes not only the danger without, but also the threat within; the heterolingual element *kuffar* (infidels) emphasises the sheikh's alienation from the society he grew up in.

In combination with the account which Lakhdar's flatmate Mounir gives of Paris – which is reminiscent of Mathieu Kassovitz's famous film *La Haine* (1995; *Hate*) – *Rue des voleurs* thus underlines the dangers of a society which is inwardly torn.[97]

Throughout the novel, Bassam – and the situation in general – become increasingly dangerous in Lakhdar's portrayals. When he thinks of Bassam, Lakhdar often pictures him in contexts of danger and violence. Even before he knows that Bassam is implicated in the attacks in Marrakesh, his description of the gruesome deed is followed by a reference to Bassam (*Rue*: 90). When Lakhdar receives an email from Bassam after the attack in Marrakesh, his imagination is fuelled:

> Je l'ai imaginé dans son Pays de Ténèbres, avec le Khidr qui portait ses messages jusqu'à moi, ce Pays de Ténèbres où il maniait le sabre, le fusil ou la bombe, enhardi par la prière, avec d'autres combattants, comme lui, le front ceint d'un bandeau, tels qu'on les voit dans les vidéos sur Internet. (*Rue*: 150)[98]

Conjuring up diverse weapons when he imagines Bassam, Lakhdar mixes contemporary imagery from web videos with an allusion to al-Khidr. The latter is, in some versions of the Alexander romance, the servant of Alexander the Great during the latter's quest into the Land of Darkness.[99] Not coincidentally, al-Khidr, the personification of good, and Lakhdar are linked by their names: both their names derive from the word *green*. As Lakhdar is a rare name in Morocco (*Rue*: 126), it further posits Lakhdar on the good side of the antithesis. Contrary to *Book of Sands*, *Rue des voleurs* does not oppose non-religious rationalism and Islamism. Instead, by means of Lakhdar, a moderate Muslim who has *green* – the colour of Islam – in his name, and his friend Bassam, who increasingly radicalises himself, the novel juxtaposes what is presented as good forms of Muslim faith and its Islamist perversion. If this can be read as an attempt to counter anti-Muslim tropes, the simplistic representation of Bassam's radicalisation nonetheless offers little differentiation of the securitised image of the allegedly dangerous Islamicate man.

In combination with the novel's epigraph and intertextual allusions to *Heart of Darkness*, the reference to the 'Pays de Ténèbres' further feeds into the notion of growing darkness in the novel. It thereby complements the protagonist's increasingly gloomy portrayal of the world:

> Un ciel d'une infinie noirceur, voilà ce qui nous attendait – aujourd'hui dans ma bibliothèque, où la fureur du monde est assourdie par les murs, j'observe la série des cataclysmes comme qui, dans un abri réputé sûr, sent le plancher vibrer, les parois trembler, et se demande combien de temps encore il va pouvoir conserver sa vie : dehors tout semble n'être qu'obscurité. (*Rue*: 272)[100]

As Lakhdar's depictions become more and more apocalyptic (*Rue*: 329), the flames of hatred and destruction constitute the only source of light: towards the end of the novel, the first-person narrator accumulates images of fire and flames to illustrate how hate and danger consume Europe (*Rue*: 42–3, 268, 278, 283, 288–9, 300, 302, 303, 334–6, 343). Although Lakhdar also briefly evokes fire as a revolutionary spark (*Rue*: 270), the rising flames are mostly used as a metaphor for spreading hate and fundamentalism: just as the Islamist group begins its attacks in Tangier, the fire imagery first appears when its members burn down their headquarters to cover their tracks. Then, they spread out, carrying the flame of hate to various places; and it is Cheikh Nouredine – whose name translates as 'the light of religion' – who acts as 'the man who fired us up', 'l'homme qui nous enflammait' (*Rue*: 311),[101] as the one who kindles this flame.

At one point in the novel, in the longish digression of a *phrase migrante*, Lakhdar explains the imminent danger in some detail. Here, he takes into consideration the negative impact of global capitalism:

> [D]ans le métro de Barcelone j'ai repensé à l'explosion de Marrakech, au Cheikh Nouredine quelque part en Arabie et à Bassam, quelque part au Pays des Ténèbres, à l'attentat de Tanger où cet étudiant avait trouvé la mort d'un coup de sabre – bien sûr, Barcelone c'était différent, c'était de la démocratie, mais on sentait que tout cela était sur le point de basculer, qu'il ne fallait pas grand-chose pour que le pays entier tombe lui aussi dans la violence et la haine, que la France suivrait, que l'Allemagne suivrait, que toute l'Europe flamberait comme le Monde arabe, et l'obscénité de cette affiche de métro en était la preuve, il n'y avait plus rien d'autre à faire pour

> Marrakech qu'investir du fric en campagnes publicitaires pour que revienne la manne perdue, même si on savait pertinemment que c'était cet argent du tourisme qui provoquait le sous-développement, la corruption et le néocolonialisme, comme à Barcelone, petit à petit, on sentait monter le ressentiment contre le fric de l'étranger, de l'intérieur ou de l'extérieur ; l'argent montait les pauvres les uns contre les autres, l'humiliation se changeait doucement en haine ; tous haïssaient les Chinois qui rachetaient un à un les bars, les restaurants, les bazars avec l'argent de familles entières provenant de régions dont on n'imagine même pas la pauvreté ; tous méprisaient les prolos britanniques qui venaient s'abreuver de bière pas chère, baiser dans des coins de portes et reprendre, encore saouls, un avion qui leur avait coûté le prix d'une pinte d'ale dans leur obscure banlieue ; tous désiraient, en silence, ces très jeunes Nordiques couleur craie que la différence de température poussait à étrenner leurs minijupes et leurs tongs en février – un quart de la Catalogne était au chômage, les journaux débordaient d'histoires terrifiantes de crise, de familles expulsées d'appartements qu'elles ne pouvaient plus payer et que les banques bradaient tout en continuant à rechercher leur dette, de suicides, de sacrifices, de découragement : on sentait la pression monter, la violence monter, même rue des Voleurs chez les pauvres des pauvres, même à Gràcia parmi les fils de bourgeois, on sentait la ville prête à tout, à la résignation comme à l'insurrection. (*Rue*: 268–70)[102]

However, like many of the other digressions, this exploration of the systemic insecurity of the global capitalist market does not only strain the first-person narration of *Rue des voleurs*, but it soon yields to sexualised speech. The anaphora in the phrases beginning with 'tous' quickly drifts off and ends on a phrase which blazons young white women. Even though their bodies might indeed be a battleground and an icon of neo-liberalism, the undifferentiated sexualised male gaze of this digression undermines its systemic relevance.

Apart from being framed in sexualised speech, this digression is flanked by the rendering of an attack in Toulouse (*Rue*: 270–2). When Lakhdar gives an account of its extremely cold-blooded violence, he evokes Bassam. Not only is Bassam thus co-textually linked to the word 'jihad' and to Islamists described by means of a vermin metaphor, but, quite literally, he is framed by representations of violence preceding and following his name:

> J'ai pensé à Bassam, perdu quelque part dans son Djihad personnel, qui avait peut-être assassiné un étudiant à coups de sabre à Tanger, parfois expliquer ne sert à rien ; il n'y a rien à comprendre dans la violence, celle des animaux, fous dans la peur, dans la haine, dans la bêtise aveugle qui pousse un type de mon âge à poser froidement le canon d'un flingue sur la tempe d'une fillette de huit ans dans une école, à changer d'arme quand la première s'enraye, avec le calme que cela suppose, le calme et la détermination, et à faire feu pour s'attirer le respect de quelques rats de grottes afghanes. (*Rue*: 271)[103]

Before Bassam accompanies Cheikh Nouredine to Barcelona, Lakhdar reiterates the sheikh's sermons on the Battle of Badr. Interspersed by quotations in Arabic, it is thus an evocation of one of the few battles mentioned in the Quran which precedes the sheikh's arrival in Barcelona. In combination with the gathering storm (*Rue*: 303) and Bassam's shaved head (*Rue*: 307), the quotation from the Quran is thus used as an instrument of negative foreshadowing. And in fact, the sheikh's arrival coincides with the diagnosis that Judit has a brain tumour (*Rue*: 306).

Drastically illustrating the power dynamics at play between Bassam and the sheikh, the novel describes how the latter goes to elegant receptions and meets with the international elite while Bassam prepares for a suicide attack. Bassam has changed so much that Lakhdar does not recognise him. He sketches him as 'un jeune type l'accompagnait [l': the sheikh], le crane rasé, une barbe noire …' (*Rue*: 307).[104] After a first warm welcome between the two friends, it becomes clear how far Bassam's transformation has proceeded: 'Bassam s'était rassis, il ne souriait plus ; il avait le regard dérangeant des aveugles ou de certains animaux aux yeux effrayés et fragiles qui paraissent toujours fixer dans le lointain' (*Rue*: 308).[105] Bassam, 'the one who smiles', has stopped smiling and hardly speaks any more.

While in Barcelona, Bassam stays at Lakhdar's place, and the autodiegetic narrator characterises him in a mix of infantilisation, pathologisation, sexualisation and securitisation.[106] For short stretches of time, Bassam seems to be his normal self. While he still gobbles his food like an animal (*Rue*: 310, 321–3) and stares at women (*Rue*: 312, 316–18), Lakhdar continues to infantilise him: 'Il n'arrêtait pas de se marrer tout seul comme un gosse, et c'était une vraie joie de revoir sa bonne grosse tête de plouc barbu sourire au monde' (*Rue*: 313);[107] '[I]l secouait la tête comme un enfant pris la main dans la confiote ...' (*Rue*: 330).[108] Once the sheikh is gone, Bassam continues, in Lakhdar's description, to behave like a lost little girl. When in his mutism, Bassam turns to Lakhdar by taking his hand, the latter, instead of trying to understand his friend, compares him to a puppy and a lost child: 'Il s'est laissé trainer comme le chiot ou l'enfant qu'il n'avait jamais cessé d'être' (*Rue*: 332).[109] If these images cast Bassam as helpless, the reference to his beard intimates that this image of the childlike simpleton is deceptive. In fact, it is contrasted with a scene in which Bassam, deeply shocked by a decadent painting (*Rue*: 314–15), breaks his mutism only to express his indoctrination and his hatred of the West. The novel thus uses alternating scenes to juxtapose instances in which Bassam ogles scantily clad women and scenes in which he expresses his fundamentalism. Thus, *Rue des voleurs* does not only illustrate how torn and full of contradictions Bassam is, but it also establishes a connection between Bassam's repressed sexuality and his radicalisation.

Throughout the novel, Bassam's inner vacillation increasingly drifts in the direction of fundamentalism. For Lakhdar, everything about his friend begins to evoke violence. Bassam's backpack makes him think of the attack in Marrakesh and foreshadows what is about to happen (*Rue*: 320). When Lakhdar tells his friend that he is happy to see him, he does so against a backdrop of continual broadcasts by Al Jazeera about diverse massacres in Syria and Palestine as well as about violent demonstrations in Greece and Spain (*Rue*: 321). When Lakhdar wants to know where Bassam has been, he does not receive any answer from his friend; instead, it is the violence on the television in the background which provides implicit answers when he turns to it 'par réflexe ...' (*Rue*: 323).[110] Bereft of any other explanations, Lakhdar thus conjures up cruel images when thinking of Bassam. Thus, he creates an increasingly stronger link between Bassam and violence – a link which also dominates his subconscious: in one of his nightmares, he dreams that 'Bassam, le regard vide, un bandeau sur le front, égorgeait Judit comme un mouton, en la tentant par les cheveux' (*Rue*: 177).[111]

Once the sheikh and Bassam have arrived in Barcelona, the motif of turning in circles – which informs the entire novel – intensifies and accelerates (for instance, *Rue*: 36, 47, 218–20, 233, 327, 329, 334, 335, 343, 347, 343, 344, 349). While this motif evokes the vicious cycle of violence, the intertext about Hassan le Fou also links it to madness. Introduced via Ibn Battuta's renderings of his travels to Mecca, this intertext is about Hassan, who goes insane after breaking a pact with a beggar. While the beggar magically enables Hassan to see his mother again, Hassan fails to meet the beggar's condition of not telling anyone about him. Having broken the pact by telling his master about the beggar, Hassan goes mad and mute and is damned to keep going in circles around the Kaaba (*Rue*: 218–19, 329, 347). As underlined by this reference to Hassan, Bassam turns in mad and mute circles, and the motif spirals and culminates into the whirling and spinning motion of the novel's last word, 'tournoyer' (*Rue*: 349).[112]

When Nouredine leaves Barcelona, the motifs of fire and turning in circles coalesce and culminate in a rhetoric of securitisation interspersed with heterolingual elements in Arabic. The sheikh whispers into Bassam's ear: '[S]ois fort, il se peut que l'Heure soit proche, لَعَلَّ السَّاعَة تَكونُ قَريباً …' (*Rue*: 331; italics in the original).[113] Looking up the citation, Lakhdar finds the Al-Ahzab sura: '*Il se peut que l'Heure soit proche. Dieu a maudit les Infidèles et leur a préparé un brasier, qu'ils y demeurent pour l'éternité, sans trouver ni allié ni secours*' (*Rue*: 333; italics in the original and followed by the Arabic original).[114] Repeated seven times, thus creating a loop, this allusion to the endless inferno for the infidel becomes the leitmotif of Lakhdar's increasingly apocalyptic and securitised rendering of the situation:

> لَعَلَّ السَّاعَة تَكونُ قَريباً, le verset se trouvait dans la sourate *Al Ahzâb*, Les Alliés ; il y était question de l'heure dernière, de l'heure du Jugement, où un feu éternel était promis aux non-croyants … Bassam devait attendre l'heure pour déclencher des flammes d'apocalypse, ce qui justifierait qu'il tourne en rond à Barcelone … (*Rue*: 334–5)[115]

Lakhdar amalgamates Bassam's turning in circles with the flames of the apocalypse or the pleasure of destruction and accentuates it with what he turns into a threatening incantation in Arabic. While at the beginning of the novel, the heterolingual Arabic elements refer to love poetry, this positive impression consequently yields to a negative and securitised reframing at the end of the novel.

When Bassam buys four mobile phones and continues to turn in circles, Lakhdar again evokes 'des coups de sabre à Tanger, des morts de Marrakech, de combats, d'exécutions sommaires dans un maquis afghan …' (*Rue*: 343).[116] As, however, Lakhdar thinks that Bassam's eyes implore him to save him, to prevent the flames from rising, he kills his friend – an act which he declares as *engagement*. During his trial, he stands up in court and keeps repeating what he is 'more':

> Je ne suis pas un assassin, je suis plus que ça.
> Je ne suis pas un Marocain, je ne suis pas un Français, je ne suis pas un Espagnol, je suis plus que ça.
> Je ne suis pas un musulman, je suis plus que ça.
> Faites de moi ce que vous voudrez. (*Rue*: 346)[117]

This questionable act and speech, however, constitute Lakhdar's only action to counteract Bassam's radicalisation. Politically, Lakhdar has resigned, probably due to the hardships from which he himself has to suffer:

> [T]out cela était un peu déprimant, j'avais l'impression que quoi qu'on fasse, les Arabes étaient condamnés à la violence et à l'oppression. (*Rue*: 259)[118]

> À la télévision, on voyait les manifestations en Égypte, en Tunisie, au Yémen, le soulèvement en Libye. C'est pas gagné, j'ai pensé. Le Printemps arabe mon cul, ça va se terminer à coups de trique, coincées entre Dieu et l'enclume. (*Rue*: 41, also 33–4)[119]

Throughout the novel, Bassam's radicalisation is thus only counterbalanced by representations of Judit's activism in the Indignados and Occupy movements, while Lakhdar prefers not to talk about politics (*Rue*: 242):

> Elle me parlait surtout de politique, à présent ; de la crise en Europe, de sa dureté, du chômage, de la misère qui remontait comme du fin fond de l'histoire de l'Espagne, disait-elle, des conflits, du racisme, des tensions, de l'insurrection qui se préparait. Elle était très liée au mouvement des Indignés, depuis quelques mois. Aussi très liée à celui des Okupas, disait-elle. L'autre jour un étudiant de vingt ans a encore perdu un œil à cause d'une balle de caoutchouc lorsque les flics ont délogé un sit-in pacifique,

disait-elle. La propagande ultra-libérale nous fait croire qu'on ne peut pas résister au diktat des marchés. Ici on ne soignera bientôt plus les pauvres, les vieux, les étrangers. Pour le moment la révolte n'éclate pas parce qu'il y a le football, le Real, le Barça ; mais quand ça ne suffira plus à compenser la frustration et la misère, ce sera l'émeute, disait-elle.

Je la regardais, j'avais envie de lui prendre la main, pas de parler de la crise. (*Rue*: 242).[120]

As a consequence, the revolutionary impetus of the Arab uprisings remains mostly invisible in *Rue des voleurs*; if at all, it is shown fleetingly in its Western adaptation through Judit. To some extent, this results from the choice of setting, Morocco and Spain. Considering the novel's choice of genre – that is, a coming-of-age story – this perspective is nevertheless problematic: *Rue des voleurs* can be read not only as Lakhdar's and Bassam's coming-of-age story, but also as a projection of two possible developments of the uprisings. While Lakhdar, portrayed as sympathetic with the West, ends up in a prison cell, Bassam embodies the Western-centric fear of what might happen in Europe if the Islamists seize control. If the choice of genre itself can thus be criticised as reverberating with the narrative of the so-called Arab Spring as a 'growing up' of allegedly atavistic countries according to Western standards of modernity,[121] the novel's outlook does not only cast Lakhdar and Bassam as gaining maturity in the West, but it also focuses more on possible threats for the West than on the uprisings themselves.

In sum, although *Rue des voleurs* does not present Bassam as the embodiment of terror in the form of a violent and overly potent man, the text still focuses on how this young man constitutes a threat to the West. In a world presented as increasingly dangerous, the novel's frame for Lakhdar, that is, his frame of liminality, gradually gives way to Bassam's frame of terror. Not only do the heterolingual elements in Arabic change from love poetry to an incantation for a suicide bomber, but in general, the *phrase migrante*, far from only mirroring Lakhdar's meandering, also changes from the sexualised to the securitised. In the end, the novel's stylistic attempts to create a transnational and liminal experience are, moreover, weakened when the stance of the autodiegetic narrator suddenly changes into a lecturing 'we'. If this undermines his credibility as a character, he is at the same time – in his role as the antithetical counterpoint to Bassam's radicalisation – reduced to a carrier of Western projections: 'Even when the concrete agents of emancipation are not themselves Westerners, they are conceived as the bearers of Western ideas, whether concerning economy, politics or culture.'[122] Despite its attempt to illustrate the insecurity of the securitised figure of the illegal alien, the novel's antithesis of protagonist and deuteragonist and their respective frames can thus be read as an Occidentalist self-assurance.[123] While the first-person narration brings the protagonist closer to the reader, the deuteragonist's frame of infantilisation, pathologisation, sexualisation and securitisation presents him as the incomprehensible and irrational utter Other.[124] Its endeavour to create diversity notwithstanding, *Rue des voleurs*, a novel which won the 2012 Prix Liste Goncourt/Le Choix de l'Orient, thus translates and aestheticises hegemonic Western representations of the suicide bomber in terms of utter Otherness.[125]

Terror and the Utter Other

> When pleasure or pain press too nearly, they are incapable of giving any delight, and are simply terrible; but at certain distances, and with certain modifications, they may be, and they are delightful, as we every day experience.[126]

With regard to their representation of the Arab uprisings and Islamist radicalisation, *Book of Sands* and *Rue des voleurs* share striking similarities. Both novels negotiate the tension between these two phenomena by means of their constellation of characters and their attendant frames: the texts juxtapose round protagonists who feel sympathetic to the West with flat deuteragonists in the form of Islamist Rage Boys. While the former are presented in wider frames of curiosity and love, the latter are pathologised, irrationalised, sexualised and securitised. They are presented in an Orientalised and securitised frame of difference, distance and danger, which relies on animal and/ or fire imagery and the use of increasingly dangerous heterolingual elements in Arabic. Both books consequently rely on a pronounced antithesis which invites understanding for the protagonist but casts the Islamist Rage Boys as the utter Other whose psychology and motivation are left unexplored.

By delving into the fates of their protagonists, both novels create idiopathic empathy with a protagonist who is sympathetic with the West, that is, a form of empathy 'which is "essentially self-referential, grounded on shared reality"'.[127] In contrast, the only explanation for their deuteragonists' radicalisation is that of repressed sexuality and/or the trauma of genital mutilation. Apart from this culturalised and sexualised genitals-centric explanation, *Book of Sands* and *Rue des voleurs* do not differentiate their deuteragonists' emotions and reasons. As a consequence, they ignore sociopolitical and socioeconomic variables in their depictions of radicalisation and instead present violence as the pathological manifestation of a backward culture.[128] What is more, because of this culturalisation, they also defy heteropathic empathy, that is, a form of empathy which 'implies an "identification with an alien body or experience"'.[129] The fact that *Book of Sands* grants its deuteragonist more focalising space than *Rue des voleurs* can be read as an endeavour to close this gap. However, due to Omar's pronounced pathologisation and irrationalisation and because of his frame of distance, the alienating elements in his representation outweigh any attempts of understanding him.

Epitomised by a static and pathologised character who, without any emotional depth, ambiguity or identificatory potential, defies heteropathic empathy, Islamist radicalisation is presented as unapproachable and unambiguous in the two novels. Not only do the texts thus present the rise of Islamist radicalisation mostly as cultural and pathological, but they also uphold feelings of proximity and distance which create a gap in empathy and ethics:

> We can be alive or dead to the sufferings of others – they can be dead or alive to us. But it is only when we understand that what happens there also happens here, and that 'here' is already an elsewhere, and necessarily so, that we stand a chance of grasping the difficult and shifting global connections in ways that let us know the transport and the constraint of what we might still call ethics.[130]

While both novels, and in particular *Rue des voleurs*, try to illustrate the insecurity of the securitised by means of their protagonists, the way in which they paint their secondary characters follows the dominant framing and established asymmetry of power with regard to security. As the novels' governing literary trope, the structural antithesis between the protagonist and the deuteragonist consequently does not only mirror epistemic asymmetries of violence in representations of terror, but it also helps to constitute the self by perpetuating dichotomous understandings of security and terror.[131] Even though one could of course argue that a dualism between protagonist and antagonist is a typical feature in novels, it is nevertheless striking that *Book of Sands*, *Rue des voleurs* (and *Ahlam* by Marc Trévidic) all fictionalise the Arab uprisings by retracing the path of radicalisation by means of a deuteragonist who is influenced by an antagonistic Islamist. Deradicalisation, on the other hand, is not represented. If the novels attempt to diversify a straightforward dichotomy between a 'good' protagonist and a 'bad' Islamist antagonist, they nonetheless reproduce a binary between the rational protagonist and the irrational, pathologised and dangerous deuteragonist who increasingly radicalises himself.

Interestingly, neither *Book of Sands* nor *Rue des voleurs* presents the result of this radicalisation in the horror of bomb blasts. Although both novels thus reduce the violence in their direct depictions of the deuteragonists, there is epistemic violence in the frames in which they present Omar and Bassam: both novels leave unchallenged the figuration of the Islamist Rage Boy – in fact, they provide a literary form to it. This figuration, which creates a distance to the dangers of terror, allows the novels to present terror from a Burkean distance. While Islamist radicalisation can function as the mover of their plot and although terror lurks in the background of the books, it does not 'press too nearly'.[132] As '[t]o live in terror is painful, but to live in terror vicariously gives you a certain kind of pleasure ...',[133] this distance allows the reader to experience terror not as horror, but as a thrill. With the modifications of stylistic embellishment, terror 'at a safe remove'[134] consequently creates tension and titillation which can serve as sources of Western entertainment. Both novels do thus not function according to an aesthetics of shock; instead, they prepare the reader in a slow but steady accelerando of radicalisation and present terror at a safe remove, as lived vicariously through the protagonist: '[T]he reader senses fear and apprehension from the safety of her fictional distance; only the characters within the novel experience terror as such. Its production within a formal aesthetic genre, the novel, offers the novel as a para-site for and of terror where everything happens at a safe remove.'[135]

Both novels thus do not just represent terror but produce terror as titillation. They do not confront the reader with it directly, by means of the protagonists, but indirectly, by means of the deuteragonists. As a result, the novels do not function as securitising in the sense that they directly spread fear and horror, but as books which narratively put in order and break down the contradictory complexities of terror by means of a deuteragonist. Where desecuritisation would mean a more complex differentiation, both novels consequently narrativise the ordering discourse of radicalised Islamists by means of titillation and thereby provide pleasure in the dangerous and Western-centric process of securitisation.

Notes

1. Mathias Énard. *Street of Thieves*. Trans. Charlotte Mandell. Rochester, NY: Open Letter, 2014. 254–5. For the purposes of close reading, the text is henceforth quoted in the French original and in the main text as *Rue* + page number. Mathias Énard. *Rue des voleurs*. Arles: Actes Sud, 2012.
2. Mathias Énard. 2014. 254.
3. Elleke Boehmer and Stephen Morton. 'Introduction: Terror and the Postcolonial'. *Terror and the Postcolonial*. Eds Elleke Boehmer and Stephen Morton. Malden and Oxford: Wiley-Blackwell, 2010. 1–24. 7.
4. Karim Alrawi. *Book of Sands: A Novel of the Arab Uprising*. Toronto: HarperCollins, 2015. Henceforth quoted in the main text as *Book of Sands* + page number.
5. That is, 'an era that has been marked by the US-led war on terror and the emergence of security as the *raison d'état*'. Stephen Morton and Stephen Bygrave. 'Introduction'. *Foucault in an Age of Terror: Essays on Biopolitics and the Defence of Society*. Eds Stephen Morton and Stephen Bygrace. Basingstoke and New York: Palgrave Macmillan, 2008. 1–13. 1.
6. Alex Houen. *Terrorism and Modern Literature: From Joseph Conrad to Ciaran Carson*. Oxford: Oxford University Press, 2002. 7.
7. Robert J. C. Young. 'Terror Effects'. *Terror and the Postcolonial*. Eds Elleke Boehmer and Stephen Morton. Malden and Oxford: Wiley-Blackwell, 2010. 307–28. 311–2.
8. Elleke Boehmer. 'Postcolonial Writing and Terror'. *Terror and the Postcolonial*. Eds Elleke Boehmer and Stephen Morton. Malden and Oxford: Wiley-Blackwell, 2010. 141–50. 144.
9. Ibid. 144.
10. Edward W. Said. 'Islam and the West are Inadequate Banners'. *The Observer*. 16 September 2001 (website – last accessed 15 December 2018).

11. Tarak Barkawi and Mark Laffey. 'The Postcolonial Moment in Security Studies'. *Review of International Studies* 32 (2006): 329–52. 329.
12. Ibid. 329.
13. Marc Botha. 'Toward a Critical Poetics of Securitization: A Response to Anker, Castronovo, Harkins, Masterson, and Williams'. *American Literary History* 28.4 (2016): 779–86. 783.
14. Eugene Victor Walter. *Terror and Resistance: A Study of Political Violence*. Oxford: Oxford University Press, 1969. 5.
15. See Charlotte Klonk. *Terror: Wenn Bilder zu Waffen werden*. Frankfurt: Fischer, 2017.
16. Elleke Boehmer. 'Postcolonial Writing and Terror'. 2010. 147.
17. Elleke Boehmer and Stephen Morton. 'Introduction: Terror and the Postcolonial'. 2010. 7.
18. Ibid. 7.
19. Judith Butler. *Precarious Life: The Powers of Mourning and Violence*. London and New York: Verso, 2004. 147; see also Daniel O'Gorman. *Fictions of the War on Terror: Difference and the Transnational 9/11 Novel*. Basingstoke and New York: Palgrave Macmillan, 2015. 8–9.
20. In fact, this figuration as a deuteragonist or secondary character appears to be on the rise: in Marc Trévidic's novel *Ahlam* (2016), the trajectory of the protagonist's brother is similar to Omar's and Bassam's radicalisation in *Book of Sands* and *Rue des voleurs*. Marc Trévidic. *Ahlam*. Paris: J. C. Lattès, 2016.
21. Pankaj Mishra. 'The Politics of Paranoia'. *The Guardian*. 17 September 2006 (website – last accessed 27 June 2017); Peter Morey and Amina Yaqin. *Framing Muslims: Stereotyping and Representation after 9/11*. Cambridge, MA: Harvard University Press. 2011. 2–3.
22. Sigmund Freud. *Civilization and Its Discontents* [1930]. *The Complete Psychological Works of Sigmund Freud – The Future of an Illusion, Civilization and its Discontents, and Other Works*. Trans. James Strachey. London: Hogarth Press, 1961. Vol. XXI, 79–80.
23. Riazat Butt. 'All the Rage – Victim of US Bloggers' Cartoon Hits Back'. *The Guardian*. 23 July 2007 (website – last accessed 8 October 2018).
24. Ibid.
25. As will be shown in the analyses below, both novels process this stereotype as an implicit norm. While their representations therefore contain striking similarities in their depiction of Islamist radicalisation, in direct comparison, *Book of Sands* paints a more differentiated picture of its deuteragonist than *Rue des voleurs*.

26. The following biographical information is gathered from: 'Book of Sands'. *HarperCollinsCanada*. No date (website – last accessed 18 December 2018); Rachel Rose. 'Karim Alrawi: What If?' *Guernica*. 16 November 2015 (website – last accessed 18 December 2018).
27. Quotation from the blurb on the cover of *Book of Sands*. 2015.
28. Elliptical sentences are frequent in the entire novel and are not linked to one character in particular. The omission of the cupola verb *to be*, which does not exist in Arabic, can be read as an effect of reality or as a stylistic device to create local colour.
29. Michel Foucault [1967]. 'Of Other Spaces: Utopias and Heterotopias'. Trans. Jay Miskowiec. *Rethinking Architecture: A Reader in Cultural Theory*. Ed. Neil Leach. New York: Routledge, 1997. 330–6. 332.
30. Pavan Kumar Malreddy. 'Post-Orientalism and Post-Multiculturalism in Contemporary Britain: Literary and Cinematic Representations of the London Bombings'. *Hard Times* 96 (2014): 32–5. 32.
31. With regard to the usage of the term 'female genital mutilation', Martha Nussbaum writes: 'Although discussions sometimes use the terms "female circumcision" and "clitoridectomy", "female genital mutilation" (FGM) is the standard generic term for all these procedures in the medical literature … The term "female circumcision" has been rejected by international medical practitioners because it suggests the fallacious analogy to male circumcision …' Martha Nussbaum. *Sex and Social Justice*. Oxford: Oxford University Press, 1999. 119.
32. Ad de Vries. 'Cockroach'. *Dictionary of Symbols and Imagery*. Amsterdam and London: North-Holland Publishing Company, 1974. 106.
33. Rawi Hage. *Cockroach*. Toronto: Anansi, 2008.
34. Caroline Wiedmer. *The Claims of Memory: Representations of the Holocaust in Contemporary Germany and France*. Ithaca and London: Cornell University Press, 1999. 19.
35. See, for instance, Julia Ebner. *The Rage: The Vicious Circle of Islamist and Far-Right Extremism*. London and New York: I. B. Tauris, 2017. 133.
36. Hamid Dabashi. *Post-Orientalism: Knowledge and Power in Time of Terror*. New Brunswick, NJ and London: Transaction, 2009. x.
37. Pankaj Mishra. 2006.
38. Kristin Husen and Wolfgang Lutz. 'Psychological and Clinical Perspectives on Trauma'. *Wor(l)ds of Trauma: Canadian and German Perspectives*. Ed. Wolfgang Klooß. Münster and New York: Waxmann, 2017. 25–37. 25–6.

39. Donatien Alphonse François de Sade [1791]. *Justine ou les Malheurs de la vertu*. Paris: Le Livre de Poche, 1973.
40. Chris Baldick. 'Magic Realism'. *Oxford Dictionary of Literary Terms*. Oxford: Oxford University Press, 2008. 194.
41. Elleke Boehmer. *Postcolonial Poetics: 21st-Century Critical Readings*. Basingstoke: Palgrave Macmillan, 2018. 69.
42. John T. Irwin. *The Mystery to a Solution: Poe, Borges, and the Analytic Detective Story*. Baltimore and London: Johns Hopkins University Press, 1994. 79.
43. Sarah Roger. *Borges and Kafka: Sons and Writers*. Oxford: Oxford University Press, 2017. 97.
44. For an example of a more differentiated and subversive portrayal of the issue of Islamist radicalisation, see Frauke Matthes's article on Feridun Zaimoğlu's 'Gottes Krieger'. Unlike the flat character of Omar who all of a sudden realises his mistake but whose deradicalisation is not shown, 'Zaimoğlu's narrator is an ambiguous figure: gradually turning away from radical Islamist ideas, he becomes consciously aware of his sexuality – and its "impurity", which he has been taught to detest.' Frauke Matthes. 'Of Kanaken and Gottes Krieger: Religion and Sexuality among Feridun Zaimoğlu's Young Muslim Men'. *Masculinities in German Culture: Edinburgh German Yearbook* 2 (2008): 250–61. 256.
45. Éric Fassin. 'National Identities and Transnational Intimacies: Sexual Democracy and the Politics of Immigration in Europe'. *Public Culture* 22.3 (2010): 507–29. 509.
46. Ibid. 509.
47. Désirée Schyns. '*Harraga* dans la littérature francophone: Boualem Sansal, Tahar Ben Jelloun, Mathias Enard et Marie Ndiaye'. *Romanische Studien* 3 (2016): 201–17. 209.
48. 'Mathias Énard'. *Actes Sud*. No date (website – last accessed 12 February 2019).
49. Oana Sabo. *The Migrant Canon in Twenty-First-Century France*. Lincoln, NE and London: University of Nebraska Press, 2018. 117.
50. 'Muslim Group for the Propagation of Koranic Thought'. Mathias Énard. 2014. 18.
51. Victor Turner defines liminal individuals as 'neither here nor there; they are betwixt and between the positions assigned and arrayed by law, custom, convention, and ceremony'. Victor Turner [1969]. *The Ritual Process: Structure and Anti-Structure*. New Brunswick, NJ and London: Aldine, 2008. 95. See also Ursula Lehmkuhl et al., eds. 'Spaces and Practices of Diversity: An

Introduction'. *Of 'Contact Zones' and 'Liminal Spaces': Mapping the Everyday Life of Cultural Translation*. Münster and New York: Waxmann, 2015. 7–27. 7.
52. Victor Turner [1969]. 2008. 95.
53. B. Carra de Vaux. 'Barza<u>k</u>h'. *Encyclopaedia of Islam*. 2nd edn. Ed. P. Bearman et al. (website – last accessed 27 February 2019).
54. Désirée Schyns. 2016. 206–7.
55. 'original sin'. Mathias Énard. 2014. 91.
56. Désirée Schyns. 2016. 207.
57. 'I've met guys who dreamed of going there, as tourists, to rent a pretty villa with a view of the sea, drink tea at the Café Hafa, smoke kif, and fuck natives, male natives for the most part but not exclusively, there are some who want to bang princesses from the *Arabian Nights* … and if they had known that the only ass I ogled before I was 18 was my cousin Meryem's they'd have fallen down laughing or wouldn't have believed me; they so associate Tangier with sensuality, with desire, with a permissiveness that it never had for us, but which is offered to the tourist in return for hard cash in the purse of misery.' Mathias Énard. 2014. 9–10.
58. 'no doubt because everyone thought there'd be sex in it, advice on positions, or weighty religious arguments so that women would allow certain practices …' Mathias Énard. 2014. 21.
59. '[M]y old man was pious, what they call a good man, a man of honor who mistreated neither his wife nor his children – aside from a few kicks in the backside now and then, which never harmed anyone.' Mathias Énard. 2014. 10.
60. 'I was generously offering him the most beautiful collection of asses on earth. Lying in the same direction, … breasts bare or not, some in thongs, others in modest one-pieces, a whole rainbow of girls unfurled before us – milk-white ones applying sunscreen; pink ones wearing hats to protect their faces; slightly tanned ones, bronze ones, black ones, many shades of ass, the triangular mounds hidden under swimsuits, breasts of all shapes and sizes and colors … a meter away from me I had, thighs slightly spread on a multicolored towel, a Nordic girl whose round ass was beginning to turn pink past the edges of her suit – you could make out her sex where the material puckered slightly, dented it into waves of softness where there peeked out, at the edge of the cloth, against the flesh, a few tiny blond hairs … I felt as if my head were between her legs and I wondered if my gaze had any effect on this cunt, so close; if, by staring at it for a long time, I could manage to make it warm, the way the sun sets fire to straw with its rays … The girl from the North scratched her lower

back, as if I had disturbed her, and I quickly looked away, by an idiotic reflex – unless Odin had provided his creatures with unheard-of abilities, the single eye that observed me from behind the garnet polyester was blind.' Mathias Énard. 2014. 240–1.
61. Michaël Ferrier. 'Mathias Énard, *Rue des voleurs*'. *Hommes et migrations* 1302 (2013): 1889–90. 189.
62. Michaël Ferrier. 2013. 189.
63. 'What prompted me to put myself in the shoes of Lakhdar is the complexity of today's world, the diversity of these cultures which mix. [I wanted to] show that when it comes to their aspirations, young Catalan people have a lot in common with those from Morocco, for instance. That Europe's destiny is nowadays inseparable from the destiny of the Arab world, that they mix.' Mathias Énard. 'L'identité est elle aussi en mouvement'. Interview by Catherine Simon. *Le Monde*. 4 September 2012 (website – last accessed 15 March 2019). My translation.
64. Désirée Schyns. 2016. 206–7.
65. Ibid. 206–7.
66. 'The TV was showing the demonstrations in Egypt, in Tunisia, in Yemen, the uprisings in Libya. It isn't over yet, I thought. Arab Spring my ass, it'll end with beatings, stuck between God and a hard place.' Mathias Énard. 2014. 32.
67. '[I]t was time to be a man, to move toward her like a man and kiss her on the mouth since that's what I wanted, what I dreamed about, and if we don't make an effort towards our dreams they disappear, nothing changes the world except hope or despair, in equal proportions, those who set themselves on fire in Sidi Bouzid, those who get beatings and bullets on Tahrir Square, and those who dare French-kiss a Spanish student in the street, obviously that has nothing to do with the others but for me, in that silence, that instant lost between two worlds, I needed as much courage to kiss Judit as to shout Qadafi! Bastard! in front of a jeep of Libyan soldiers or to yell Long Live the Republic of Morocco! alone smack in the middle of the Dar-el-Makhzen in Rabat …' Mathias Énard. 2014. 66–7.
68. Joseph Conrad [1902]. *Heart of Darkness*. London: Penguin, 1994. 110.
69. Wolfgang Klooß. 'Die Metaphorik des Kolonialismus: Joseph Conrads "Heart of Darkness" als Problem literarischer Wirklichkeitserfassung um die Jahrhundertwende'. *Germanisch-Romanische Monatsschrift* 31 (1981): 74–92.
70. Apart from Lakhdar's job with Cruz, the novel alludes to the insecurity of refugees through Mounir, the protagonist's flatmate in Barcelona. Mounir

is a refugee from Tunisia who, via Lampedusa, first comes to Paris, then to Barcelona. He tells Lakhdar of the shortage of dwellings and food for refugees. After he was attacked in France, he has taken to carrying a knife, and makes a living by pickpocketing tourists. Although he has a great dislike of Islamists, he cracks jokes which demonstrate how blurry the lines between the securitisation and insecurity of the figure of the illegal alien can become in the absence of better alternatives: 'Non, répondait-il, si Al-Qaida permet d'égorger les Infidèles, je ne vois pas pourquoi il serait interdit de les détrousser, et il partait d'un grand éclat de rire' (*Rue*: 268). 'No, he replied, if Al-Qaida allows infidels to be beheaded, I don't see why it's forbidden to pickpocket them, and he let out a big laugh.' Mathias Énard. 2014. 203.

71. For the controversial debate on how to read *Heart of Darkness*, see Chinua Achebe. 'An Image of Africa: Racism in Conrad's "Heart of Darkness"'. *Massachusetts Review* 18 (1977): 782–94.
72. Désirée Schyns. 2016. 207.
73. Ibid. 209.
74. 'the intellectual of the Street of Thieves'. Mathias Énard. 2014. 210.
75. 'I was getting a little foretaste of Paradise, may God forgive me, I lacked only the houris.' Mathias Énard. 2014. 199.
76. 'He had met the Group of Thought at Friday prayers, with his father. After seeing them for a while, they had gotten acquainted, and there you have it. They're the right kind of people, said Bassam. They come from Arabia and they're loaded.' Mathias Énard. 2014. 19.
77. '[T]he group saw the Arab revolts as the long-awaited green tide. Finally, genuine Muslim countries would stretch from the Atlantic Ocean to the Persian Gulf, they dreamed about them at night.' Mathias Énard. 2014. 26.
78. For racist undertones of images of waves, tides and floods, see for instance Siegfried Jäger. *BrandSätze: Rassismus im Alltag*. Duisburg: Diss-Studien, 1992. 15; François Héran. 'Les migrations à rebours des idées reçues'. Interview by Laure Cailloce. *CNRS: Le Journal*. 10 December 2018 (website – last accessed 20 May 2019).
79. Renaud Camus. *Le Grand Remplacement: Introduction au remplacisme global*. Neuilly-sur-Seine: David Reinharc, 2011. For the book's enormous influence in extreme right-wing circles and on racist terrorists such as Anders Breivik and Brenton Tarrant, see for instance Felix E. Müller. '"Le Grand Remplacement": Dieses Buch inspiriert rechtsradikale Terroristen'. *Neue Zürcher Zeitung*. 6 April 2019 (website – last accessed 20 May 2019).

80. 'The Group was like a pack of caged animals – they kept pacing in circles, waiting for night and the time for action.' Mathias Énard. 2014. 27.
81. 'neighborhood cleanup'. Mathias Énard. 2014. 27.
82. On page 37, Bassam is also 'en tête'. 'Bassam, anxious to avenge his broken nose on the first person to come along, was on the prowl for fights. They went out in bands of a dozen each, armed with cudgels and pickax handles after a belligerent, eloquent sermon by Sheikh Nureddin, which talked of the campaigns of the Prophet, the Battle of Badr, the Battle of the Trench, the fight against the Jewish tribe of the Banu Qaynuqa; about Hamza the hero, the glory of the martyrs in Paradise, and about the beauty, the great beauty of dying in battle. Then, very heated after this theoretical warm-up, they would move out into the night almost at a run, with Bassam's nerves and cudgel in the lead.' Mathias Énard. 2014. 28.
83. 'Bassam hit him hard, on the shoulder, it made a dull sound, he shouted in pain, ... Bassam pummeled his ribs with his cudgel, very spiritedly, the bookseller shouted again, swore profusely, Bassam started up again on his thigh, aiming for the bone, the man began groaning. Bassam was smiling, brandishing his stick. I wondered for an instant if he was going to smash my face in as well.' Mathias Énard. 2014. 29–30.
84. 'Bassam'. *QuranicNames*. No date (website – last accessed 18 March 2019).
85. 'Bassam had a stolid peasant's head, round, with little eyes. He went to the mosque every day, with his old man.' Mathias Énard. 2014. 11.
86. Mathias Énard. 2014. 37.
87. 'He was overexcited, as usual. He kept pacing in circles like a puppy around its mother's basket. – "What's happened to you now?" I asked. "One more guy to beat up?" – "No, this time it's bigger than that." – "Is it the Prophet's sword?" – "Stop your blasphemies, you degenerate. It's time for revenge." I thought for a minute that he was joking, but after I turned on the light I could see that his weaselly eyes shone with a strange madness, in the center of his thick peasant's head ... He fed me some vague paranoid theory according to which only an attack that would shock people's sensibilities would get things underway by precipitating the West, the population, and the Palace into confrontation. It was all Sheikh Nureddin, with hardly any Bassam. He had a tiny pea in place of a brain ... What's more, I knew very well that, in truth, he couldn't care less about political Islam.' Mathias Énard. 2014. 37.
88. 'But his eyes had lit up. That made a big impression, in his head.' Mathias Énard. 2014. 38.

89. 'weakness for stories about houris, who were always virgins you could fuck for eternity on the shores of Kawthar, the Lake of Abundance in the hereafter'. Mathias Énard. 2014. 38.
90. 'Bassam was literally licking his chops, his fat tongue slid over his upper lip to gather the last bits of chocolate shavings …' Mathias Énard. 2014. 42.
91. 'empty eyes, his blind man's eyes, his dog's eyes. It was Nureddin who answered for him: he was with me, completing his training.' Mathias Énard. 2014. 234.
92. 'His beaten mongrel's gaze returned to his plate, was he thinking of war, no, he must've been content to chew, his head empty.' Mathias Énard. 2014. 245.
93. 'If all of Sheikh Nureddin's recruits were as easy to manipulate as Bassam, the victory of Islam won't happen very soon.' Mathias Énard. 2014. 39.
94. 'Bassam was watching me with envy, Sheikh Nureddin had taken out the bills without hiding anything, Bassam had the right to another kind of pay: violence and danger.' Mathias Énard. 2014. 61.
95. '[H]e had the same round head and childlike face as Bassam, it could have been him.' Mathias Énard. 2014. 104.
96. 'But when I thought about it carefully I was also aware that, *a contrario*, just because he liked girls or dreamed of Germany and America didn't prevent anything whatsoever. I knew that Sheikh Nureddin had grown up in France, and when I had spoken with him about it he appreciated some aspects of the country and he acknowledged that, if not for living in the midst of *kuffar*, infidels, it was better to live in France than in Spain or Italy, where, he said, Islam was scorned, crushed, reduced to poverty.' Mathias Énard. 2014. 105.
97. Oana Sabo. 2018. 121.
98. 'I pictured him in his Land of Shadows, with the Khidr who carried his messages to me, that Land of Shadows where he wielded the sword, gun, or bomb, emboldened by prayer, with other fighters, strips of cloth tied around their heads, as they appear in videos online.' Mathias Énard. 2014. 114.
99. Brannon M. Wheeler. 'Moses or Alexander? Early Islamic Exegesis of Qur'ān 18:60–65'. *Journal of Near Eastern Studies* 57.3 (1998): 191–215. 200.
100. 'A sky of infinite blackness, that was what was waiting for us – today in my library, where the fury of the world has been muffled by the walls, I watch the series of cataclysms like one who, in a supposedly safe shelter, feels the floor vibrating, the walls trembling, and wonders how much longer he'll be able to preserve his life: outside, everything seems to be nothing but darkness.' Mathias Énard. 2014. 206.
101. 'the man who fired us up …' Mathias Énard. 2014. 236.

102. '[I]n the Barcelona subway I thought again of the explosion in Marrakesh, of Sheikh Nureddin somewhere in Arabia, and of Bassam, somewhere in the Land of Darkness, of the attack in Tangier where that student had met death by sword – of course, Barcelona was different, it was a democracy, but you felt it was all at a tipping point, that it wouldn't take much for the whole country to fall into violence and hatred as well, that France would follow, then Germany, and all of Europe would catch fire like the Arab world; the obscenity of this poster in the subway was proof of it, there was nothing else for Marrakesh to do than invest money in ad campaigns so that their lost manna would return, even if they knew perfectly well that it was the money from tourism that provoked underdevelopment, corruption and neo-colonialism, just as in Barcelona, little by little, you felt resentment against foreign cash mounting, cash from within as well as from without; money pitted the poor against each other, humiliation was slowly changing into hatred; everyone hated the Chinese, who were buying up the bars, restaurants, markets, one by one with the money of entire families who came from regions whose poverty couldn't even be imagined; everyone despised the British louts who came to quench their thirst with cheap beer, fuck in doorways, and, still drunk, take a plane back that had cost them the price of a pint of ale in their obscure suburb; everyone silently desired those very young Nordic girls the color of chalk who, because of the difference in temperature, broke out their miniskirts and flip-flops in February – one quarter of Catalonia was out of work, the papers overflowed with terrifying stories about the crisis, about families kicked out of apartments they couldn't pay for anymore, which the banks sold off cheaply while still continuing to claim their debt, about suicides, sacrifices, discouragement: you could feel the pressure mounting, violence mounting, even on the Street of Thieves among the poorest of the poor, even in Gràcia among the sons of the middle class, you could feel the city ready for anything, for resignation as well as for insurrection.' Mathias Énard. 2014. 203–4.

103. 'I thought of Bassam, lost somewhere in his own personal Jihad, who might have killed a student with a sword in Tangier, sometimes explaining serves no purpose; there's nothing to understand in violence, the violence of animals, mad from fear, from hatred, from blind stupidity that motivates a guy my age to coolly place the barrel of a gun to the temple of a little eight-year-old girl in a school, to change his weapons when the first one jams, with the calm that implies determination, and to fire in order to win the respect of some rats in Afghan caves.' Mathias Énard. 2014. 205.

104. 'a young guy was with him, with a shaved head and a black beard …' Mathias Énard. 2014. 232.
105. 'Bassam was sitting down again, he had stopped smiling; he had the disturbing gaze of a blind man or certain animals with frightened, fragile eyes which always seem to be staring off into the distance.' Mathias Énard. 2014. 233.
106. Claudia Brunner. *Wissensobjekt Selbstmordattentat: Epistemische Gewalt und okzidentalistische Selbstvergewisserung in der Terrorismusforschung*. Wiesbaden: VS Verlag, 2011. 220–340.
107. 'He kept cracking up in delight on his own like a kid, and it was a real joy to see his big fat bearded yokel's head smiling at the world.' Mathias Énard. 2014. 237.
108. '[H]e shook his head like a child caught with his hand in the cookie jar …' Mathias Énard. 2014. 250.
109. 'He let himself be dragged along like the puppy or child he had never stopped being.' Mathias Énard. 2014. 252.
110. 'reflexively …' Mathias Énard. 2014. 245.
111. 'Bassam, his eyes empty, a band of cloth around his forehead, was slitting Judit's throat like a sheep's, holding her by the hair.' Mathias Énard. 2014. 134.
112. 'wheel'. Mathias Énard. 2014. 265.
113. '[B]*e strong, the Hour may be near,* لَعَلَّ السَّاعَةَ تَكُونُ قَرِيباً …' Mathias Énard. 2014. 251. Italics in the original.
114. '*It could be that the Hour is near. God has cursed the Infidels and has prepared a burning furnace for them, where they will remain for eternity, without finding either ally or aid.*' Mathias Énard. 2014. 253. Italics in the original.
115. 'لَعَلَّ السَّاعَةَ تَكُونُ قَرِيباً, the verse was in the Al Ahzab Sura, "The Allies"; it was about the final hour, the hour of Judgment, when an eternal fire was promised for non-believers … Bassam must be waiting for the time to spark the flames of the apocalypse, which would explain why he was going round in circles in Barcelona …' Mathias Énard. 2014. 254.
116. 'the sword attack in Tangier, the dead in Marrakesh, the fighting, the summary executions in the Afghan underground …' Mathias Énard. 2014. 261.
117. 'I am not a murderer, I am more than that. / I am not a Moroccan, I am not a Frenchman, I'm not a Spaniard, I'm more than that. / I am not a Muslim, I am more than that. / Do what you will with me.' Mathias Énard. 2014. 263.
118. '[I]t was all a little depressing, I felt that whatever we did, the Arabs were condemned to violence and oppression.' Mathias Énard. 2014. 196.

119. 'The TV was showing the demonstrations in Egypt, in Tunisia, in Yemen, the uprisings in Libya. It isn't over yet, I thought. Arab Spring my ass, it'll end with beatings, stuck between God and a hard place.' Mathias Énard. 2014. 32.
120. 'She spoke to me mostly of current politics; of the crisis in Europe, its hardness, of unemployment, of poverty that was coming back, as if from the depths of Spanish history, she said, of conflicts, racism, tensions, the insurrection that was being prepared. She had gotten very involved in the Movement of the Indignants, for some months. Also very involved in the Spanish Occupy movement, *los Okupas*, she said. Repression had never been so violent. The other day a twenty-year-old student lost an eye from being hit with a rubber bullet when the cops broke up a peaceful sit-in, she said. Spain is heading for its end, Europe too. Ultra-liberal propaganda would have us believe we can't resist the diktat of the markets. Here they won't take care anymore of the poor, the old, the foreigners. Right now the revolution is delayed because of soccer, Real, Barça; but when that's not enough to make up for frustration and poverty, then there'll be riots, she said. I watched her, I wanted to take her hand, not talk about the crisis.' Mathias Énard. 2014. 183.
121. See, for instance, Lorella Ventura. 'The "Arab Spring" and Orientalist Stereotypes: The Role of Orientalism in the Narration of the Revolts in the Arab World'. *Interventions* 19.2 (2017): 282–97; Stefan Borg. 'The Arab Uprisings, the Liberal Civilizing Narrative and the Problem of Orientalism'. *Middle East Critique* 25.3 (2016): 211–27; Dipesh Chakrabarty. *Provincializing Europe: Postcolonial Thought and Historical Difference*. Princeton: Princeton University Press, 2000.
122. Tarak Barkawi and Mark Laffey. 2006. 350.
123. Claudia Brunner. 2011. 15.
124. Philipp Sarasin uses the term of the 'ganz anderen Anderen' in *Geschichtswissenschaft und Diskursanalyse*. Frankfurt: Suhrkamp, 2003. 49. Quoted in: Claudia Brunner. 2011. 22.
125. Claudia Brunner. 2011. 32.
126. Edmund Burke [1757]. *A Philosophical Enquiry into the Origin of Our Ideas of the Sublime and the Beautiful*. Ed. Paul Guyer. Oxford: Oxford University Press, 2015. 34.
127. Jill Bennett. 'The Limits of Empathy and the Global Politics of Belonging'. *Trauma at Home: After 9/11*. Ed. Judith Greenberg. Lincoln, NE and London: University of Nebraska Press, 2003. 132–38. 134. Quoted in: Daniel

O'Gorman. *Fictions of the War on Terror: Difference and the Transnational 9/11 Novel*. Basingstoke and New York: Palgrave Macmillan, 2015. 17.
128. In this, the figuration of Islamist Rage Boy is reminiscent of what Dag Tuastad calls the 'new barbarism' thesis, which casts violence as 'the product of backward cultures' while 'omit[ting] political and economic interests and contexts'. Dag Tuastad. 'Neo-Orientalism and the New Barbarism Thesis: Aspects of Symbolic Violence in the Middle East Conflict(s)'. *Third World Quarterly* 24.4 (2003): 591–9. 591.
129. Ibid. 591.
130. Judith Butler. 'Precarious Life, Vulnerability, and the Ethics of Cohabitation'. *The Journal of Speculative Philosophy* 26.2 (2012): 134–51. 150.
131. Claudia Brunner. 2011. 32.
132. Edmund Burke [1757]. 2015. 34.
133. Robert J. C. Young. 2010. 313.
134. Ibid. 319.
135. Ibid. 319.

6

THE ARAB UPRISINGS BETWEEN INEQUALITY, INSECURITY AND IDENTITY

In the ten years since the beginning of the Arab uprisings, the so-called Arab Spring and its repercussions have not only become the object of considerable media coverage and innumerable academic analyses, they have also often been fictionalised. In fact, there have been so many fictional adaptations of the uprisings that what the Egyptian author Youssef Rakha calls the 'Arab Spring Industry'[1] now also constitutes a segment on the Western literary market. This segment includes a small number of texts – mostly in translation or written by diasporic writers – which paint a differentiated picture of the uprisings and their continuing revolutionary potential.[2] Most Western fictionalisations of the uprisings, however, barely grant any representational space to the revolutions themselves, and hardly any of the texts prioritise the revolutionary claims for bread, freedom and social justice. Instead, these texts are often deeply preoccupied with a self-referential processing of the uprisings. This processing frequently manifests in the books' predominantly unsuccessful attempts at distancing themselves from Orientalist and Neo-Orientalist forms of representation. Although most of the books try to overcome such forms of representation, they often replicate the very stereotypes which they try to surmount. In fact, this tendency is so strong – and marketable – that it is also discernable in some works by diasporic authors.

Through their transnational and comparatist design, the preceding close readings of the works of non-diasporic and diasporic authors have not only unfolded striking similarities of narrative structures and configurations which transcend the Orientalist literary traditions of individual countries, but they have also revealed the transnational impact of Neo-Orientalism. While most of the Western representations of the Arab uprisings struggle to transcend inveterate clichés and dichotomous modes of representing the Islamicate Other, they still rely on stereotypes which cast the Other as allegedly affect-driven, prone to violence, lust and passivity, backward or as incapable of establishing democracy or rule of law – even if often in an ironic or self-referential way. Moreover, most of the works adopt frames of insecurity, difference and distance to depict the Arab uprisings. As a consequence, although the texts feature narrative attempts to overcome individual stereotypes, this endeavour proves futile because the overarching frames of insecurity and distance in which they present these stereotypes remain mostly unchallenged. Fundamental reframings in different contexts of meaning are thus the exception rather than the rule. This lack of reframings does not only hinder a deconstruction or de-essentialising of dichotomies, but – as the figuration of the Islamist Rage Boy most starkly illustrates – it also fosters a securitisation of the Orient and an Orientalisation of insecurity.

Taken together, the close readings consequently show that whereas most Western and some diasporic fictionalisations of the Arab uprisings can be read as attempts to overcome the paradigm of Orientalism, these texts still adopt a poetics which relies on dichotomous ideas of proximity and distance. While the demands of the literary market thus indicate an interest in books which can be marketed as open-minded cosmopolitan or as 'authentic' diasporic literature, securitisation takes a subtle but nonetheless pernicious form here: in the guise of seemingly tolerant literature, it provides and reiterates an imaginary which purports to overcome itself but which instead further inscribes itself through a Neo-Orientalist poetics.

Interestingly, *Frühling der Barbaren* can be read as a meta-comment on this Neo-Orientalist ambivalence. Firstly, through its ironic use of intertexts, the novella illustrates how the construct of the Orient exists mainly as a bourgeois or capitalist form of art or entertainment which conceals systemic injustice. Secondly, by subverting its own novella form and by turning its protagonist's refusal to assume responsibility into the actual focal point of its story, *Frühling der Barbaren* can also be read as a critique of the narrative situation in works such as Adam Thirlwell's *Kapow!* and Jochen Beyse's *Rebellion*: in both texts, the narrators distance themselves from their own representations by referring to their alcohol and drug use and by means of postmodern narrative strategies, most importantly irony.[3] In contrast, *Frühling der Barbaren* centres on an artful criticism of this avoidance of narratorial responsibility, and questions the ideas of proximity and distance which importantly influence the way in which the precarity of others is perceived in terms of injustice. As a result of this reframing, *Frühling der Barbaren* presents insecurity not as a consequence of backwardness, the inability to establish democracy or Islamist fundamentalism; instead, the novella depicts insecurity as a consequence of the neo-liberal system, and highlights how in this system, it is not just Western security which is at stake.

However, such questioning of the Western-centric, classist concept of security remains an exception. In most Western – and also some of the diasporic – fictionalisations, the Arab uprisings serve as a foil against which the West's own insecurities are negotiated, while the revolutionary claims have been suppressed by a Neo-Orientalist discourse of insecurity.

Literature, Insecurity and Inequality

If the discussion about freedom versus security remains virulent in liberal societies, this debate is often externalised by means of the Islamicate Other. In this, aestheticised discourses of insecurity frequently serve as a means of refracting internal, systemic problems into a pronounced and marketable Othering. However, the adverse consequences of the neo-liberal project do not only affect those who refract their own insecurities into a poetics of the securitised Other. As those who are erroneously suspected of constituting a threat also often suffer from high precarity, this predominance of a Western-centric and classist concept of security, perpetuated by traditional security studies and also informing the first investigation of a poetics of insecurity,[4] is urgently in need of postcolonial alternatives.[5]

In such a critique of the predominance of biased discourses of insecurity, the domain of literature is interesting in several regards. As Ziauddin Sardar proffers, '[n]ovelists are no longer just novelists – they are also global pundits shaping our opinions on everything from art, life, and politics to civilisation as we know it.'[6] As discussed in Chapter One, this special role of literary figures plays an important part in Neo-Orientalist discourse and its demands for 'authenticity'. What is more, literature and security are also connected in their relationship to the realm of the fictional: if for a long time, security thinking has operated with the principle of risk, not least since the 9/11 attacks, scenario techniques have become more important.[7] While the principle of risk is based on probability and prognosis, scenario techniques – which engage in the consideration of different conceivable futures – are not centred on probability, but on possibility. Evoking possible catastrophes not to prevent them, but to better prepare for their aftermath, scenario techniques do not only enter the realm of the fictional by imagining possible futures, but in this, they rely on the principle of verisimilitude. As especially in scenarios of future threats, the real thus operates according to the rules of the fictional,[8] the fictional is where the realms of security and literature overlap.

In Neo-Orientalist refractions of the Arab uprisings, this overlap between security and literature manifests itself in a poetics of insecurity. At the level of stylistics, this poetics of insecurity relies on difference, distance and danger, on animal and fire imagery and on the use of increasingly dangerous heterolingual elements in Arabic. In its postmodern inflection, the poetics of insecurity tries to challenge unequivocal representations of insecurity. Rather than as a given fact, insecurity is thus presented in ambiguous terms. On the one hand, if the stylistic devices used were not such well-established postmodern devices, this attempt to create uncertainty about stereotypes could be read as an extension of the issue of insecurity from the level of content to the level of form. On the other hand, it could also be read as an attempt to subvert the alleged stability of images associated with insecurity and to thus undermine the security paradox. This paradox results from the fact that, so as to create acceptance for drastic measures used in the name of security, there is in fact an increased representation of alarming images or measures which create more insecurity. Due to the recognition value of well-known representational structures, these images, in turn, provide some reassurance and a deceptive impression of security.

In addition to these narratological insights, the preceding analyses more importantly are geared towards a critical deconstruction of aestheticised discourses of insecurity and their reliance on a pronounced Othering. By showing how a poetics of insecurity, marketable though it is on the Western literary market, serves to refract the adverse consequences of the neo-liberal project onto the allegedly problematic Other, they have not only demonstrated the role of aesthetics in securitisation. By examining the inextricable link between securitisation and Othering, between security and difference,[9] they also serve as a reminder that security is a not only a highly racialised and gendered, but also a highly classist concept.

For this classist dimension of security, it is hardly surprising that security concerns can easily be co-opted in reductionist analyses of identity politics. Indeed, Western fictionalisations of the Arab uprisings are a prime example of how a strong focus on identity and alterity often obliterates questions of economic inequality.[10] Because of this, and as explained in Chapter One, securitisation – especially when aestheticised in the form of a poetics of insecurity – can in fact serve as a means used to play off different precarious groups against each other.[11] Far from causing creative discomfort only, a poetics of insecurity is thus complicit not only in the co-optation of some postcolonial writing, but it is also instrumental in upholding a focus on the security of the few while being without caring – *sine cura*, as the etymology of security reads[12] – about 'most of the world'.[13]

Notes

1. Quoted in Nahrain Al-Mousawi. 'Literature After the Arab Spring'. *Middle East Institute*. 5 February 2016 (website – last accessed 15 March 2021).
2. For an overview of the literary adaptations of the Arab uprisings published on the Western market, see Chapter Two.
3. For a critique of postmodern simulacra in representations of the Egyptian revolution, see Caroline Rooney. 'Popular Culture and the Arab Spring'. *The Edinburgh Companion to the Postcolonial Middle East*. Eds Anna Ball and Karim Mattar. Edinburgh: Edinburgh University Press, 2018. 407–26. 420; Maha El Said. 'Alternating Images: Simulacra of Ideology in Egyptian Advertisements'. *Popular Culture in the Middle East and North Africa*. Eds Walid El Hamamsy and Mounira Soliman. New York and Abingdon: Routledge, 2013. 211–30. 226.
4. Johannes Voelz. *The Poetics of Insecurity: American Fiction and the Uses of Threat*. Cambridge: Cambridge University Press, 2018. A brief caveat regarding systemic injustice notwithstanding (19), *The Poetics of Insecurity* does not consider the connection between discourses of insecurity, structural discrimination and

precarity. While the study takes a 'post-rank social order' (17) as its starting point and thus backgrounds the classist dimension of security thinking, the 'subject of security' (15) whom the book presupposes does not include the many of the world. So although *The Poetics of Insecurity* tries to foreground the issue of agency, it follows the conceptualisation of security in traditional security studies in its limited consideration of who acts and is affected by security thinking. Thus neglecting questions of precarity by focusing on vulnerability only, the study conceptualises vulnerability and uncertainty as resources: 'Since the imaginary appeal of security arises from the manifold opportunities that grow out of our vulnerabilities, vulnerability itself becomes a prized resource for the imagination' (188).
5. Mark Laffey and Suthaharan Nadarajah. 'Postcolonialism'. *Contemporary Security Studies*. Ed. Alan Collins. Oxford: Oxford University Press, 2016. 122–38.
6. Ziauddin Sardar. 'The Blitcon Supremacists'. *The Guardian*. 9 December 2006 (website – last accessed 15 March 2021).
7. Susanne Krasmann. 'Die Regierung der Sicherheit – Über das Mögliche und das Fiktive'. *Foucaultblog*. 5 December 2013 (website – last accessed 15 March 2021).
8. Ibid.
9. For more on the relationship between security and difference, see Anja Krause and Sigrid Ruby, eds. *Sicherheit und Differenz in historischer Perspektive / Security and Difference in Historical Perspective*. Baden-Baden: Nomos, forthcoming.
10. Walter Benn Michaels. 'Let Them Eat Diversity: On the Politics of Identity'. Interview by Bhaskar Sunkara. *Jacobin*. 1 January 2011 (website – last accessed 5 January 2021).
11. Zygmunt Bauman. *Strangers at Our Door*. Cambridge: Polity Press, 2016. 17–18.
12. 'Security'. *Oxford English Dictionary*. No date (website – last accessed 29 September 2017); Giorgio Agamben. 'De l'État de droit à l'État de sécurité'. *Le Monde*. 23 December 2015 (website – last accessed 22 September 2017).
13. Partha Chatterjee. *The Politics of the Governed: Reflections on Popular Politics in Most of the World*. New York: Columbia University Press, 2004.

REFERENCES

Aarseth, Espen J. *Cybertext: Perspectives on Ergodic Literature*. Baltimore: Johns Hopkins University Press, 1997.

Abdel Aziz, Basma. *Here Is a Body*. Trans. Jonathan Wright. Cairo: Hoopoe, 2021.

Abdel Aziz, Basma [2013]. *The Queue*. Trans. Elisabeth Jaquette. New York: Melville House, 2016.

'About'. *Visual Editions.* No date (website – last accessed 15 January 2021).

Achebe, Chinua. 'An Image of Africa: Racism in Conrad's "Heart of Darkness"'. *Massachusetts Review* 18 (1977): 782–94.

Agamben, Giorgio. 'De l'État de droit à l'État de sécurité'. *Le Monde.* 23 December 2015 (website – last accessed 22 September 2017).

Agamben, Giorgio. *Homo Sacer: Die souveräne Macht und das nackte Leben*. Trans. Hubert Thüring. Frankfurt: Suhrkamp, 2002.

Agamben, Giorgio. *Homo Sacer: Sovereign Power and Bare Life*. Trans. Daniel Heller-Roazen. Stanford: Stanford University Press, 1998.

Agamben, Giorgio. 'On Security and Terror'. Trans. Soenke Zehle. *Libcom.org.* 24 September 2006 (website – last accessed 28 August 2017). Originally published in *Frankfurter Allgemeine Zeitung.* 20 September 2001.

Ahmed, Sara. *The Cultural Politics of Emotion*. 2nd edn. Edinburgh: Edinburgh University Press, 2014.

Al Aswani, Alaa [2018]. *Die Republik der Träumer*. Trans. Markus Lemke. Munich: Hanser, 2021.

Al Aswani, Alaa. *On the State of Egypt: What Caused the Revolution*. Trans. Jonathan Wright. Edinburgh: Canongate, 2011.

Al Aswani, Alaa [2018]. *The Republic of False Truths*. Trans. S. R. Fellowes. London: Faber & Faber, 2021.

Al Aswani, Alaa [2002]. *The Yacoubian Building*. Trans. Humphrey T. Davies. Cairo: The American University in Cairo Press, 2004.

Albakry, Mohammed and Rebekah Maggor, eds. *Tahrir Plays: Plays From the Egyptian Revolution*. Chicago: University of Chicago Press, 2016.

Alexander, Anne and Mostafa Bassiouny. *Bread, Freedom, Social Justice: Workers and the Egyptian Revolution*. London: Zed Books, 2014.

Al Khamissi, Khaled [2006]. *Taxi*. Trans. Jonathan Wright. London: Aflame Books, 2008.

Al Khamissi, Khaled and Stefan Weidner. 'Arabischer Frühling'. Trans. Günther Orth. *Qantara.de*. 19 May 2011 (website – last accessed 10 January 2020).

Al-Mousawi, Nahrain. 'Literature After the Arab Spring'. *Middle East Institute*. 5 February 2016 (website – last accessed 15 March 2021).

Alrawi, Karim. *Book of Sands: A Novel of the Arab Uprising*. Toronto: HarperCollins, 2015.

Altwaiji, Mubarak. 'Neo-Orientalism and the Neo-Imperialism Thesis: Post-9/11 US and Arab World Relationship'. *Arab Studies Quarterly* 36.4 (2014): 313–23.

Al-Zubaidi, Layla, Matthew Cassel and Nemonie Craven Roderick, eds. *Writing Revolution: The Voices from Tunis to Damascus*. London: I. B. Tauris, 2013.

Amar, Paul. 'Middle East Masculinity Studies: Discourses of "Men in Crisis", Industries of Gender in Revolution'. *Journal of Middle East Women's Studies* 7.3 (2011): 36–70.

Amar, Paul. 'Turning the Gendered Politics of the Security State Inside Out? Charging the Police with Sexual Harassment in Egypt'. *International Feminist Journal of Politics* 13.3 (2011): 299–328.

Amin-Khan, Tariq. 'New Orientalism, Securitisation and the Western Media's Incendiary Racism'. *Third World Quarterly* 33.9 (2012): 1595–610.

Aravamudan, Srinivas. 'East–West Fiction as World Literature: The *Hayy* Problem Reconfigured'. *Eighteenth-Century Studies* 47.2 (2014): 195–231.

Aschauer, Wolfgang. 'Die Wahrnehmung von Umbrüchen, Ungleichheiten und Unsicherheiten als neue Erklärungsfaktoren der Fremden- und Islamfeindlichkeit in Europa'. *Identität und Inklusion im europäischen Sozialraum*. Eds Elisabeth

Klaus, Clemens Sedmak, Ricarda Drüeke and Gottfried Schweiger. Wiesbaden: VS Verlag, 2010. 87–112.

Ateş, Seyran. *Der Islam braucht eine sexuelle Revolution: Eine Streitschrift*. Berlin: Ullstein, 2009.

Atia, Nadia. 'Queering the Arab Spring: Belonging in Saleem Haddad's *Guapa*'. *Wasafiri* 34.2 (2019): 54–60.

Bachmann, Ingeborg [1978]. *Das Buch Franza / Requiem für Fanny Goldmann. Texte des 'Todesarten'-Projekts*. Eds Monika Albrecht and Dirk Göttsche. Munich: Piper, 2004.

Baker, Mona, ed. *Translating Dissent: Voices from and with the Egyptian Revolution*. New York and Abingdon: Routledge, 2016.

Baldick, Chris. 'Magic Realism'. *Oxford Dictionary of Literary Terms*. Oxford: Oxford University Press, 2008. 194.

Ball, Anna, and Karim Mattar. 'Dialectics of Post/Colonial Modernity in the Middle East: A Critical, Theoretical and Disciplinary Overview'. *The Edinburgh Companion to the Postcolonial Middle East*. Eds Anna Ball and Karim Mattar. Edinburgh: Edinburgh University Press, 2019. 3–22.

Barkawi, Tarak and Mark Laffey. 'The Postcolonial Moment in Security Studies'. *Review of International Studies* 32 (2006): 329–52.

Barthes, Roland. *Mythologies*. Paris: Seuil, 1957.

'Bassam'. *QuranicNames*. No date (website – last accessed 18 March 2019).

Bauman, Zygmunt. *Strangers at Our Door*. Cambridge: Polity Press, 2016.

Beck, Ulrich. *Risikogesellschaft: Auf dem Weg in eine andere Moderne*. Frankfurt: Suhrkamp, 1986.

Behdad, Ali and Juliet Williams. 'Neo-Orientalism'. *Globalizing American Studies*. Eds Brian T. Edwards and Gaonkar Dilip Parameshwar. Chicago: University of Chicago Press, 2010. 283–99.

Ben Jelloun, Tahar. *By Fire: Writings on the Arab Spring*. Trans. Rita S. Nezami. Evanston: Curbstone/Northwestern University Press, 2016.

Ben Jelloun, Tahar. *Cette aveuglante absence de lumière*. Paris: Seuil, 2001.

Ben Jelloun, Tahar. *L'Étincelle: Révoltes dans les pays arabes*. Paris: Gallimard, 2011.

Ben Jelloun, Tahar. *L'Islam expliqué aux enfants*. Paris: Seuil, 2002.

Ben Jelloun, Tahar. *Par le feu: Récit*. Paris: Gallimard, 2011.

Ben Jelloun, Tahar [2011]. *Par le feu*. Stuttgart: Klett, 2014.

Ben Jelloun, Tahar. 'Que peut la littérature, le cas du printemps arabe?' Opening speech of the International Literature Festival Berlin 2011. 10 August 2011 (website – last accessed 22 October 2017).

Bennett, Jill. 'The Limits of Empathy and the Global Politics of Belonging'. *Trauma at Home: After 9/11*. Ed. Judith Greenberg. Lincoln, NE and London: University of Nebraska Press, 2003. 132–138.

Bertrand, Sarah. 'Can the Subaltern Securitize? Postcolonial Perspectives on Securitization Theory and Its Critics'. *European Journal of International Security* 3.3 (2018): 281–99.

Beyse, Jochen. *Rebellion: Zwischenbericht*. Zurich and Berlin: Diaphanes, 2013.

Bhattacharyya, Gargi. *Dangerous Brown Men: Exploiting Sex, Violence and Feminism in the Age of Terror*. London and New York: Zed Books, 2008.

Biskamp, Floris. *Orientalismus und demokratische Öffentlichkeit: Antimuslimischer Rassismus aus Sicht postkolonialer und neuerer kritischer Theorie*. Bielefeld: Transcript, 2016.

Blandfort, Julia. 'Die Arabischen Revolutionen aus frankophoner Perspektive: Intellektuelle Interventionen als transkultureller Diskurs? Zur Einleitung'. *HeLix* 9 (2016): 1–21.

Bloch, Werner. 'Egypt's Culture on Four Wheels'. *Qantara.de*. 13 March 2011 (website – last accessed 10 January 2020).

Boehmer, Elleke. *Postcolonial Poetics: 21st-Century Critical Readings*. Basingstoke: Palgrave Macmillan, 2018.

Boehmer, Elleke. 'Postcolonial Writing and Terror'. *Terror and the Postcolonial*. Eds Elleke Boehmer and Stephen Morton. Malden and Oxford: Wiley-Blackwell, 2010. 141–50.

Boehmer, Elleke and Stephen Morton. 'Introduction: Terror and the Postcolonial'. *Terror and the Postcolonial*. Eds Elleke Boehmer and Stephen Morton. Malden and Oxford: Wiley-Blackwell, 2010. 1–24.

Boer, Inge E. *Disorienting Vision: Rereading Stereotypes in French Orientalist Texts and Images*. Ed. Mieke Bal. Amsterdam and New York: Rodopi, 2004.

'Book of Sands'. *HarperCollinsCanada*. No date (website – last accessed 18 December 2018).

Borg, Stefan. 'The Arab Uprisings, the Liberal Civilizing Narrative and the Problem of Orientalism'. *Middle East Critique* 25.3 (2016): 211–27.

Botha, Marc. 'Toward a Critical Poetics of Securitization: A Response to Anker, Castronovo, Harkins, Masterson, and Williams'. *American Literary History* 28.4 (2016): 779–86.

Brunner, Claudia. *Wissensobjekt Selbstmordattentat: Epistemische Gewalt und okzidentalistische Selbstvergewisserung in der Terrorismusforschung*. Wiesbaden: VS Verlag, 2011.

Buch, Hans Christoph. *Tod in Habana*. Frankfurt: Frankfurter Verlagsanstalt, 2007.
Bude, Heinz. *Gesellschaft der Angst*. Hamburg: Hamburger Edition, 2015.
Burke, Edmund [1757]. *A Philosophical Enquiry into the Origin of Our Ideas of the Sublime and the Beautiful*. Ed. Paul Guyer. Oxford: Oxford University Press, 2015.
Butler, Judith. *Frames of War: When is Life Grievable?* London: Verso, 2009.
Butler, Judith. *Precarious Life: The Powers of Mourning and Violence*. London and New York: Verso, 2004.
Butler, Judith. 'Precarious Life, Vulnerability, and the Ethics of Cohabitation'. *The Journal of Speculative Philosophy* 26.2 (2012): 134–51.
Butt, Riazat. 'All the Rage – Victim of US Bloggers' Cartoon Hits Back'. *The Guardian*. 23 July 2007 (website – last accessed 8 October 2018).
Buzan, Barry, Ole Wæver and Jaap de Wilde: *Security: A New Framework for Analysis*. Boulder: Lynne Rienner, 1998.
'Camel'. *The Penguin Dictionary of Symbols*. Alain Gheerbrant and Jean Chevalier. Trans. John Buchanan-Brown. London: Penguin, 1996. 149.
Camus, Renaud. *Le Grand Remplacement: Introduction au remplacisme global*. Neuilly-sur-Seine: David Reinharc, 2011.
Carra de Vaux, B. 'Barzakh'. *Encyclopaedia of Islam*. 2nd edn. Ed. P. Bearman et al. (website – last accessed 27 February 2019).
Cartwright, Mark. 'Dido'. *Ancient History Encyclopedia*. 29 June 2016 (website – last accessed 1 March 2018).
Casanova, Pascale. *The World Republic of Letters*. Cambridge, MA: Harvard University Press, 2004.
Cesari, Jocelyne. *Securitization and Religious Divides in Europe: Muslims in Western Europe after 9/11: Why the Term Islamophobia is More a Predicament than an Explanation*. Submission to the Changing Landscape of Citizenship and Security – 6th PCRD of European Commission. Paris, 2006.
Chakrabarty, Dipesh. *Provincializing Europe: Postcolonial Thought and Historical Indifference*. Princeton: Princeton University Press, 2000.
Chassany, Anne-Sylvaine. 'France: The Permanent State of Emergency'. *Financial Times*. 2 October 2017 (website – last accessed 4 October 2017).
Chatterjee, Partha. *The Politics of the Governed: Reflections on Popular Politics in Most of the World*. New York: Columbia University Press, 2004.
Cheng, Jennifer E. 'Islamophobia, Muslimophobia or Racism? Parliamentary Discourses on Islam and Muslims in Debates on the Minaret Ban in Switzerland'.

Discourse and Society 26.5 (2015): 562–86. Accessed in web format with page numbers 1–15.
Chrisafis, Angelique. 'Ben Ali Will Not Attend Tunisia Trial for Theft and Fraud'. *The Guardian*. 17 June 2011 (website – last accessed 15 January 2018).
Conrad, Joseph [1902]. *Heart of Darkness*. London: Penguin, 1994.
Cuddon, J. A. 'Novella'. *Dictionary of Literary Terms & Literary Theory*. 3rd edn. London et al.: Penguin, 1999. 600–1.
Cuddon, J. A. 'Orientalism'. *Dictionary of Literary Terms & Literary Theory*. 3rd edn. London et al.: Penguin, 1999. 618–22.
Dabashi, Hamid. *Post-Orientalism: Knowledge and Power in Time of Terror*. New Brunswick, NJ and London: Transaction, 2009.
Dabashi, Hamid. *The Arab Spring: The End of Postcolonialism?* London and New York: Zed Books, 2012.
Danielewski, Mark Z. *House of Leaves*. New York: Pantheon Books, 2000.
Danielewski, Mark Z. *Only Revolutions*. New York: Pantheon Books, 2006.
Decker, Oliver, Johannes Kiess and Elmar Brähler. *Die enthemmte Mitte: Autoritäre und rechtsextreme Einstellung in Deutschland*. Gießen: Psychosozial-Verlag, 2016.
'Der Leser spielt mit'. *Neue Zürcher Zeitung*. 9 October 2015 (website – last accessed 15 January 2021).
Dietze, Gabriele. 'Ethnosexismus: Sex-Mob-Narrative um die Kölner Sylvesternacht [sic]'. *Movements* 1 (2016): 177–85.
Dietze, Gabriele. 'Sexualitätsdispositiv Revisited: Die Figuration des "Arabischen Mannes" als Abwehrfigur neoliberaler Freiheit'. *Der inspizierte Muslim*. Ed. Schirin Amir-Moazami. Bielefeld: Transcript, 2018. 215–45.
Dressler, Markus, Armando Salvatore and Monika Wohlrab-Sahr. 'Islamicate Secularities: New Perspectives on a Contested Concept'. *Historical Social Research* 44.3 (2019): 7–34.
Eberl, Oliver. *Naturzustand und Barbarei: Begründung und Kritik staatlicher Ordnung im Zeichen des Kolonialismus*. Hamburg: Hamburger Edition, 2021.
Ebner, Julia. *The Rage: The Vicious Circle of Islamist and Far-Right Extremism*. London and New York: I. B. Tauris, 2017.
Economic Diversification in Africa: A Review of Selected Countries. OECD/United Nations: OECD Publishing, 2011.
Edmunds, June. 'The "New" Barbarians: Governmentality, Securitization and Islam in Western Europe'. *Contemporary Islam* 6.1 (2012): 67–84.

Ehrenberg, Alain [1998]. *Das erschöpfte Selbst: Depression und Gesellschaft in der Gegenwart*. Trans. Manuela Lenzen and Martin Klaus. Frankfurt and New York: Campus Bibliothek, 2015.

El-Aswad, el-Sayed. 'Images of Muslims in Western Scholarship and Media after 9/11'. *Digest of Middle East Studies* 22.1 (2013): 39–56.

Elias, Norbert. *Über den Prozeß der Zivilisation*. Vol. 1. Frankfurt: Suhrkamp, 1976.

El Qasri, Jamal. 'Le Degré zéro de l'émotion dans *Par le feu* de Tahar Ben Jelloun'. *HeLix* 9 (2016): 61–8.

El Said, Maha. 'Alternating Images: Simulacra of Ideology in Egyptian Advertisements'. *Popular Culture in the Middle East and North Africa*. Eds Walid El Hamamsy and Mounira Soliman. New York and Abingdon: Routledge, 2013. 211–30.

El Shafee, Magdy [2008]. *Metro*. Trans. Chip Rossetti. New York: Macmillan, 2012.

Énard, Mathias. 'L'identité est elle aussi en mouvement'. Interview by Catherine Simon. *Le Monde*. 4 September 2012 (website – last accessed 15 March 2019).

Énard, Mathias. *Rue des voleurs*. Arles: Actes Sud, 2012.

Énard, Mathias. *Street of Thieves*. Trans. Charlotte Mandell. Rochester, NY: Open Letter, 2014.

Fabian, Johannes. *Time and the Other: How Anthropology Makes Its Object*. New York: Columbia University Press, 1983.

Farris, Sara R. *In the Name of Women's Rights: The Rise of Femonationalism*. Durham, NC: Duke University Press, 2017.

Fassin, Éric. 'National Identities and Transnational Intimacies: Sexual Democracy and the Politics of Immigration in Europe'. *Public Culture* 22.3 (2010): 507–29.

Fekete, Liz. 'Enlightened Fundamentalism? Immigration, Feminism and the Right'. *Race & Class* 48.2 (2006): 1–22.

Ferrier, Michaël. 'Mathias Énard, *Rue des voleurs*'. *Hommes et migrations* 1302 (2013): 1889–90.

Feurer, Martina. *Psychoanalytische Theorien des Denkens: S. Freud – D. W. Winnicott – P. Aulagnier – W. R. Bion – A. Green*. Würzburg: Königshausen & Neumann, 2011.

Forderer, Christof. 'Der rasende Stillstand'. *Taz*. 8 September 2012 (website – last accessed 15 July 2018).

Foucault, Michel. *Folie et déraison: Histoire de la folie à l'âge classique*. Paris: Gallimard, 1972.

Foucault, Michel [1967]. 'Of Other Spaces: Utopias and Heterotopias'. Trans. Jay Miskowiec. *Rethinking Architecture: A Reader in Cultural Theory*. Ed. Neil Leach. New York: Routledge, 1997. 330–6.

Foucault, Michel. *Wahnsinn und Gesellschaft: Eine Geschichte des Wahns im Zeitalter der Vernunft*. Trans. Ulrich Köppen. Frankfurt: Suhrkamp, 1973.

'Frankreich macht den Ausnahmezustand zum Gesetz'. *Deutsche Welle*. 3 October 2017 (website – last accesssed 4 October 2017).

Freud, Sigmund. *Civilization and Its Discontents* [1930]. *The Complete Psychological Works of Sigmund Freud – The Future of an Illusion, Civilization and its Discontents, and Other Works*. Trans. by James Strachey. London: Hogarth Press, 1961.

Gerlach, Julia. *Der verpasste Frühling: Woran die Arabellion gescheitert ist*. Bonn: Bundeszentrale für politische Bildung, 2016.

Gibbons, Alison. '"Take that you intellectuals!" and "kaPOW!" Adam Thirlwell and the Metamodernist Future of Style'. *Studia Neophilologica* (2015): 29–43.

Gozlan, Martine. *Tunisie, Algérie, Maroc: La colère des peuples*. Paris: L'Archipel, 2011.

'Gruppenvergewaltigung Essen / Vertuscht: Lauenburger Gang ist ein großer Muslimclan'. *Rapefugees.net*. 15 February 2018 (website – last accessed 26 September 2018).

Haddad, Saleem. *Guapa*. London: Europa Editions, 2016.

Haddad, Saleem. 'On the Arab Spring and Writing About the Queer Arab Experience'. Interview by Stuart Waterman. *Lambda Literary*. 21 May 2016 (website – last accessed 15 January 2021).

Hafez, Farid, ed. *Islamophobia Studies Yearbook*. Vienna: New Academic Press, 2012.

Hage, Rawi. *Cockroach*. Toronto: Anansi, 2008.

Hamilton, Omar Robert. *The City Always Wins*. London: Faber & Faber, 2017.

Hansen, Lene. 'The Little Mermaid's Silent Security Dilemma and the Absence of Gender in the Copenhagen School'. *Millenium: Journal of International Studies* 29.2 (2000): 285–306.

Hark, Sabine, and Paula-Irene Villa. *Unterscheiden und herrschen: Ein Essay zu den ambivalenten Verflechtungen von Rassismus, Sexismus und Feminismus in der Gegenwart*. Bielefeld: Transcript, 2017.

Hassan, Waïl S. *Immigrant Narratives: Orientalism and Cultural Translation in Arab American and Arab British Literature*. Oxford: Oxford University Press, 2011.

Hatfield, Elaine, and Richard L. Rapson. 'Lust'. *The Oxford Companion to Emotion and the Affective Sciences*. Eds David Sander and Klaus R. Scherer. Oxford: Oxford University Press, 2009.

Heidemann, Birte. '"We Are the Glue Keeping the Civilization Together": Post-Orientalism and Counter-Orientalism in H. M. Naqvi's *Home Boy*'. *Journal of Postcolonial Writing* 48.3 (2012): 289–98.

Héran, François. 'Les migrations à rebours des idées reçues'. Interview by Laure Cailloce. *CNRS: Le Journal*. 10 December 2018 (website – last accessed 20 May 2019).

Hernández, Alberto. '"Kapow!" An Experimental Collaborative Book of Upside-Down Texts and Fold-Out Pages'. *The Publishing Lab*. 8 May 2013 (website – last accessed 27 March 2015).

Hiebler, Heinz. *Hugo von Hofmannsthal und die Medienkultur der Moderne*. Würzburg: Königshausen & Neumann, 2003.

Hitchcock, Peter. 'Immolation'. *The Routledge Companion to Literature and Human Rights*. Eds Sophia A. McClennen and Alexandra Schultheis Moore. Abingdon and New York: Routledge, 2016. 86–94.

Hodgson, Marshall G. S. *The Venture of Islam: Conscience and History in a World Civilization Vol. 1: The Classical Age of Islam*. Chicago: University of Chicago Press, 1974.

Hofer-Krucker Valderrama, Stefan. 'Die perpetuierte Katastrophe: Globalisierung und ihre Schattenseiten in Jonas Lüschers *Frühling der Barbaren*. Mit einigen literaturdidaktischen Anmerkungen'. *Globalisierung – Natur – Zukunft erzählen* (2015): 39–57.

Houellebecq, Michel. *Soumission*. Paris: Flammarion, 2015.

Houen, Alex. *Terrorism and Modern Literature: From Joseph Conrad to Ciaran Carson*. Oxford: Oxford University Press, 2002.

Huggan, Graham. 'African Literature and the Anthropological Exotic'. *The Postcolonial Exotic: Marketing the Margins*. London: Routledge, 2001. 34–57.

Huntington, Samuel P. 'The Clash of Civilizations?' *Foreign Affairs* 72.3 (1993): 22–49.

Huntington, Samuel P. *The Clash of Civilizations and the Remaking of World Order*. New York: Simon & Schuster, 1996.

Husen, Kristin and Wolfgang Lutz. 'Psychological and Clinical Perspectives on Trauma'. *Worl(d)s of Trauma: Canadian and German Perspectives*. Ed. Wolfgang Klooß. Münster and New York: Waxmann, 2017. 25–37.

Hutcheon, Linda. *The Politics of Postmodernism*. London and New York: Routledge, 1989.

Hütter, Yvonne. 'Ethics and Aesthetics in Jonas Lüscher's *Barbarian Spring*'. *Primerjalna književnost* 40.2 (2017): 149–63.

Illouz, Eva. *Consuming the Romantic Utopia: Love and the Cultural Contradictions of Capitalism*. Berkeley and Los Angeles: University of California Press, 1997.
Irwin, John T. *The Mystery to a Solution: Poe, Borges, and the Analytic Detective Story*. Baltimore and London: Johns Hopkins University Press, 1994.
Irwin, Robert. 'How and Why the West Misrepresents the East'. *The Times Literary Supplement*. 19 August 2011 (website – last accessed 18 February 2015).
'Islamophobia'. *Oxford English Dictionary*. No date (website – last accessed 28 August 2017).
Izzo, Sara. '*Témoin actif und traducteur de l'invisible*: Tahar Ben Jellouns Konzept der literarischen Intervention im "Arabischen Frühling"'. *HeLix* 9 (2016): 69–83.
Jäger, Siegfried. *BrandSätze: Rassismus im Alltag*. Duisburg: Diss-Studien, 1992.
'Jochen Beyse'. *Diaphanes*. No date (website – last accessed 7 December 2020).
'Jonas Lüscher'. *C. H. Beck*. No date (website – last accessed 25 April 2020).
Kabbani, Rana. *Imperial Fictions: Europe's Myths of Orient*. London, San Francisco and Beirut: SAQI, 2008.
Kahlweiß, Luzie H. and Samuel Salzborn. '"Islamophobie" als politischer Kampfbegriff: Zur konzeptionellen und empirischen Kritik des Islamophobiebegriffs'. *Jahrbuch für Extremismus- und Terrorismusforschung 2011/2012* (II). Ed. Armin Pfahl-Traughber. Brühl: Fachhochschule des Bundes für öffentliche Verwaltung, 2012. 248–63.
'Kapow! by Adam Thirlwell'. *Visual Editions*. No date (website – last accessed 24 September 2018).
Keller, Sarah. 'Feminismus im Licht des Umsturzes in Ägypten'. *Arabischer Frühling? Alte und neue Geschlechterpolitiken in einer Region im Umbruch*. Eds Dagmar Filter, Jana Reich and Eva Fuchs. Herbolzheim: Centaurus, 2013. 112–32.
Khadra, Yasmina. *Die letzte Nache des Muammar al-Gaddafi*. Trans. Regina Keil-Sagawe. Hamburg: Osburg, 2015.
Khadra, Yasmina. *La dernière nuit du Raïs*. Paris: Julliard, 2015.
Khadra, Yasmina. *The Dictator's Last Night*. Trans. Julian Evans. London: Gallic, 2015.
Khalil, Kays. *Hit the Floor*. Fachhochschule Düsseldorf, 2006.
Kiefer, Sascha. *Die deutsche Novelle im 20. Jahrhundert: Eine Gattungsgeschichte*. Cologne, Weimar and Vienna: Böhlau, 2010. 472–3
Kleinpass, Susanne. 'Storytelling in Zeiten der Finanzkrise'. *Praxis Deutsch* 255 (2016): 33–6.
Klonk, Charlotte. *Terror: Wenn Bilder zu Waffen werden*. Frankfurt: Fischer, 2017.

Klooß, Wolfgang. 'Die Metaphorik des Kolonialismus: Joseph Conrads "Heart of Darkness" als Problem literarischer Wirklichkeitserfassung um die Jahrhundertwende'. *Germanisch-Romanische Monatsschrift* 31 (1981): 74–92.

Krasmann, Susanne. 'Die Regierung der Sicherheit – Über das Mögliche und das Fiktive'. *Foucaultblog*. 5 December 2013 (website – last accessed 15 March 2021).

Krause, Anja and Sigrid Ruby, eds. *Sicherheit und Differenz in historischer Perspektive / Security and Difference in Historical Perspective*. Baden-Baden: Nomos, forthcoming.

Kristeva, Julia. *Crisis of the European Subject*. New York: Other Press, 2000.

Kumar, Deepa. 'Framing Islam: The Resurgence of Orientalism during the Bush II Era'. *Journal of Communication Inquiry* 34.3 (2010): 254–77.

Laffey, Mark and Suthaharan Nadarajah. 'Postcolonialism'. *Contemporary Security Studies*. Ed. Alan Collins. Oxford: Oxford University Press, 2016. 122–38.

Lau, Lisa. 'Re-Orientalism: The Perpetation and Development of Orientalism by Orientals'. *Modern Asian Studies* 43.2 (2009): 571–90.

Lehmkuhl, Ursula, Hans-Jürgen Lüsebrink and Laurence McFalls, eds. 'Spaces and Practices of Diversity: An Introduction'. *Of 'Contact Zones' and 'Liminal Spaces': Mapping the Everyday Life of Cultural Translation*. Münster and New York: Waxmann, 2015. 7–27.

Lewis, Bernard. *The Crisis of Islam: Holy War and Unholy Terror*. London: Phoenix, 2004.

Lewis, Bernard. 'The Roots of Muslim Rage: Why So Many Muslims Deeply Resent the West, and Why Their Bitterness Will Not Easily Be Mollified'. *The Atlantic*. 1 September 1990 (website – last accessed 18 February 2015).

Lewis, Bernard. *What Went Wrong? The Clash between Islam and Modernity in the Middle East*. New York: Harper Perennial, 2002.

Lewis, Mary Anne. 'Between Francophonie and World Literature in French: Tahar Ben Jelloun's Evolving Authority'. *The Journal of North African Studies* 21.2 (2016): 301–9.

Littell, Jonathan. *Carnets de Homs*. Paris: Gallimard, 2012.

Littell, Jonathan. *Notizen aus Homs*. Trans. Dorit Gesa Engelhardt. Munich: Hanser, 2012.

Littell, Jonathan [2012]. *Syrian Notebooks: Inside the Homs Uprising*. Trans. Charlotte Mandell. London: Verso, 2015.

Loginov, Michail. 'Islamophobie, Islam- und Muslimfeindlichkeit: Versuch einer konsensfähigen Definition'. *forum kriminalprävention*. January 2016.

Lubrich, Naomi. 'The Art of Tahrir Square: Adam Thirlwell's Kapow!' *Jewish Museum Berlin*. 1 February 2013 (website – last accessed 14 April 2015).

Lüscher, Jonas. *Barbarian Spring*. Trans. Peter Lewis. London: Haus Publishing, 2014.

Lüscher, Jonas. 'Den Widerstand der Welt erfahren – Interview mit Jonas Lüscher'. Interview by Gregor Szyndler. *Zeitnah*. 3 June 2013 (website – last accessed 21 April 2019).

Lüscher, Jonas [2013]. *Frühling der Barbaren*. Munich: btb, 2015.

Lynx Qualey, Marcia. 'The Drama of Protest'. *Qantara*. 20 December 2016 (website – last accessed 15 January 2021).

Maani, Sama. 'Der Begriff Islamophobie. Interview mit Sama Maani'. Interview by Nikolai Schreiter and Nikola Staritz. *Malmoe*. 12 May 2015 (website – last accessed 25 November 2016).

Maani, Sama. 'Warum wir Linken über den Islam nicht reden können'. *Der Standard*. 10 January 2017 (website – last accessed 3 January 2020).

Malreddy, Pavan Kumar. 'Introduction: Orientalism(s) after 9/11'. *Journal of Postcolonial Writing* 3 (2012): 233–40.

Malreddy, Pavan Kumar. 'Post-Orientalism and Post-Multiculturalism in Contemporary Britain: Literary and Cinematic Representations of the London Bombings'. *Hard Times* 96 (2014): 32–5.

Mann, Thomas [1912]. *Der Tod in Venedig*. Frankfurt: Fischer, 1992.

'Marc Trévidic'. *Internationales Literaturfestival Berlin*. No date (website – last accessed 30 March 2019).

'Marc Trévidic'. *Rowohlt*. No date (website – last accessed 19 January 2021).

Marrouchi, Mustapha. 'Willed from the Bottom Up: The Postcolonial Turned Revolutionary'. *The Journal of North African Studies* 18.3 (2013): 387–401.

Massumi, Brian. *Politics of Affect*. Cambridge: Polity Press, 2015

Matar, Hisham. *The Return: Fathers, Sons and the Land in Between*. New York: Viking, 2016.

'Mathias Énard'. *Actes Sud*. No date (website – last accessed 12 February 2019).

Mattar, Karim. 'Edward Said and the Institution of Postcolonial Studies'. *The Edinburgh Companion to the Postcolonial Middle East*. Eds Anna Ball and Karim Mattar. Edinburgh: Edinburgh University Press, 2018. 23–42.

Matthes, Frauke. 'Of Kanaken and Gottes Krieger: Religion and Sexuality among Feridun Zaimoğlu's Young Muslim Men'. *Masculinities in German Culture: Edinburgh German Yearbook* 2 (2008): 250–61.

Matzner, Alexandra. 'Museum Barberini: Picasso. Das späte Werk. Aus der

Sammlung Jacqueline Picasso'. *ARTinWords*. 6 March 2019 (website – last accessed 9 May 2019).

Mbembe, Achille. 'Necropolitics'. *Public Culture* 15.1 (2003): 11–40.

McAloon, Jonathan. 'Middle Immaturity: Adam Thirlwell, Kapow!' *Jonniemcaloon.com*. 17 July 2012 (website – last accessed 8 March 2015).

McNally, David. 'Tunisia and the Global Crisis'. *SocialistWorker.org*. 24 January 2011 (website – last accessed 15 December 2017).

Mehrez, Samia, ed. *Translating Egypt's Revolution: The Language of Tahrir*. Cairo: The American University in Cairo Press, 2012.

Michaels, Walter Benn. 'Let Them Eat Diversity: On the Politics of Identity'. Interview by Bhaskar Sunkara. *Jacobin*. 1 January 2011 (website – last accessed 5 January 2021).

Mishra, Pankaj. 'The Politics of Paranoia'. *The Guardian*. 17 September 2006 (website – last accessed 27 June 2017).

Mitchell, Amy, Heather Brown and Emily Guskin. 'The Role of Social Media in the Arab Uprisings'. *Pew Research Center*. 28 November 2012 (website – last accessed 28 January 2019).

Moghul, Haroon. 'Why Arab and Muslim Are Not Synonymous'. *The Huffington Post*. 10 November 2010 (website – last accessed 13 February 2017).

Moore, Lindsey. *Narrating Postcolonial Arab Nations: Egypt, Algeria, Lebanon, Palestine*. New York and Abingdon: Routledge, 2018.

Moore, Lindsey. '"What Happens After Saying No?" Egyptian Uprisings and Afterwords in Basma Adel Aziz's *The Queue* and Omar Robert Hamilton's *The City Always Wins*'. *CounterText* 4.2 (2018): 192–211.

Morey, Peter. 'Applications of Neo-Orientalism and Islamophobia in Recent Writing'. *Orientalism and Literature*. Ed. Geoffrey P. Nash. Cambridge: Cambridge University Press, 2019. 269–85.

Morey, Peter. *Islamophobia and the Novel*. New York: Columbia University Press, 2018.

Morey, Peter, and Amina Yaqin. *Framing Muslims: Stereotyping and Representation after 9/11*. Cambridge, MA: Harvard University Press, 2011.

Morton, Stephen, and Stephen Bygrave. 'Introduction'. *Foucault in an Age of Terror: Essays on Biopolitics and the Defence of Society*. Eds Stephen Morton and Stephen Bygrave. Basingstoke and New York: Palgrave Macmillan, 2008. 1–13.

Mosebach, Martin. *Mogador*. Reinbek: Rowohlt, 2016.

Mouley, Sami. 'The Effects of the Global Financial Crisis and Combined Transition Factors Associated with the Post-Revolutionary Period: The Case of

Tunisia'. *Mediterranean Yearbook* 2013. Barcelona: European Institute of the Mediterranean, 2013. 230–4.

Müller, Felix E. '"Le Grand Remplacement": Dieses Buch inspiriert rechtsradikale Terroristen'. *Neue Zürcher Zeitung*. 6 April 2019 (website – last accessed 20 May 2019).

Mullin, Corinna and Brahim Rouabah. 'Requiem for Tunisia's Revolution?' *Jadaliyya*. 22 December 2014 (website – last accessed 2 February 2015).

Mutman, Mahmut. 'From Orientalism to Islamophobia'. *Orientalism and Literature*. Ed. Geoffrey P. Nash. Cambridge: Cambridge University Press, 2019. 255–68.

Nachtwey, Oliver. *Die Abstiegsgesellschaft – Über das Aufbegehren in der regressiven Moderne*. Berlin: Suhrkamp, 2016.

Nachtwey, Oliver. 'Transnationale Protestbewegungen in der Abstiegsgesellschaft – die Occupy-Proteste in Deutschland'. *Working Paper der DFG-KollegforscherInnengruppe Postwachstumsgesellschaften* 4 (2014).

Nazemroaya, Mahdi Darius. 'Dictatorship and Neo-Liberalism: The Tunisian People's Uprising'. *GlobalResearch*. 19 January 2011 (website – last accessed 18 January 2018).

Nehrlich, Thomas. '*Es hat mehr Sinn und Deutung, als du glaubst*'. *Zu Funktion und Bedeutung typographischer Textmerkmale in Kleists Prosa*. Hildesheim: Olms, 2012.

Nesselhauf, Jonas. 'SpielGeldSpiel – Der Spekulant als Reflektionsfigur in der deutschen Gegenwartsprosa'. *Germanica* 55 (2014): 81–96.

Nussbaum, Martha. *Sex and Social Justice*. Oxford: Oxford University Press, 1999.

O'Gorman, Daniel. *Fictions of the War on Terror: Difference and the Transnational 9/11 Novel*. Basingstoke and New York: Palgrave Macmillan, 2015.

Olesen, Thomas. '"We are all Khaled Said": Visual Injustice Symbols in the Egyptian Revolution, 2010–2011'. *Advances in the Visual Analysis of Social Movements*. Eds Nicole Doerr, Alice Mattoni and Simon Teune. Bingley: Emerald Group Publishing Limited, 2013. 3–25.

Park, Mungo [1799]. *Travels in the Interior Districts of Africa*. Ware: Wordsworth, 2002.

'Pegida-Chef wegen Volksverhetzung angezeigt'. *Zeit online*. 10 January 2016 (website – last accessed 26 September 2018).

Platzgumer, Hans. *Trans-Maghreb: Novelle vom Bauträger Anton Corwald*. Innsbruck: Limbus, 2012.

Polaschegg, Andrea. *Der andere Orientalismus: Regeln deutsch-morgenländischer*

Imagination im 19. Jahrhundert. Berlin and New York: Walter de Gruyter, 2005.

Prince, Mona [2012]. *Revolution Is My Name.* Trans. Samia Mehrez. Cairo: The American University in Cairo Press, 2014.

Puar, Jasbir K. *Terrorist Assemblages: Homonationalism in Queer Times.* Durham, NC and London: Duke University Press, 2007.

Reidy, Julian. '"Wie der Geist zum Kamele ward": Zu einem Leitmotiv in Jonas Lüschers *Frühling der Barbaren*'. *Colloquium Helveticum* 45 (2016): 157–73.

de Rochebrune, Renaud. 'Et il est comment le dernier Rachid Boudjedra'. *JeuneAfrique.* 29 June 2014 (website – last accessed 17 January 2021).

Roger, Sarah. *Borges and Kafka: Sons and Writers.* Oxford: Oxford University Press, 2017.

Rooney, Caroline. 'Popular Culture and the Arab Spring'. *The Edinburgh Companion to the Postcolonial Middle East.* Eds Anna Ball and Karim Mattar. Edinburgh: Edinburgh University Press, 2018. 407–26.

Rose, Rachel. 'Karim Alrawi: What If?' *Guernica.* 16 November 2015 (website – last accessed 18 December 2018).

Runnymede Trust. *Islamophobia: A Challenge for Us All.* London, 1997.

Rushdie, Salman [2015]. *Two Years Eight Months & Twenty-Eight Nights.* London: Vintage, 2016.

Sabo, Oana. *The Migrant Canon in Twenty-First-Century France.* Lincoln and London: University of Nebraska Press, 2018.

de Sade, Donatien Alphonse François [1791]. *Justine ou Les Malheurs de la vertu.* Paris: Le Livre de Poche, 1973.

Saffari, Siavash, Roxana Akhbari, Kara Abdolmaleki and Eveyln Hamdon, eds. *Unsettling Colonial Modernity in Islamicate Contexts.* Newcastle upon Tyne: Cambridge Scholars Publishing, 2017.

Said, Edward W. [1981]. *Covering Islam: How the Media and the Experts Determine How We See the Rest of the World.* New York: Vintage, 1997.

Said, Edward W. 'Islam and the West are Inadequate Banners'. *The Observer.* 16 September 2001 (website – last accessed 15 December 2018).

Said, Edward W. *Orientalism* [1978]. Ed. with new Afterword and Preface. London: Penguin, 2003.

Saleh, Fakhri. 'Rethinking World Literature: The Arabic Novel in Non-Western Eyes'. *Qantara.* 6 May 2011 (website – last accessed 28 June 2018).

Samiei, Mohammed. 'Neo-Orientalism? The Relationship Between the West and Islam in Our Globalised World'. *Third World Quarterly* 31.7 (2010): 1145–60.

'The Return'. *HishamMatar.com*. No date (website – last accessed 17 January 2021).

Thirlwell, Adam. 'An Interview with Adam Thirlwell'. Interview by Alison Gibbons. *Contemporary Literature* 55.4 (2014): 610–34.

Thirlwell, Adam. 'Interview: Adam Thirlwell'. Interview by Ted Hodgkinson. *Granta*. 19 June 2012 (website – last accessed 28 March 2015).

Thirlwell, Adam. *Kapow!* London: Visual Editions, 2012.

Thirlwell. Adam, ed. *Multiples: 12 Stories in 18 Languages by 61 Authors*. London: Granta Books, 2013.

Ticineto Clough, Patricia, and Jean Halley, eds. *The Affective Turn: Theorizing the Social*. Durham, NC: Duke University Press, 2007.

Toumi, Amel. 'It Takes But a Spark …' *The Arab Review*. No date (website – last accessed 22 March 2015).

Tourage, Mahdi. *Rūmī and the Hermeneutics of Eroticism*. Leiden and Boston: Brill, 2007.

Treisman, Deborah. 'This Week in Fiction: Tahar Ben Jelloun'. *The New Yorker*. 6 September 2013 (website – last accesed 26 April 2015).

Trévidic, Marc. *Au coeur de l'anti-terrorisme*. Paris: J. C. Lattès, 2011

Trévidic, Marc. *Ahlam*. Paris: J. C. Lattès, 2016.

Trévidic, Marc. 'On manque d'hommes pour neutraliser les terroristes'. Interview by Frédéric Helbert. *Paris Match*. 30 September 2015 (website – last accessed 19 January 2021).

Trévidic, Marc. *Terroristes: Les 7 pilliers de la déraison*. Paris: J. C. Lattès, 2013.

Tromans, Nicholas. 'Introduction'. *The Lure of the East: British Orientalist Painting*. Ed. Nicholas Tromans. New Haven: Yale University Press, 2008. 10–21.

Tuastad, Dag. 'Neo-Orientalism and the New Barbarism Thesis: Aspects of Symbolic Violence in the Middle East Conflict(s)'. *Third World Quarterly* 24.4 (2003): 591–99.

Turner, Victor [1969]. *The Ritual Process: Structure and Anti-Structure*. New Brunswick, NJ and London: Aldine, 2008.

Varisco, Daniel Martin. *Reading Orientalism: Said and the Unsaid*. Seattle and London: University of Washington Press, 2007.

Ventura, Lorella. 'The "Arab Spring" and Orientalist Stereotypes: The Role of Orientalism in the Narration of the Revolts in the Arab World'. *Interventions* 19.2 (2017): 282–97.

Virilio, Paul. *L'Inertie polaire*. Paris: Christian Bourgois, 1990.

Virilio, Paul. *Rasender Stillstand* [1990]. Trans. Bernd Wilczek. Frankfurt am Main: Fischer, 1997.

Sarasin, Philipp. *Geschichtswissenschaft und Diskursanalyse*. Frankfurt: Suhrkamp, 2003.

Sardar, Ziauddin. 'The Blitcon Supremacists'. *The Guardian*. 9 December 2006 (website – 15 March 2021).

Sarrazin, Thilo [2010]. *Deutschland schafft sich ab: Wie wir unser Land aufs Spiel setzen*. Munich: Deutsche Verlags-Anstalt, 2016.

Schaffner, Anna Katharina. *Exhaustion: A History*. New York: Columbia University Press, 2016.

Schanda, Susanne. *Literatur der Rebellion: Ägyptens Schriftsteller erzählen vom Umbruch*. Zurich: Rotpunktverlag, 2013.

Scheiwiller, Staci Gem. *Liminalities of Gender and Sexuality in Nineteenth-Century Iranian Photography*. New York and Abingdon: Routledge, 2017.

Schyns, Désirée. '*Harraga* dans la littérature francophone: Boualem Sansal, Tahar Ben Jelloun, Mathias Enard et Marie Ndiaye'. *Romanische Studien* 3 (2016): 201–17.

'Security'. *Oxford English Dictionary*. No date (website – last accessed 29 September 2017).

Sivanandan, Ambalavaner. 'Poverty Is the New Black'. *Race & Class* 43.2 (2001): 1–5.

Slimani, Leïla. 'Gegen die Angst'. Interview by Khuê Phạm. *Zeit Magazin*. 23 August 2018. 14–20.

Sonderquist, K. Brian. *The Isolated Self: Truth and Untruth in Søren Kierkegaard's* On the Concept of Irony. Copenhagen: C. A. Reitzel, 2007.

Soueif, Ahdaf. *Cairo: Memoir of a City Transformed*. London: Bloomsbury, 2012.

Spivak, Gayatri Chakravorty. 'Can the Subaltern Speak?' *Colonial Discourse and Post-Colonial Theory: A Reader*. Eds Patrick Williams and Laura Chrisman. New York: Columbia University Press, 1994. 66–111.

Sterne, Laurence [1759–67]. *The Life and Opinions of Tristram Shandy, Gentleman*. Oxford: Oxford University Press, 1983.

Stiglitz, Joseph E. 'The 99 Percent Wakes Up'. *The Daily Beast*. 5 February 2012 (website – last accessed 2 February 2015). Excerpt originally published in *From Cairo to Wall Street: Voices from the Global Spring*. New York: The New Press, 2012.

'Stories'. *Adamthirlwell.com*. No date (website – last accessed 2 June 2017).

Surber, Peter. 'Krisen-Showdown in der Oase'. *Saiten*. 8 January 2015 (website – last accessed 8 March 2018).

'Tahar Ben Jelloun'. *Gallimard.fr*. No date (website – last accessed 29 April 2020).

Voelz, Johannes. *The Poetics of Insecurity: American Fiction and the Uses of Threat*. Cambridge: Cambridge University Press, 2018.
de Vries, Ad. 'Cockroach'. *Dictionary of Symbols and Imagery*. Amsterdam and London: North-Holland Publishing Company, 1974. 106.
Wade, Laura. *Posh*. London: Oberon Books, 2010.
Walkowitz, Rebecca L. 'Epilogue: Multiples'. *Born Translated: The Contemporary Novel in an Age of World Literature*. New York: Columbia University Press, 2015. 235–45.
Walter, Eugene Victor. *Terror and Resistance: A Study of Political Violence*. Oxford: Oxford University Press, 1969.
Wardleworth, Nina. 'The Roman Maghrébin in the Aftermath of the Arab Spring'. *Contemporary French and Francophone Studies* 20.1 (2016): 141–9.
Watson, Scott D. '"Framing" the Copenhagen School: Integrating the Literature on Threat Construction'. *Millenium: Journal of International Studies* 40.2 (2012): 279–301.
Wheeler, Brannon M. 'Moses or Alexander? Early Islamic Exegesis of Qur'ān 18: 60–65'. *Journal of Near Eastern Studies* 57.3 (1998): 191–215.
Wiedmer, Caroline. *The Claims of Memory: Representations of the Holocaust in Contemporary Germany and France*. Ithaca and London: Cornell University Press, 1999.
Willis, Michael J. *Politics and Power in the Maghreb: Algeria, Tunisia and Morocco from Independence to the Arab Spring*. Oxford: Oxford University Press, 2014.
Wilson, G. Willow. *Alif the Unseen*. London: Corvus, 2012.
Wilson, G. Willow. *Cairo*. New York: Vertigo, 2007.
Wilson, G. Willow. *The Butterfly Mosque: A Young American Woman's Journey to Love and Islam*. New York: Grove, 2010.
Yamaguchi, Kenichi. 'Rationalization and Concealment of Violence in American Responses to 9/11: Orientalism(s) in a State of Exception'. *Journal of Postcolonial Writing* 48.3 (2012): 241–51.
Yazbek, Samar [2011]. *A Woman in the Crossfire: Diaries of the Syrian Revolution*. Trans. Max Weiss. London: Haus, 2012.
Yazbek, Samar. *The Crossing: My Journey to the Shattered Heart of Syria*. Trans. Nashwa Gowanlock and Ruth Ahmedzai Kemp. London: Rider, 2015.
Yazbek, Samar. 'Waiting for Death: I Will Not Carry Flowers to My Grave'. Trans. Anne-Marie McManus. *Jadaliyya*. 2 April 2011 (website – last accessed 15 January 2021).

Yeğenoğlu, Meyda. *Colonial Fantasies: Towards a Feminist Reading of Orientalism*. Cambridge: Cambridge University Press, 1998.
Young, Robert C. 'Terror Effects'. *Terror and the Postcolonial*. Eds Elleke Boehmer and Stephen Morton. Malden and Oxford: Wiley-Blackwell, 2010. 307–28.
Žižek, Slavoj. *The Year of Dreaming Dangerously*. London and New York: Verso, 2012.

INDEX

9/11 attacks, 2, 3, 6, 15
2005 London bombings, 16

Abdel Aziz, Basma, 35–6, 37
Abu Ghraib prison, 10
affect-driven behaviour, 6, 138–42
affective masculinity, 22–3, 138–40, 141
  and *Kapow!*, 101–6, 108, 113–17, 117
Agamben, Giorgio, 11
agency, 126–9
aggression, 103, 105
Ahlam (Trévidic), 42–3, 58, 206
Al Aswani, Alaa, 36–7
Al Khamissi, Khaled, 35, 109
Algeria, 41, 42, 124–6, 135, 137
Alif the Unseen (Wilson), 44
allochronic time, 59, 60, 61, 62, 68–9
  and *Book of Sands*, 172–3
  and *Kapow!*, 119
Alrawi, Karim, 45, 159; see also *Book of Sands: A Novel of the Arab Uprising*
alterity, 7–9, 12; *see also* Othering
Amar, Paul, 110, 113
Andalusia, 7
animal imagery, 161, 163–4, 168, 191, 194–5
anti-Muslim racism, 4, 10, 13, 14–18, 21

Arab uprisings (Arab Spring), 3, 4–6, 34–6, 87–8, 223
  and Egypt, 33–5
  and *Frühling der Barbaren* (*Barbarian Spring*), 69–70, 84–6
  and *Kapow!*, 102, 107–14, 118, 119–20, 121–2
  and literature, 20–3, 35–7, 39–42, 220–2
  and media, 54–5
  and popular culture, 37–9
  and *Rebellion: Zwischenbericht*, 124, 131, 132, 137, 138, 139
  and time, 59
  and Western fictionalisations, 42–7
  see also *Book of Sands: A Novel of the Arab Uprising* (Alrawi); *Par le feu* ('By Fire') (Ben Jelloun); *Rue des voleurs* (*Street of Thieves*) (Énard)
Arab world, 8, 27n54
Arabian Nights, The, 8, 62, 68, 104, 122–3
Arabic language, 41, 189
Arendt, Hannah, 122
Atia, Nadia, 41
authoritarianism, 2, 35–6

Bachmann, Ingeborg
  Das Buch Franza (*The Book of Franza*), 83–4

Bachmann, Lutz, 143n11
backwardness, 2, 5, 6, 58, 61–2, 103
Badr, Battle of, 199
Baker, Mona, 38
Balkans, 7
Barbarian Spring see *Frühling der Barbaren (Barbarian Spring)* (Lüscher)
Barbary pirates, 8
Barkawi, Tarak, 157
Bauman, Zygmunt, 12
beards, 19, 114–15, 165, 191, 200
Ben Ali, Zine El Abidine, 55, 62, 64, 66, 85
Ben Jelloun, Tahar, 45, 56–8, 68
  Partir (Leaving Tangier), 189
  see also *Par le feu* ('By Fire') (Ben Jelloun)
Berbers, 76, 78, 81–2
Beyse, Jochen see *Rebellion: Zwischenbericht ('Rebellion: Status Report')* (Beyse)
Bhat, Shakeel Ahmad, 158
Bible, the, 9
birds, 160, 163–4, 165, 168, 179
Biskamp, Floris, 17
Blockupy movement, 4, 54
Boehmer, Elleke, 44
bombers, 19
Book of Sands: A Novel of the Arab Uprising (Alrawi), 22, 39, 44, 155, 159
  and Omar, 164–80
  and Tarek, 160–4
  and utter Other, 204–7
Borges, Jorge Luis, 175–6
Borkenau, Franz, 70
Bouazizi, Mohamed, 34, 93n70
  and *Par le feu* ('By Fire'), 57–8, 62, 67–9, 87
Boudjedra, Rachid, 40, 41–2
Bowles, Paul, 186, 188
Boyle, T. C.
  Water Music, 82
Buch, Hans Christoph
  Tod in Habana ('Death in Habana'), 137
Bullingdon Club (Oxford), 83
burkas, 19, 102, 115

Burke, Edmund, 121
Burroughs, William, 188
Burton, Richard
  The Arabian Nights, 104
Bush, George W., 105
Butler, Judith, 55–6, 158
Butterfly Mosque: A Young American Woman's Journey to Love and Islam, The (Wilson), 44
Buzan, Barry, 10
Byzantine Empire, 7

Cairo (Egypt), 124–6, 137, 138; see also Tahrir Square
Cairo (Wilson), 44
Cairo: Memoir of a City Transformed (Soueif), 33–4, 35, 39
camels, 54, 77–80, 83–4
Camus, Albert, 59
  L'Étranger (The Stranger), 59, 124, 126, 135, 136, 137
Camus, Renaud, 2, 191
capitalism, 13, 36, 197–8
  and *Frühling der Barbaren (Barbarian Spring)*, 54, 55–6, 84–5
  see also cultural capitalism
Carnets de Homs (Syrian Notebooks: Inside the Homs Uprising) (Littell), 40
Casanova, Giacomo, 188
Cesari, Jocelyne, 14–15
Cette aveuglante absence de lumière (This Blinding Absence of Light) (Ben Jelloun), 68
Chateaubriand, François-René de, 121
child labour, 77–8, 86
children, 160
China, 7
Choukhri, Mohamed
  For Bread Alone, 186, 188, 189
Christianity, 8, 9, 104
City Always Wins, The (Hamilton), 40
civil liberties, 11–12
civil society, 66, 67
civilisation, 71, 72, 103–4
clichés see stereotypes
cockroaches, 169–71, 177, 179
Cold War, 10

colonialism, 3, 104, 188
  and *Rebellion: Zwischenbericht*, 130–1, 132, 133–4
  see also postcolonialism
coming-of-age stories, 43, 180, 190, 203
Conrad, Joseph
  Heart of Darkness, 187–8, 196
Constant, Benjamin
  De l'Esprit de conquête et de l'usurpation, 121–2
Copenhagen School, 10
corporeality, 192–4
corruption, 55, 63, 64, 65
crime, 19
Crossing: My Journey to the Shattered Heart of Syria, The (Yazbek), 39
Crusades, 8
cultural capitalism, 80–6
culture, 16; *see also* popular culture
currency, 62

Dabashi, Hamid, 4–5
danger, 2, 3, 4, 115, 195–8
Danielewski, Mark Z., 123
death, 59–60; *see also* self-immolation
Delacroix, Eugène
  Femmes d'Alger dans leur appartement (*Women of Algiers in Their Apartment*), 125
democracy, 2, 5, 6, 62, 132
deradicalisation, 179–80, 206
Dernière Nuit du Raïs, La (*The Dictator's Last Night*) (Khadra), 42
desecuritisation, 117–24, 141
despotism, 62, 63–9
deuteragonists, 156, 158–9, 204–7
  and *Book of Sands*, 164–80
  and *Rue des voleurs* (*Street of Thieves*), 190–204
diasporic writers, 39–42, 45, 220
dictatorships, 4, 55
Dinet, Etienne
  L'Orient vu de l'Occident, 14
discrimination, 13, 15–17
dissidents, 35, 36
drugs, 176–7
dystopias, 35–6

effeminacy, 143n7
Egypt, 4, 7, 33–4, 35, 38–9
  and literature, 35–7, 39–40, 44
  see also *Book of Sands: A Novel of the Arab Uprising* (Alrawi); Cairo; *Kapow!* (Thirlwell); *Rebellion: Zwischenbericht* ('Rebellion: Status Report') (Beyse)
El Shafee, Magdy
  Metro, 39
Elias, Norbert
  Über den Prozeß der Zivilisation (*The Civilising Process*), 103–4
emergency, states of, 11
empathy, 204–5
Énard, Mathias see *Rue des voleurs* (*Street of Thieves*)
Enfant de sable, L' (*The Sand Child*) (Ben Jelloun), 56
English language, 39–40, 45–6
Enlightenment, 103
epistemic modality, 121
ergodic elements, 139
essays, 38
Étincelle: Révoltes dans les pays arabes, L' ('The Spark') (Ben Jelloun), 43
Étranger, L' (*The Stranger*) (Camus), 59, 124, 126, 135, 136, 137
exoticism, 76–8
experts, 42–3
exploitation, 13

Fabian, Johannes, 59
family, 183–4
fanaticism, 2, 10
Fanon, Frantz, 17
fascism, 2
fatherhood, 160
fear *see* danger; securitisation
Fekete, Liz, 103
female genital mutilation, 171–2, 173–5, 180
film, 38
financial crisis, 54, 55, 67
fire imagery, 197, 201–2
Foer, Jonathan Safran
  Tree of Codes, 123
foreshadowing, 195, 199

Foucault, Michel, 94n77
Fourteenth of January Front, 84–5
framing, 70–2; *see also* negative framing
France, 11, 42–3, 56–7
French language, 40, 45–6, 56, 189
French Revolution, 121, 156
Freud, Sigmund, 7
Frühling der Barbaren (Barbarian Spring) (Lüscher), 22, 42, 53–4, 69–70
   and insecurity, 221–2
   and Orientalism, 74–86
   and precarity, 55–6, 87–8
   and truth, 70–4
fundamentalism, 2, 62, 155–6, 171
   and *Rue des voleurs (Street of Thieves)*, 181, 195, 197, 200

Gaddafi, Muammar, 40, 42, 55
Gallimard, 40, 46, 56
gender equality, 18, 101–2; *see also* women
gender inequality, 10, 43–4, 109–13, 132–3
geography, 3, 118
German language, 45–6
Germany, 7, 36–7, 103
Gibbons, Alison, 118, 120, 121, 123
globalisation, 3, 54–5, 67
   and *Frühling der Barbaren (Barbarian Spring)*, 86, 88
   and *Kapow!*, 118, 119
Goncourt Academy, 56
Gozlan, Marianne, 68
graffiti, 38
grammar, 121, 127, 128–30; *see also* stylistics
Grand Remplacement, Le (Camus), 213n79
graphic novels, 38, 39, 44
Guapa (Haddad), 40–2

Haddad, Saleem, 34–5, 40–2
Hage, Rawi
   Cockroach, 171
Haine, La (Hate) (film), 196
Hall, Stuart, 17
Hamilton, Omar Robert, 39–40
harassment *see* sexualised violence
harems, 105
HarperCollins, 46

Hassan le Fou, 201
hate speech, 2
Here Is a Body (Abdel Aziz), 36
heterochrony, 118, 119, 120, 121, 123, 136–8
heterolingualism, 118
   and *Book of Sands*, 162–3, 166–7
   and *Rue des voleurs (Street of Thieves)*, 189, 201, 203
Hobbes, Thomas, 11
Hodgson, Marshall G. S.
   The Venture of Islam, 23n2
homonationalism, 18, 41
homophobia, 18, 144n30
homosexuality, 40, 41–2, 182–3
hostage crisis, 3
Houellebecq, Michel
   Soumission, 20
House of Leaves (Danielewski), 123
Huntington, Samuel P., 10, 105

Ibn Battuta, 188, 201
illegal aliens, 181
immigration, 13, 15, 21
   and affective masculinity, 103, 105
   and vermin imagery, 171
   see also refugees
imperialism *see* colonialism
India, 7
Indignados, 4, 54, 180, 202–3
inequality, 12, 222–4; *see also* gender inequality
injustice, 18, 54–5, 61–2, 63, 161–2
insecurity, 5, 11–14, 19–20, 45, 221–4, 118
Insight (magazine), 14
International Literature Festival (Berlin), 43, 57
intertextuality, 140
   and *Book of Sands*, 175–6
   and *Frühling der Barbaren (Barbarian Spring)*, 81–2, 83–4
   and *Kapow!*, 116–17, 121–3
   and *Par le feu* ('By Fire'), 62
   and *Rebellion: Zwischenbericht*, 128–9, 136–7
   and *Rue des voleurs (Street of Thieves)*, 186, 187–9, 196–7, 201

Iran, 3, 62
irony, 1, 22, 36, 87, 140, 141–2
　and *Kapow!*, 115–16
　and *Rue des voleurs* (*Street of Thieves*), 183–4
Islam, 2–3, 6–9, 10, 12, 19, 104
　and Ben Jelloun, 57
　and framing, 17–18
　and society, 32n112
　and time, 58
　see also anti-Muslim racism; Islamicate man; Islamicate Other; Islamophobia
Islamic State, 3, 5
Islamicate man, 102–6, 114–17, 135–6, 138–9
　and *Book of Sands*, 164–70, 171–2, 177–80
　see also Islamist Rage Boys
Islamicate Other, 1–2, 3, 18, 19–20, 221
Islamist Rage Boys, 19, 22, 43, 158–9, 206, 221
　and *Rue des voleurs* (*Street of Thieves*), 155, 181–2, 190–204
Islamophobia, 14–15, 17
Izzo, Sara, 68–9

Japan, 7
Jasmine Revolution, 43
jihadism, 2, 19, 198–9

Kabbani, Nizar, 188, 189
Kafka, Franz
　Die Verwandlung (*The Metamorphosis*), 171
Kapow! (Thirlwell), 22, 42, 46, 106
　and affect-driven behaviour, 138–40
　and gender equality, 101–2
　and gender inequality, 109–13
　and masculinity, 113–17
　and Orientalism, 140–2
　and repressed lust, 107–9
　and stylistics, 117–24
Khadra, Yasmina, 42
al-Khidr, 196
Kosovo, Battle of, 8
Kraft (Lüscher), 69
Künstlernovelle, 137

Laffey, Mark, 157
layout, 123
Lewis, Bernard, 10
　'The Roots of Muslim Rage', 105
Lewis, Mary Anne, 68
LGBTIQ, 18
Libya, 4, 40, 42
liminality, 181, 182, 186–7, 188, 189–90, 203
literary Neo-Orientalism, 19–23, 222–4
Littell, Jonathan, 40
Lüscher, Jonas see *Frühling der Barbaren* (*Barbarian Spring*) (Lüscher)
lust, 107–9, 115, 116–17, 139

madness, 201; see also mental illness
magic realism, 44, 172, 174–6
Mahfouz, Naguib, 188
Maistre, Joseph de, 121
male gaze, 101, 116, 181, 198
Mandeville, Sir John, 7
Mann, Thomas
　Der Tod in Venedig (*Death in Venice*), 137
Marie Antoinette, Queen 121
marketing, 36–7
masculinity see affective masculinity; Islamicate man
Matar, Hisham, 39, 40, 42
mathematics, 162, 166
media, 2, 54–5, 84, 134
　and Arab uprisings, 4, 5, 110
　see also social media
Mehrez, Samia, 38, 39
Melville, Herman, 188
Menezes, Jean Charles de, 16
mental illness, 71, 72–4, 94n77
Messadi, Mahmoud
　Die Genese des Vergessens, 80–1
Middle East, 9, 27n54, 58–9; see also Arab uprisings; Syria
Mishra, Pankaj, 171
misogyny, 18
Mogador (Mosebach), 58
Moore, Lindsey, 35, 37
　Narrating Postcolonial Arab Nations, 47

Morocco, 56; see also *Rue des voleurs* (*Street of Thieves*) (Énard); Tangier
Mosebach, Martin, 58
Moulessehoul, Mohammed *see* Khadra, Yasmina
Mubarak, Hosni, 36, 39
Muhammad, Prophet, 104
Muslim Brothers, 84–5
'Muslim Misery Memoirs', 37
Muslims *see* Islam
mutism, 190, 194, 200, 201

Nazism, 171
necropolitics, 59–60
negative framings, 1–2, 34–5
neo-liberalism, 3, 11, 84, 86
Neo-Orientalism, 2–4, 26n35, 55, 221
   and anti-Muslim racism, 14–17
   and Arab uprisings, 4–6
   and insecurity, 11–14
   and *Kapow!*, 138–9
   and literature, 19–23, 43, 44, 45–7
   and Others, 6–7
nepotism, 64–5
North Africa, 9, 58–9; *see also* Algeria; Arab uprisings; Egypt; Libya; Morocco; Tunisia
Nuit sacrée, La (*The Sacred Night*) (Ben Jelloun), 56
Nuwâs, Abû, 188

Occupy Wall Street movement, 4, 54, 202–3
oil crisis, 3
Oman, 62
Only Revolutions (Danielewski), 123
oppression, 37, 54, 161–2
Orientalism, 3, 4, 5, 7–9
   and *Frühling der Barbaren* (*Barbarian Spring*), 54, 74–86, 88
   and lust, 107–9
   and masculinity, 113–17
   and *Par le feu* ('By Fire'), 58–62, 66, 69, 87
   and *Rebellion: Zwischenbericht*, 126
   and *Rue des voleurs* (*Street of Thieves*), 183, 184

and Said, 6, 26n30
and security, 221–2
and sensuality, 104–6
and stereotypes, 37
see also Neo-Orientalism
Othering, 6–7, 12, 14, 103, 223–4
   and *Book of Sands*, 166
   and *Frühling der Barbaren* (*Barbarian Spring*), 70–4
   and securitisation, 9–10
   and Western fiction, 45, 46
   see also Islamicate Other; utter Other
Ottoman Empire, 8

Par le feu ('By Fire') (Ben Jelloun), 22, 39, 43, 55, 57–8
   and despotism, 63–9
   and precarity, 87–8
   and time, 58–62
Paris attacks, 43
Park, Mungo
   Travels in the Interior Districts of Africa, 82
patriarchy, 37
PEGIDA, 143n11
perspective, 6, 23, 38, 40–2
   and Arab uprisings, 54
   and female, 39, 43
   and *Frühling der Barbaren* (*Barbarian Spring*), 84
   and *Kapow!*, 118, 121, 122
   and *Par le feu* ('By Fire'), 55, 67
   and *Rue des voleurs* (*Street of Thieves*), 203–4
   and terrorism, 157–8
   and Western, 8–9, 34
phrase migrante ('migrant sentence'), 185, 195, 197–8, 203
Picasso, Pablo, 125
Platzgumer, Hans, 42
plays, 38, 39
poetics, 18, 20, 21, 22, 26n35, 45, 56, 221
   and insecurity, 19, 32n117, 141, 222–4
   and precarity, 87–8
poetry, 38, 39
polar inertia, 134
Polaschegg, Andrea, 7

police, 61, 63, 64, 66
politics, 2, 5, 10, 109–13, 114; *see also* right-wing extremism
Polo, Marco, 7
popular culture, 37–9
postcolonialism, 47
poverty, 13, 61–2, 64, 65, 66–7
precarity, 22–3, 55–6, 187
    and *Frühling der Barbaren* (*Barbarian Spring*), 69–70, 74–88
    and *Par le feu* ('By Fire'), 63, 64, 65–7
Prince, Mona, 39
Printemps ('Spring') (Boudjedra), 40, 41–2
private space, 109–13
projection, 134–6, 138–42
prostitution, 176–7, 186
publishers, 46

Qasr El Nil Bridge (Cairo), 161
Qatar, 62
Qotb, Sayyid, 191
queer *see* homosexuality; LGBTIQ
Queue, The (Abdel Aziz), 35–6, 37
Quran, 104, 166, 188, 199

racialisation, 6–7, 184–5
racism, 4, 13, 131; *see also* anti-Muslim racism
radicalisation, 22, 155–6, 204–7
    and *Book of Sands*, 164–5, 167–70, 171–2, 177–80
    and *Rue des voleurs* (*Street of Thieves*), 190–3, 196, 200–3
rage, 130–4, 136
Rage Boys *see* Islamist Rage Boys
Rakha, Youssef, 220
rape, 113, 114, 173–4
'rapefugees', 2, 103, 143n11
rationality, 71, 72, 73–4
reason, 71, 72
Rebellion: Zwischenbericht ('Rebellion: Status Report') (Beyse), 22, 42, 106, 124–6
    and affect-driven behaviour, 139–40
    and heterochrony, 136–8
    and literary form, 148n78

    and Orientalism, 140–2
    and rage, 130–4
    and representation, 126–30
    and sublimation, 134–6
reform, 58–9
refugees, 12, 13, 19, 188, 212n70
religion *see* Christianity; Islam
representation, 126–30
repression, 104, 107–9
Republic of False Truths, The (Al Aswani), 36
responsibility, 126–30, 139–40, 141–2
Return: Fathers, Sons and the Land in Between, The (Matar), 40, 42
Revolution Is My Name (Prince), 39
revolutionary models, 34, 35, 38, 121–2
right-wing extremism, 10, 131, 143n11, 171, 213n79
rights, 10, 11–12
Rue des voleurs (*Street of Thieves*) (Énard), 22, 43, 154–5, 180–2
    and Bassam, 190–204
    and Lakhdar, 182–90
    and utter Other, 204–7
rule of law, 2, 5, 6, 62
Rumi
    'The Woman Who Discovered Her Maidservant Having Improper Relations with an Ass', 116–17
Runnymede Trust Commission on British Muslims, 14, 30n85
Rushdie, Salman, 68
    Two Years Eight Months & Twenty-Eight Nights, 1–2, 44

Said, Edward, 6, 7, 15, 104–5, 157
    Orientalism, 26n30
Salih, Tayeb, 188
Saracen, 8
Sardar, Ziauddin, 222
Saudi Arabia, 62
scanners, 11
scenario techniques, 223
secularism, 103
securitisation, 4, 6, 9–10, 205–7, 221
    and *Rue des voleurs* (*Street of Thieves*), 203–4

securitisation (*cont.*)
  and Western fiction, 45, 46
  see also desecuritisation; insecurity
self-immolation, 34
  and *Par le feu* ('By Fire'), 57, 59, 60, 64, 67, 87
sexism, 2, 6, 43
  and *Kapow!*, 110–12, 116, 138–9
sexualised violence, 37
  and *Kapow!*, 109, 110, 112–13, 114
sexuality, 101–3, 104–6, 115
  and *Book of Sands*, 166–8, 171–2, 176–7
  and *Rebellion: Zwischenbericht*, 135
  and *Rue des voleurs* (*Street of Thieves*), 155, 184–6, 193–4, 198, 200
  see also homosexuality; LGBTIQ; lust
Shidyaq, Ahmad Faris
  al-Saq ala al-Saq fim a huwa al-faryaq, 109
short stories, 38
Sicily, 7
al-Sisi, Abdel Fattah, 40
Sivanandan, Ambalavaner, 13
skin colour, 16, 184–5
Slimani, Leïla, 43–4
social media, 60, 163
Soueif, Ahdaf, 33–4, 35, 39
Spain, 4, 181, 182, 200–1; *see also* Indignados
Spanish language, 189
Spartacus (film), 62
spatial levels, 118, 120, 136–7, 140
Spivak, Gayatri Chakravorty, 105
state, the, 11, 55, 63, 66
stereotypes, 1, 2, 5, 6, 141, 220
  and backwardness, 58
  and beards, 115
  and democracy, 132
  and effeminate Oriental male, 143n7
  and *Frühling der Barbaren* (*Barbarian Spring*), 74–7, 79, 84
  and Islamicate Other, 221
  and Islamist Rage Boys, 158–9
  and masculinity, 102–3, 105
  and *Par le feu* ('By Fire'), 64
  and patriarchy, 37

  and *Rebellion: Zwischenbericht*, 135
  and *Rue des voleurs* (*Street of Thieves*), 184, 186
Sterne, Laurence
  The Life and Opinions of Tristram Shandy, Gentleman, 123
Stiglitz, Joseph E., 4
stylistics, 117–24, 131
  and *Rue des voleurs* (*Street of Thieves*), 185, 187, 203
sublimation, 134–6
surveillance, 11
Syria, 4, 34–5, 39, 40

taboos, 104
Tahrir Square (Cairo), 4, 113, 119–20, 164, 170
Tahrir Tales: Plays from the Egyptian Revolution, 39
Taksim Gezi Park (Istanbul), 4
Tangier, 180–1, 182–3, 184, 186
Taxi (Al Khamissi), 35, 109
telecommunications, 11
temporality *see* time
terrorism, 1, 5, 10, 21, 156–9, 206–7
  and France, 42–3
  and racism, 16
  and *Rue des voleurs* (*Street of Thieves*), 155, 181, 196, 198–9, 200
  see also 9/11 attacks
testimonies, 38
theatre *see* plays
Thirlwell, Adam *see Kapow!* (Thirlwell)
time, 58–62, 68–9, 140
  and *Book of Sands*, 172–3
  and *Kapow!*, 119, 121
  and *Rebellion: Zwischenbericht*, 136–8
Tod in Kairo ('Death in Cairo'), 106, 124, 126–9, 131–4, 135, 136, 137, 138
tourism, 79–80, 84
Trans-Maghreb: Novelle vom Bauträger Anton Corwald ('Trans-Maghreb: A Novella about Anton Corwald, Building Constructor') (Platzgumer), 42
Translating Dissent: Voices from and within the Egyptian Revolution, 38

Translating Egypt's Revolution: The Language of Tahrir, 38
Trévidic, Marc, 42–3, 58
Trump, Donald, 2, 105
truth, 70–4
Tunisia, 4, 22, 34, 43; see also *Frühling der Barbaren (Barbarian Spring)* (Lüscher); *Par le feu* ('By Fire') (Ben Jelloun)
Turkey see Ottoman Empire; Taksim Gezi Park (Istanbul)
turning in circles motif, 200–2
Twitter, 163
Two Years Eight Months & Twenty-Eight Nights (Rushdie), 1–2, 44

unemployment, 13
utter Other, 204–7

Vázquez, Àngel, 188
Victorian era, 104
video games see *Tod in Kairo*
Vienna, 7
violence, 2, 6, 54, 205–6
  and *Book of Sands*, 172–4, 177
  and *Frühling der Barbaren (Barbarian Spring)*, 86
  and masculinity, 105
  and *Rebellion: Zwischenbericht*, 124, 127–30, 131–2, 139
  and *Rue des voleurs (Street of Thieves)*, 192, 198–9, 200–1
  and the state, 63, 66
  see also sexualised violence; terrorism

Virilio, Paul
  L'Inertie polaire (Polar Inertia), 134
Visual Editions, 46, 123

Wade, Laura
  Posh, 83
Wæver, Ole, 10
'Waiting for Death: I Will Not Carry Flowers to My Grave' (Yazbek), 39
Walter, Eugene Victor, 157
War on Terror, 10
Wilde, Jaap de, 10
Wilson, G. Willow, 44
Woman in the Crossfire: Diaries of the Syrian Revolution, A (Yazbek), 39
women, 18, 19, 37, 43–4
  and *Book of Sands*, 166–9, 171–5, 176–9
  and *Rue des voleurs (Street of Thieves)*, 184–5
  see also gender equality; gender inequality; sexism
Writing Revolution: From Tunis to Damascus, 38

xenoracism, 13

Yacoubian Building, The (Al Aswani), 36
Yazbek, Samar, 39
Yemen, 62

Zaimoğlu, Feridun
  'Gottes Krieger', 210n44
Zapata, Emiliano, 121
Žižek, Slavoj, 4, 140

EU representative:
Easy Access System Europe
Mustamäe tee 50, 10621 Tallinn, Estonia
Gpsr.requests@easproject.com

www.ingramcontent.com/pod-product-compliance
Lightning Source LLC
Chambersburg PA
CBHW070324240426
43671CB00013BA/2353